First Edition – May, 2024

ISBN 978-1-7382180-0-4

A Frank Acknowledgement

I am grateful to the newspaper reporters, local historians and archivists who have kept the story of the Sells-Floto Circus elephants alive for the past ninety-eight years, most particularly because they have provided me with so many different versions to choose from, making the one appearing in this book as likely as any.

Thank you to Stanton Hooper for his thorough (with pictures) explanations of the workings of a 1926 McLaughlin-Buick, to Anna Majkowski for those incredibly useful maps of early Cranbrook, to Joey Bell for navigating the editing maize, Evan Brynne for the cover design, and Cranbrook History Centre archivist Dave Humphrey for answering sundry questions about everything from Fernie to Yahk.

Thank you to Margaret Teneese of the Ktunaxa Interpretive Centre and to Chrystal Williams, ?aquam Culture and Language Coordinator, Ktunaxa Nation.

My deep gratitude to Iona Whishaw for her encouragement and advice.

This book was produced by The Nelson History Theatre Society with funding from the Province of British Columbia Gaming Branch.

FRANK AND THE ELEPHANTS
A Romance of the Rockies

For Family and Friends
And particularly Ilene

The Story

My grandfather, Frank Burton, died at the age of ninety-eight when he fell off a ladder and broke his neck. Those of us who knew and loved him, though shocked and saddened, were not entirely surprised by the manner of his passing. We'd always known he was "a mite clumsy" – a judgment originally passed by Granny Jenny's own grandfather and frequently brought out by Frank himself in matter-of-fact explanation for various bruises, sprains and occasional fractures sustained over the years. This time he'd leaned out too far while clearing a bunch of leaves clogging an eaves trough at the back of his house. At least it was quick because he was just one story up and didn't have far to fall.

That a ninety-eight-year-old should still be living in his own house was unusual enough, you might say. That he should be up a ladder clearing clogged leaves from an eavestrough was downright criminal – on the part of his relatives who should never have allowed him up there in the first place. Sure, easy for you to say. You're not Frank's relative. You haven't lived with, near, or around that stubborn old mule all your life. I have – almost. In fact, I was there, at the bottom of the ladder yelling, "Grampa, for Christ's sake get off that goddamn ladder and let me...." when it happened. Truth be known, and I'll carry this to *my* grave, it was me, coming around the corner of the house and yelling it, that caused him to defiantly reach out for that last and farthest bunch of leaves with a to-hell-with-you look on his face. That look, suddenly turning to surprise, then the beginnings of "Oh shit!" and finally panic as he scrambled to keep his balance, will be my last memory of Grampa Frank.

Not quite true. There was Frank in his coffin four days later, no longer surprised. He looked resigned if anything and slightly eager like he always did when somebody else was talking, waiting for his chance to jump in. Granny J had refused to allow the undertaker to colour him up so there was no pretense that he was 'just sleeping' but we all agreed he still looked great. All his life he had possessed dazzling good looks and even death had scarcely diminished them.

Frank could have made his fortune in Hollywood had looks and personality been all there was to it. He had thick brown hair, most of which he kept to the end, a high forehead, soft hazel eyes exactly the right distance from the top of a straight nose, a wide mouth, perfect teeth – also all kept – and a jaw that outlined the strong bones beneath. He tanned well in the summer and even looked good with a moustache.

He was forty-four when I was born so I didn't know him at the height of his beauty, but I was familiar with photographs taken in his 20's and 30's, even had one in my apartment during the years before I moved back to Cranbrook. As a matter of fact, it was a picture from the one and only time he had ventured onto the stage. "Not his shining hour," Granny J told me. "Spencer Tracy said know your lines and don't bump into the furniture. It was some English thing the Little Theatre was doing, and Frank was supposed to be the hero. You'd think he could manage that – being something of a hero in real life. But he didn't know his lines very well and he bumped into just about everything that couldn't get out of his way."

Nobody seemed to mind very much though," she added with a sad little smile, "because, well, because it was Frank."

The photo, perched on a shelf above my stereo, always drew admiring attention, especially, but not exclusively, from female visitors. His eyes were open then, of course allowing the warmth of his personality to shine through. "Irresistible" was the word most often used. Some just whistled. One said, "Nice. Looks a bit like you." By which I could tell she liked me and was willing to stretch the truth to show it. We got married a couple of years later.

After the funeral we gathered at the farmhouse for a reading of Frank's letter to the family. It had been a bright autumn day, the kind always called 'crisp' and the white lace curtains were slanting in with the slight breeze. Several of us, on coming in, had gone straight across to make sure the windows were open. Grampa Frank was out there in his fresh grave on the other side of town and nobody wanted to shut him out.

The letter was written in Frank's shaky script, showing it was a recent creation, and addressed to my father as his "oldest surviving heir." The phrase was typical of Frank since it was purely decorative, the kind he was fond of. We're a long-lived and healthy family. My father, his brother and four sisters, their wives, and husbands, us grandchildren – I, at fifty-four, the oldest – and great and great-great-grandchildren are all still here. We were almost all there too, crowded into the parlor. The implication that there were still others who *didn't* survive is altogether misleading. It was my father who pointed this out, noting too that Jenny, as Frank's widow, was the real heir when it came to the house, the savings etc. All the letter was meant to do was distribute a few of his personal possessions according to Frank's wishes.

I noticed a faint, almost shamefaced, look of satisfaction on Dad's face when he got the elephant gun. It was the only piece of real interest, the rest being pictures, books, odds and ends that one of us had admired some time or other and Frank had tucked away in his memory. But the elephant gun was a well-known object, massive and immaculately maintained, hauled out as exhibit A every time Frank found someone new to tell his story to.

I got the story.

"As promised," Dad read, "Frankie gets the story. You are now free to tell it as many times as you want. Tell it straight, just like I always did." This got a laugh. "There's adventure, history, romance, and humour. Hell, you're the writer in the family, make it into a book. You could probably get a grant from the Columbia Basin Trust.

To be clear, I'm not a writer. I'm an engineer. I've written a few technical papers for professional journals about truss stress and things like that and had a minor success with an introductory level textbook - as Frank well knew. It was his little dig at me because he guessed I'd always wanted to be a real writer but lacked the courage – or maybe the imagination. Years ago, when he discovered I'd been telling his story to some friends at university, he called me up in Toronto one night in a real lather about it.

"Goddamn it, Frankie," he yelled, "That's *my* story! You want to tell a story, make up your own. Or go live one. Tell your friends if they want to hear my story, they should come to *me*! You can tell it after I'm dead, not a minute sooner!" Now, given the inheritance and the fact that I'm at least partly responsible for his death, I don't really have much choice. Not if I want to sleep at night.

Frank was a great storyteller and had a large collection of local tales and personal anecdotes which he'd produce whenever he was reminded "of the time when..." And off he'd go, sometimes for an hour or more, other times tossing out a quick snippet which he'd cut short with a look that said, "I can't stand around jawing all day for your benefit" although this became rarer the older he got.

But Frank's Story, as we called it, capitals included, and now mine by right of inheritance, was in an altogether different category. It's verifiably true, for one thing and, like Frank said, it's got everything – an elephant stampede, a nail-biter election campaign, star-crossed lovers, and a happy ending. I think, but I can't be absolutely certain, that I have heard every single word of it at least once. Most of it I've heard dozens of times, but I also know that other family members have heard some of it way more often. And later I found out there were things Frank never talked about at all.

Sitting there in the parlour surrounded by Frank's heirs and feeling the weight of narrative responsibility descending upon me, I suddenly realized how much of it we had all taken for granted and how little we *really* knew about a world that had existed a quarter century before I was born. What was the weather like that summer? Frank rarely mentioned it. What did this city look like back then? Were the streets paved, the sidewalks wood or cement? I can't remember a single descriptive word about the Victoria Café where Frank used to start his day, or about Mavis and her surprising career. I'd never seen a picture of Eva or Ned Harris, had no idea how to drive a McLaughlin-Buick nor what happened to Mike Wilson. And finally, what it was like all those years ago to live in a world whose centre was Cranbrook, B.C.

After growing up thinking I knew Frank's Story as well as it could be known, I realized how infinitely better Frank knew it - or Granny J knew it, for that matter. Behind every word was a detailed picture that Frank was seeing but I never had. I had imagined that summer of 1926 as a world just like my own, like watching an old play brought up to date and performed in modern dress. I realized how much work it was going to be to tell it so that even *I* understood it, let alone anybody else.

When we got home from the reading, my wife Ellen said, "You know you're going to have to do it.". She knew it wasn't an idle suggestion on his part, it was a command from the dead. By telling it to a few friends with the pride of family ownership, I had declared myself the keeper of Frank's legacy. The way he saw it, I was his road to immortality.

That was over a decade ago and I've been limping along that long and winding thoroughfare ever since. Actually, for the first year or so I just stood there. I told myself I was thinking about it, working out the details, but I was really trying to think of a way out, hoping everybody would just forget about it. Not a chance. Not a week went by without somebody asking, "How's the book coming, Frankie?" Frankie. I was even named after him.

Then one day Ellen saw me staring at a blank Word document and said, "It doesn't have to pour out like Charles Dickens, you know. Try making notes in point form like you did for Fundamentals." She was referring to my previous magnus opus, Fundamentals of Stress, the success of which prompted me to quit my job, move back home and start my own business.

"Write down all the parts you remember and then collect all the parts everyone else remembers. Decide which ones are consistent with known facts, which ones contradict each other, and which are most likely to be true. Then fill in the blanks. Treat it like a work of fiction if you have to. I'm sure Frank did."

That kept me busy off and on for years. I still had my business to run and with the family scattered across several provinces and a few continents, it took a while. And then there was the research once I'd figured out where all the blanks were –and there were plenty. Granny J got me started. At first, I had thought she wasn't interested or, since she was ninety-six herself when Frank died, had forgotten all about it. Turns out she was just being nice.

"I wasn't certain you really felt the call,' she said, after Ellen had told her of my struggles, "but I know Frank will appreciate it." Note the 'will' - not 'would have'. She was convinced he was up there watching over us and I think she was probably right. I could feel him breathing down my neck.

A lot of blanks got filled in fairly quickly after that. It was from Granny J that I learned about Doc King's voice and speaking style - somewhere between Richard Nixon and John Diefenbaker. She set me straight about Mr Mac too. I had him pegged for a Scottish accent but no, "he was as Canadian as rye whiskey which, by the way, he kept hidden in a jar on the top shelf of our pantry. I found it one afternoon after he'd forgotten to put it away – made me quite tipsy. There were considerably fewer Presbyterian teetotallers than you might suppose. Even the Reverend Mackay couldn't resist Mrs. McKinnon's fruit cake." I had her help for about a year. Now they are both looking down.

What follows is the result of intermittent research interspersed with stretches of procrastination. I got a lot of it from Granny J before she died, lots more from local sources or history books. The rest I just plain made up based on what seemed likely. As for which parts Frank made up, your guess is as good as mine.

The Fight

"Cranbrook," Frank used to say, "is a working man's town." To which Granny J always added "and woman's, Frank."

"Cranbrook's problem," he'd continue, after a barely perceptible roll of his eyes "is the fact that it's situated in one of the most beautiful pieces of real estate on earth and by way of contrast the town itself has never been much to look at." True enough. Just the usual small-town architecture, a few houses prettier than the rest, a few buildings downtown on Baker St. with some fancy brickwork, and that's about it. The rest was just rail lines, lumber yards, and warehouses.

"At some point back in the seventies we gave up altogether and put in that goddamn strip mall – a mile and a half of Kentucky Fried Chicken and gas stations. It's an embarrassment."

I grew up here too and didn't know what he was talking about until I went away for a few years and saw a bit of the world. The interesting thing, though, is Frank never did. After he came west at seventeen, he lived the rest of his life in Cranbrook, never went back east, went to Vancouver twice and nowhere else all his long life. But he saw what most of his fellow citizens never saw – or would admit to. Cranbrook was not, is not, nor ever will be, much of a town. If you're looking for anything out of the ordinary here, you have to look at the people or the scenery.

The first thing you see, fifteen miles to the northeast, are The Steeples rising forty-five hundred feet straight up from the floor of the Kootenay Valley like the walls of a giant's castle. In the summer when I was a kid, we used to drive to Fort Steele, then down past the Wild Horse River and the old gold rush diggings to the Norbury Lakes. It's a park now, but in those days, it was just a mix of range land and lodge pole pine around two pretty little lakes. If it had been an early spring you could swim in them by late April. They are shallow and warmed by the sun.

But if you come back a few weeks later, in June or early July, they'll be as cold as ice. That's because the snowpack melts and runs straight down through hidden channels into a whole series of small crystal pools scattered along the valley floor.

The valley itself is mostly second growth conifer forest and grass land– the best parts being the low ridges of Ponderosa pines, one of the most beautiful trees in the world. They are tall and straight with fat, reddish- brown trunks that can go up a hundred feet or more clear of any branches, with bark that you can break off in your hand like the pieces of a jigsaw puzzle. In the heat of summer, after a few weeks of cloudless blue skies, the grass and needles beneath are as dry and crackling as week-old breadcrumbs. Somewhere among them are the scattered bones of an elephant.

The townsite of Cranbrook was laid out in the middle of a few square miles of natural pastureland called Joseph's Prairie. Over the years it grew on the proceeds from mining, lumber, and the railway. It got its start, in fact, in 1898 when Colonel Baker bribed the CPR with several city blocks of real estate in exchange for putting their terminus here instead of the then-flourishing town of Fort Steele – now a ghost town tourist attraction. Like Frank said, it's a working...person's... town, plain and down to earth, practical and not given to architectural flourishes.

We seldom got the whole story from beginning to end but it always began at the same place - his fight with Mike Wilson. THE FIGHT, as Frank pronounced it with a portentous bass rumble, was more of a quick scuffle. It took place in a lumber yard following a few choice words never repeated in front of Granny J - only suggested with a grin and a wink – then some posturing, a little footwork and lastly a sudden exchange of blows - one each. Frank always claimed he'd had the better of it because Mike got his in first and he hadn't gone down while Frank's punch caused Mike to briefly hit the dirt – giving him the opportunity, as he freely admitted, to walk away in triumph.

The superficial reason for the fight was that Frank didn't like the way Mike was bossing him around and told him so. But since Mike, as assistant foreman and son of the owner, really *was* Frank's boss, the real reason had to be Jenny Macpherson.

Jenny – and this is gospel as far as Frank's Story goes – was the prettiest girl in British Columbia – probably in the entire Dominion although naturally he couldn't absolutely swear to it. If we were sitting in the parlour at the time, he would direct our attention to a photo in a silver wire frame on the mantle. This showed a slender young woman of eighteen wearing a man's battered fedora slightly too large for her and decorated with fishing flies. The hat belonged to her grandfather and guardian, Mr. Mac, who had popped it onto her head a moment before the Courier photographer clicked the shutter. The occasion was the weighing in of entries at the Moyie Lake fishing derby. Besides the beautiful, grinning Jenny herself, the picture contained a large rainbow trout hanging upside down from a scale and sporting a rosette which declared that Jenny, or possibly the fish, had won second prize. Her grin is not directed at the fish but out to the side towards Frank and Mike who were both hovering around her like moths. This was in March, when everything was still up for grabs and most of the smart money was on Mike.

Frank came away from the fight with a shiner on his left eye and no job. Jobs were easy to come by in Cranbrook in 1926 so he wasn't too worried – at least from the point of view of getting a new one. There was the CPR Tie and Timber Branch, The Cranbrook Sash and Door Company, and any number of lumber yards. The wage for a forest worker was about fifty cents an hour, forty-four hours a week. That was good pay for a twenty-year-old living in a boarding house with nothing much to spend it on. The worry came from what Jenny would say.

The fight must have taken place on Thursday, July 29th because next morning Frank was in the Victoria Café at the corner of Baker and Fenwick, intending to brag about his exploit to his best friend Bob. It was well after eight o'clock when he walked in. Being temporarily unemployed he hadn't bothered to set his alarm, had overslept and missed breakfast. Mrs.

McKinnon kept very strict hours and wasn't about to reward sloth even for her favourite boarder. Bob was sitting at a table by the front window, alternately keeping an eye out for Ernie Pinkerton, the manager of The Imperial Bank, and reading the latest edition of The Herald. It came out every Thursday afternoon which is how I know the exact date.

Bob and Frank had struck up a friendship at the Star Theatre's showing of *Singed Wings*. It was billed as a tragedy about a Spanish dancer and a jealous clown, but both found it so ridiculous that their laughter and shouted comments, exchanged over several rows of seats, resulted in their ejection at the end of the third reel. Since then, they had spent most of their off hours either exploring the countryside in Bob's uncle's Model A Ford or taking advantage of whatever social opportunities the city afforded.

Bob had recently been hired as a teller and was wearing his brown checked suit with starched collar and red bowtie. He was tall, thin, almost spindly, with a long, pointed nose and a receding hairline which he tried to hide by combing his hair forward. He had bright, intelligent eyes and a pleasant smile, making up for his deficiencies.

Pinkerton had made it clear that promotion depended upon 'keenness' which in the end boiled down to getting to the bank before he did. Bob had made the happy discovery that his manager strolled to work along Garden Ave. and up Baker. By quickly paying his bill, ducking out the back door and jogging through the alleys crossing Hanson and Armstrong Streets, he could slip through the back door well ahead of his boss. "It's a trick I learned from studying The Three Little Pigs," he'd say.

The friends had once been regulars at The Victoria, meeting every Friday morning at six for bacon and eggs and coffee. Committed to getting ahead in the world, they would forgo their boarding house breakfasts, each bringing a copy of the weekly paper and sharing the news both local, national, and occasionally international. Cranbrook had two papers; The Courier (Liberal) and The Herald (Conservative). Lately, however, since Bob's new job allowed him to keep bankers' hours while Frank's job at the lumber yard started at 5:30, this arrangement had fallen by the wayside.

"Hiya Frank, "Bob grinned, "Thought I might see you. Nice shiner."

Frank examined his reflection in the window. "Geeze, does it show? Me and Mike had a little set to yesterday down at the yard. You should see him."

"I did. Says he fired you."

"Sure he fired me - or he would have if I hadn't quit first. Ever since Jenny broke up with him and took up with me it's been 'Burton this and Burton that' til I told him where to stick it. Then push came to shove - you know how it is."

"Dames!" said Bob.

"But that's not the worst of it. This was my fifth, wait a minute, sixth job in three years and you know Jenny. Wants me to settle down, get steady. Says I need to find myself. Well, Geeze, I'm right here ain't I?"

Frank was very proud of that little joke and always laughed when he told it. Jenny would tell him not to say ain't in front of the children and remind him that she had definitely *not* taken up with him and that he had been on probation, hanging by a thread.

"A real cliff hanger," Frank would say with a smirk.

Bob held up his copy of The Herald. As a banker, of course, he couldn't afford to be caught reading The Courier. "Says here Doc King is running again. You'd think he'd have had enough after that customs scandal. The Herald says the Liberals are all crooks and he doesn't stand a chance this time around."

"Well, they would. But you can bet The Courier's got him back in the cabinet already. Morning Mavis," - this last addressed to the waitress, a pretty brunette about a year older than the boys and a real knockout with Clara Bow curls and Gloria Swanson's eyes. She was the reason they had chosen The Victoria for their Friday rendezvous, and it was to hear her sing that they had gone to the Elks' Christmas Show– where Frank had first seen Jenny MacPherson.

"Hello boys," Mavis said. Her tone was very big sister. "Long time no see. I was beginning to think I'd lost my admirers. Better stick to flap jacks. Hung Lee lost fifty bucks at the poker table last night and the pepper's flying." She flicked the edge of Bob's paper with a bright red fingernail. "Circus is coming to town – top of six." Mavis had ambitions to ride her looks and voice out of Cranbrook and was always on the lookout for anything connected to 'showbiz'. She kept a copy of Broadway Nights under the counter by the cash machine.

Bob flipped through the paper and began to read. "Friday, August 6th. Sells-Floto Circus..."

CRANBROOK
FRIDAY, AUGUST 6

SELLS
FLOTO
CIRCUS

2 SHOWS
DAILY
2 & 8 P.M.

THE CIRCUS BEAUTIFUL

AND

"Poodles" Hannaford, England's Own — a British Subject — and without a doubt the Greatest Riding Comedian that the World has ever seen.

TOGETHER WITH
THE WORLD'S
GREATEST
MOST MAGNIFICENT
SPECTACLE
1000 PEOPLE
HORSES, ELEPHANTS AND
JUNGLE BORN MAN KILLERS,
INCLUDING ALSO SEVERAL
HUNDRED GORGEOUS SINGING
AND DANCING GIRLS
ZOO-CIRCUS-HIPPODROME
400 ARENIC STARS

EARTH'S BEST
AND ONLY
EXCLUSIVE CIRCUS

NO STREET PARADE. TICKETS ON SALE CIRCUS DAY ONLY AT CRAN-BROOK DRUG AND BOOK STORE

What the heck's a riding comedian?"

"Probably falls off a lot," Frank offered, which turns out to be true. There's a clip on Youtube of Poodles doing exactly that (Slapstick Clips – Circus Daze 1928).

"So, let's make it a double-date Bob - that'll make a

hundred and two gorgeous girls. But don't you say anything yet. I'm not asking until I get another job."

"I could put in a word at the bank."

"No thanks. Banks rattle me. Speaking of which, isn't that Old Pinky trotting across Baker?"

Bob sprang to his feet and headed for the door accidentally on purpose colliding with Mavis who was bringing their orders. "Frank's paying," he said, taking advantage of her encumbered state to kiss her nose.

The Girl

Despite his eternal optimism, sunny disposition, and a stomach full of flap jacks, it must have been an anxious moment for Frank, sitting there and wondering what next. A hard-working young man could get by well enough in those days thanks to a booming economy after the flat post-war years. No shortage of jobs. But with all the boys coming back from the war and then the thousands of new immigrants, the bosses had the upper hand.

The working man got squeezed so hard he – it was mostly he, of course - had to go out on strike and then the Mounties showed up with clubs. Unions were still a long way off. Frank could get a job at a factory back in Ontario or in a lumber yard or a mine out here, and work until he dropped. But get ahead? Get married and have kids so as to give them a decent education? How the hell was a fellow supposed to do that?

Frank grew up poor in Whitby, just outside of Toronto along with an older brother named Ted. He had an older sister too, younger than Ted, but she died while he was still a baby. Ted was seven years older, big for his age, good at everything and Frank worshipped him.

Their father joined up in 1915, mostly to escape family life and left Ted in charge, which was fine by Frank. But then, two years later, Ted ran off and joined up too – the same regiment as his father. He left a note, "Gone to find Dad. You're the man of the house now, Frankie. Take care of Mom, love Ted."

By that time, the British had decided attrition was the only way to win the war and recruits were shoved into any battalion that needed beefing up. After a couple of month's training, Ted ended up in a different outfit altogether and never saw his father. He was blown apart by an artillery shell his first day at the front.

Their dad was one of the men who made it home but in no shape for work. "His nerves were shot and he took to drink," was all Frank ever said about it. One day he disappeared. Frank's mother waited around for a couple of months and then went to live with her parents on a rock farm near Belleville. She told him he was welcome to come along but Frank had spent a summer there during the war and declined. He was seventeen years old, had just finished high school and decided to head west.

After working the midway at the C.N.E. to earn some travelling money he took a train to Saskatoon and stayed just long enough to experience the first half of a prairie winter. Then, seeing his name on a train schedule, he got back on board and headed farther west to a town named Frank.

He saw the Rockies for the first time as the sun came up just east of Fort McLeod, a bright row of teeth across the horizon. The tracks carried him over the prairies beside the Old Man River past Brocket, Pincher Station, and the ruins of the Leitch Collieries where Passburg used to be, a rickety post office among the dilapidated shacks. The foothills began to rise up around him, a solitary mound here and there, until the valley grew narrower, mountains both sides and so into the Crowsnest Pass, Bellevue and finally Frank.

He was feeling kind of tickled to be going to a town with his name on it. Standing in the corridor with his bag, waiting to hop out, he ducked down to look out the window as the train started to slow. Nothing but rock both sides, right up against the tracks – giant boulders, grey as storm clouds.

Turns out Frank used to be a mining town, a real boomer. They built it smack up against a mountain with the mine drilled right into the side. Starting in '01 they went at it for two years, a thousand men digging away and hauling out the insides. The winter of '03 was even wetter than usual and in April it got January cold. Then, early in the morning, while everybody was asleep, almost a hundred million tons of rock came down off the side of the mountain in less than two minutes. Buried the whole east end, mine buildings, tracks, stores, and a dozen houses – eighty or so people killed. They never settled on the exact number. Three weeks later they had the tracks fixed up, re-opened the mine a while later and started digging away for another fifteen years.

By the time Frank got there it was just about played out – a dirty little town taking its time dying. He spent one night in the hotel and couldn't sleep a wink. Next day he got back on the train and didn't stop until he was in the clear – Cranbrook.

It was love at first sight. Something about those mountains behind him and a lot of blue sky up ahead. New beginnings.

For the next couple of years, new beginnings were about as far as Frank got. He worked his way through a string of lumber yards, the freight depot, and the night shift at the CPR station, quitting after a few months, always hoping the next one would be more to his taste. By the fall of '25, realizing he was fast running out of options, he made himself a promise to stick to the next one no matter what. At least for a year or two, while he built up his capital.

So when Mike Wilson mentioned they were hiring at his father's lumber mill, he jumped at it. Through the rest of summer and all of fall, things seemed to settle down until friendly relations with his boss went sideways after he caught sight of Jenny at the Elks' Christmas Show.

The following Sunday which might have been the 12th of December, Frank startled Mrs. McKinnon by arriving for breakfast washed, shaved, combed, and wearing his best (his only) suit and tie. "Now don't tell me you're off to church," she said, "though I'll not stop you."

"Knox," Frank replied with a grin.

Mrs. McKinnon was a plump, handsome widow in her early forties. Her husband had been killed at Vimy and her only romantic outlet, apart from the weekly serial in The Herald, was speculating about the 'amorous escapades' of her young men. "The choir was singing at the Elks' show Friday night, I recall," she said complacently. "It'll be a lassie you saw. Well, it's often enough a lad such as yourself chases a petticoat and finds the

Lord. No doubt I'll be seeing you there myself by and by."

Knox Presbyterian was across town at the corner of Louis and Armstrong (!), a stiff walk on a cold December morning. Frank felt his virtue rise with every step. He had often passed it on his way to work, an uninspiring wooden structure with a squat tower he had never been tempted to enter. He arrived early in order to secure a place near the front and pretended to be absorbed in a prayer book while waiting for the show to begin. In front of him two elderly ladies were arranging vases of flowers around the altar table.

Frank had been raised an Anglican and consequently tended to look down on Presbyterians as somehow wrongheaded although he couldn't have said why. He had some vague notion that they believed it was already settled who got into heaven and who didn't. It made him wonder why they bothered, although he found out later it was a bit more complicated than that. He liked Knox though. It was cosy in a dim sort of way. There wasn't any stain glass like at St. John's where he went with his mother, just ordinary windows running all down one side - with curtains on them.

Behind the altar was an alcove with a simple cross. Off to the left a passageway led to the choir rooms and vestry. In the distance he heard laughter and snatches of hymns. He leaned back and closed his eyes, trying to look pious. But it was a Sunday morning, and he did what he always did at that time and drifted off to sleep.

Ten minute later, a sudden burst of organ music playing the opening bars of Angels from the Realms of Glory brought him wide awake and halfway to his feet only to be pushed back down by Mike Wilson's hand on his shoulder.

"Where the hell did you come from?" Frank whispered through the fog.

"Hardly from there. From the same place you did, I suspect. My nice warm bed."

"I thought you were Anglican," the truth beginning to dawn.

"My family is. I'm not so particular. I didn't know you were a church goer at all."

"I saw a vision Friday night at the talent show. Now I'm a believer."

Mike's face instantly darkened with suspicion. He scowled. A snarl twisted his lips. "If you're saying what I think you're saying you can forget it. She's taken."

As if on cue, the choir began to file in, singing as they came. Since the back row entered first, Jenny was leading the way looking small but very angelic in her powder blue robes.

There being no room for fisticuffs in a church – especially Presbyterian – the boys settled in for a silent battle of wills. Frank just wanted her to notice him and he could see that she did. She knew Mike would be there and looked their way. Frank quickly turned to Mike and said something about the weather with an expression on his face like we were best pals. Then they sat rigidly side by side, a pair of mute statues, eyes fixed on poor Jenny. Frank could tell she didn't like it, so he looked up at the ceiling in a spiritual kind of way, paying close attention to the sermon and singing at the top of his lungs whenever a hymn came along. When they passed around the basket he ostentatiously dropped in a whole dollar. Jenny didn't notice but Mrs. McKinnon did and gave him an extra slice of pie at supper.

Frank was not entirely satisfied with his morning's work, however, because it had forced him to see Mike in a whole new light. As a friend and co-worker, he hadn't paid much attention to his looks or thought how he might or might not appeal to the opposite sex. If asked, he would have wished him luck in that department. But with the sudden revelation that Mike considered himself as having some sort of claim on Jenny, their relationship changed dramatically. He was obliged, as well as he could, to look at Mike from a woman's point of view. What he saw was disturbing. Frank was not unaware of his own physical attractions but had never put much stock in them, preferring to rely on his wit and charm which he slightly overrated. What he couldn't deny, though, was that Mike was a formidable opponent.

First of all, he was a year older which matters more at the young end of the spectrum. He was also noticeably taller, had an extra couple of inches on his biceps, a strong jaw, wavy brown hair immaculately cut and slicked back with just the right touch of Brilliantine. His suit looked like it was tailor made too and must have cost at least forty dollars. He looked, in fact, especially with a pipe in his mouth, like something out of the Eaton's catalogue.

Jenny watched from the back of the choir with maidenly interest. Mike Wilson had been coming to church for the past few weeks and she had glanced in his direction as always, prepared to give him her usual friendly but cool smile. This time, sizing the situation up as per the heroine of a Victorian novel, she could see that something was amiss. Mike looked absolutely savage while the unknown young man had a very smug expression on his face. To tell you the truth she was not terribly impressed by his looks. As regards his character, that is, although he certainly was handsome in a wild Heathcliff kind of way. And, needless to say, she had no idea the goings-on had anything to do with her.

Frank had memories of gatherings in the church hall after service and had nurtured hopes of striking up a conversation with Jenny over tea and jam sandwiches. But while the collection basket was being passed around, Mike made it clear that any attempt to "horn in" would end badly.

"See that old buzzard over there?" he whispered, nodding towards an elderly hawk -beaked worshipper sitting across the aisle. "That's her grandfather. A few Sundays ago I caught her alone for a minute after the service and told her how much I enjoyed the choir. The usual stuff and innocent enough, right? Before she could open her mouth, I was snagged, backed into a corner and interrogated about my views on predestination and whether, in my opinion, we find grace through faith or good works."

"What did you say?"

"Told him I wasn't sure and would value his guidance. He dragged me over to a bookshelf and hauled out The History of The Reformation in Scotland and The First Blast of the Trumpet Against the Monstrous Regiment of Women both by some old geezer by the name of John Knox. Interesting reading," he added with a wicked smile. "I'll lend them to you."

Mike was betting his rival would decide the game was not worth the candle and back off. He was almost right. Frank spent the rest of Sunday reminding himself of his mother's consolation for unrequited love, "There's more fish in the sea than ever came out of it," and he went off to bed inclined to take his rod elsewhere. But as young men everywhere have discovered, darkness and the warmth of blankets are wonderful aphrodisiacs and he awoke next morning with a powerful thirst for theology.

Deciding to approach the dragon indirectly, but properly armed, Frank dropped by the church Tuesday after work to tell the Reverend McKay how much he had enjoyed his sermon and to ask for study suggestions. As luck would have it, the minister was somewhat short-sighted and didn't recognize him. The fact that Frank was wearing greasy overalls and a frayed toque no doubt helped. As they passed a notice board on their way to the church's modest library, the minister was reminded of the weekly meetings of the Young Presbyterians Social and Literary Club and asked Frank if he would like to attend.

"Is Mike Wilson a member?"

"No he is not," the Reverend declared with a tight smile, handing him a copy of An Admonition to the Faithful. "I'm afraid that young man is not serious when it comes to spiritual matters. In the first place, his family is Anglican. In the second, he gives almost exclusive attention to a particular young lady in our choir, much good it will do him." Frank remembered Mrs. McKinnon's homily about the chasing of petticoats but kept it to himself.

His plan was to carry out a campaign behind Mike's back by way of the weekly meetings of the Social and Literary Club.

He had expected it to be hard slogging but was pleasantly surprised to find a group of young people, mostly his own age, who were obviously there for the same reasons. The one exception was Jenny herself without whom the evenings would have consisted almost entirely of plans for skating parties by the young men and readings of romantic poetry by the young ladies. She steadfastly insisted on a half hour by the clock of "spirited spiritual discussion" for which Frank, at least, was grateful as it allowed him to make small inroads into the mysteries of Presbyterianism as well as to demonstrate his willingness to be her pupil. John Knox he had tossed aside within minutes.

On the first Thursday evening, Frank sat quietly listening without adding much to the conversation and dividing his attention equally among the members. By the conclusion of the following week's deliberations, however, while soliciting Jenny's interpretation of a particularly obscure article of doctrine, he guided her toward a piece of furniture at the far end of the room which, in any other setting, would have been called a love seat. There they remained for the rest of the evening, including the final singsong during which he pressed his shoulder against hers as they leaned together over their songbook.

Upon his return home, Frank was interrogated by Mrs. McKinnon. "I suppose it's Miss Macpherson you have your eyes on," she said. "There's no harm in aiming high but remember, this is a small town and a young man's character can be tarnished in an instant. It's my understanding that Mike Wilson is courting her too so you've a steep hill to climb. I won't say you've no chance…. I for one have my doubts about young Wilson. There's something not quite sincere about him, I'm thinking."

Frank rather enjoyed having his pursuit of Jenny a topic of private conversation with Mrs. McKinnon but keeping it secret from Mike Wilson himself proved impossible. He was caught red-mitted New Year's Day at an SLC skating party on the outdoor rink at the Gyro Club community playground. Frank had been wobbling across the ice, working up his courage to take

Jenny's hand, when Mike came skating up, his own arm akimbo, and expertly swept her off. "You know Mike" she said brightly, over her shoulder, as they glided smoothly away.

So began a running battle over the next six months with small victories on each side. Early in January, Mike injured his leg at work which left the skating parties to Frank although he was never able to offer her more than a stiff and tentative arm. In fact, it was Frank who needed the support. As she confided to Eileen, "He finds it a trifle humiliating, of course, as all young men would but truth to tell, he is so infuriatingly handsome, I'm glad to have something to keep me occupied and my mind off my weak knees!"

By way of consolation, Mike was allowed to accompany Jenny to a women's hockey game in early February between the Cranbrook Canucks and the champion Fernie Swastikas and to drive her home afterwards. The picture of the two of them together in the dark, side by side, in Mike's very own 1922 Studebaker Roadster was agony to Frank. The reality was scarcely any better for Jenny who had foolishly decided to wear her best coat which was far too thin. Mike, of course, very gallantly offered various ways to keep her warm which she was sorely tempted to accept. Then he drove her home with the top down, thinking… well you know what he was thinking.

When they got home Mr. Mac was sitting on the porch wrapped in an old bear skin, so Jenny hopped out without giving Mike so much as a handshake. She thought him quite as nice as Frank in a different way and he certainly had better prospects. Who knows what might have happened if her grampa hadn't been on the watch.

By the way, you might wonder why there was a women's hockey team called the Swastika's. Turns out it had not yet achieved its sinister reputation being a spiritual symbol recognized all over the world among Hindus, Buddhists, Celts, ancient Greeks, Romans - you name it. Jenny wasn't sure who won the game.

And so it went. In March: The Gryo Club's musical comedy

production of The Beauty Shop – Mike; The Great War Mike Veteran's Association's St. Patrick's Day Dance – Frank. In April: the St. Eugene Hospital Ball – Mike; The Kimberley Follies – Frank. In May: The Fort Steele Spring Picnic – Mike; The Empire Day Celebrations – Frank. In June: Professor Utall's Animal Show – Mike; The Cranbrook-Nelson Lacrosse game – Frank. And in between, several threesomes to the Star Theatre because that as the only way Mr. Mac would allow his granddaughter to sit unchaperoned in the dark.

For his part, Frank had no idea what, if any, progress Mike was making towards their mutual goal of getting Jenny to declare a winner. On his side there had been a kiss or two but mostly on the wholesome side - received on the cheek rather than given on the lips. On the positive side, they shared acres of moral and theological common ground – as demonstrated by Frank's willingness to agree to any statement of Jenny's exhibiting the slightest degree of certainty. But on the other side, he came to realize, there was his character – his character, that is, as Jenny insisted on reading it. Putting it plainly, she wondered if he had any. And by character Jenny meant the likelihood of his being a good husband, a good father, and, most importantly, his being willing and able to support this future family for the rest of their lives. If he had learned anything from those Thursday evenings of spirited spiritual discussion, it was that.

The Car

One of Frank's most admirable qualities was his willingness to tell a story against himself. More often than not it had something to do with the way his impulsiveness had collided, quite literally, with his clumsiness. It was a source of pride and he considered it his most distinguishing characteristic. Whenever he managed to perform a particularly choice example, he couldn't wait to tell somebody about it. And the funny thing is, nine times out of ten, it worked out in his favour.

That last Friday in July at the Victoria Café is an excellent case in point. After Bob had rushed off to work, Frank finished both orders of flap jacks and coffee (thirty-two cents times two) followed by a third cup (free), traced his signature with his forefinger through the remaining maple syrup, licked it, and left eight dimes in the shape of a smile beside his plate. "See ya, Mavis," he called out, plucking his hat from the rack by the door and flipping it into the air, ducking slightly to catch it on his head. As he bent over to retrieve it from the floor, he simultaneously reached out for the doorknob while darting an embarrassed glance behind him, hoping no one had noticed. His foot catching the edge of the mat, he stumbled forward, carried headlong by the swing of the door. He righted himself with an upward curving motion that took in first the hips, then the bosom and finally the startled face of Mrs. Roberts, the mayor's wife. In order to avoid knocking her to the ground, he grabbed her upraised hand, which she had flung up in self-defence and slipped his right arm around her waist as he waltzed her backwards into the street.

Once he had disentangled himself from Mrs. Roberts, offering his apologies while straightening her hat, Frank tipped his own and headed up the street. He'd noticed an ad in The Herald touting the economic benefits of the brewing industry. Prohibition had been voted out in 1921, having lasted less than four years. Three years later there had been a referendum on making it legal to sell beer by the glass. It turned out that an overall majority had voted against such a radical notion but, by the terms of the referendum, districts in favour – East Kootenay included - were allowed to go ahead anyway. Then the government decided, what the heck, everybody should have beer parlours because a majority of districts had decided in favour. Where there's a will, there's a way.

Naturally this got the prohibitionists riled up. Now there was talk of a second referendum which was why the Amalgamated Breweries of British Columbia were spending their hard-earned money on ads in the Herald and lots of other papers across the province.

It was probably just a coincidence and entirely accidental that the Cranbrook Brewery had burned down almost a year ago, not the work of a crazed teetotaller as some suspected. It had been rebuilt almost immediately at the north end of town but most of the brewers had since left. The ad reminded Frank that they were looking for apprentices. He wasn't sure what Jenny would think about him becoming a brewer or about beer in general, but he figured he could cross that bridge when he came to it – which, as it turned out, he never did.

Taking the most direct route, Frank should have gone up Fenwick Ave. to Angus, across to Cranbrook St. and north to the brewery. Had he done so there's every reason to believe this story would never have happened. Instead, he decided to walk a few blocks west, along Baker, because he couldn't resist the fun of stopping by Bob's bank to report his encounter with Mrs. Roberts.

On his way, he passed Hanson's Garage. Just pulling up in front were two brand new coal black McLaughlin-Buick sedans. Frank always had a soft spot for McLaughlin-Buicks because they were Canadian built and the factory was located in Oshawa, a few miles from where he grew up.

A short wiry man with red hair and a face to match stepped out from the passenger side of the first car. He was wearing a hound's tooth jacket with an empty left sleeve pinned up to the shoulder. "Hello Frankie," he said with a soft Irish lilt. "Got the new '27 models hot off the train this morning. Come to buy or just admire? You'd best hurry - this one's already taken." He tapped the car beside him, a top-of-the-line six-cylinder Brougham sedan complete with ornamental landau hinges curved around its rear windows.

"Hello Mr. Gourley," Frank said. "I don't suppose you'd take a cheque?"

Sean Gourley was an Ulsterman who had emigrated to Canada before the war. He'd won local fame as a footballer before returning to Derry to enlist with the 10th Irish Division in 1915. After losing an arm at Gallipoli he'd returned to Cranbrook. Now he managed the hometown Cranbrook Flyers, which Frank longed to join.

"Didn't I hear something about somebody being out of a job?" he asked. "Or do you have a gold bar hidden somewheres I don't know about. This sweetheart costs nineteen hundred and twenty. Of course, that includes all taxes, bumpers front and rear, spare tire, tube, tire cover and a full tank of gas."

Frank whistled. "I'll start saving. I suppose Mike told you about our little tiff."

"Well, son if he hadn't, your eye surely would. He didn't look so pretty neither. But I'll ask you two to quit that nonsense right now. We need him this Sunday."

It was a sore point with Frank that Mike had made the team that summer and he hadn't. "Sorry Frankie," Sean had told him, "I admire your enthusiasm. Maybe you and me can work up a variety act – me with no left arm and you with two left feet."

Sean now said "Wait a second. How'd you like a job driving this beauty? Mr. Hanson's on the Liberal committee and he's lending her for the campaign. They're looking for a driver. I suppose you can drive. You've got a license?"

"No, but I've got a buck," Frank said. Getting a driver's licence in 1926 was as easy as filling out a form and putting down a dollar You didn't even need to prove you could drive - on the assumption, I guess, that you wouldn't likely waste a dollar if you couldn't.

"To drive for money you need a chauffeur's license," Sean said. "That'll take two character references and another dollar. You wouldn't be the only one after the job, by the way. I better give you a few pointers if you're serious. Let them know you're familiar with all the special features. She's got the counter-poised crank shaft with torsion balancer, vacuum ventilator, and our exclusive giant tooth transmission...."

Half an hour later, armed with a full tank of technical details, Frank hurried over to the Liberal constituency office beside The Continental Hotel. Inside he found Harry Bennett, Dr. King's office manager, addressing four men, all holding cloth caps adorned with the metal badge of a licenced chauffeur. "Dr. King will be in Monday morning at nine and can interview you then. Hello, son. You here about the driving job too?"

The men turned to look at Frank, then at each other. They smiled and filed out. "Well, I was," Frank replied, "but it looks like..."

"Hold your horses, now. Between you and me, I'd say you have as good a chance as any of those boys. Dr. King is not just looking for a driver. He wants someone to talk to as much as anything. You're a friendly fellow and I've noticed people like you."

"Maybe you've noticed I can't seem to keep a job too."

"Yep. Duly noted," Harry laughed. "Although it's not considered wise to mention it at a job interview. Mrs. McKinnon tells me you'll settle down eventually and may even amount to something.... someday. Her good opinion goes a long way with me. She told me you have excellent table manners and always carry the dishes into the kitchen after supper. No guarantees but I'd advise you to show up Monday morning bright and early."

Frank spent the rest of the day getting his driver's license, lining up a couple of references– the Rev. MacKay and Mrs. McKinnon – and taking Bob's uncle's Ford for a spin to refresh his skills. He laid low for the weekend, making sure to stay out of Jennie's way as she would probably have heard about his fight with Mike. He was tempted to skip church too but decided against it because he didn't want to make matters worse. Seeing the look she gave him from the back of the choir, he kept his head down and slipped quietly out afterwards.

Later that day the Reverend MacKay stopped by the boarding house to drop off Frank's reference letter and pay a social call on Mrs. McKinnon. On Sunday afternoons she was known to welcome visitors with tea and an excellent, brandy-moistened fruit cake which, despite his being the standard-bearer of Presbyterian abstinence, he was never known to refuse. He found Frank and fellow boarder Jimmy Wainwright in the kitchen already enjoying their second slices.

"Ah now here's bad luck.... not you, Reverend," laughed Mrs. McKinnon, handing him a plate. "For the lads. Just the fat end left and me about to slice it between them."

"Then I've arrived in the nick of time. I doubt so much cake would be good for them," he replied solemnly withdrawing an envelope from his jacket pocket. "I've brought your letter, Frank. Since its purpose is to say good things about you, I'm afraid it's very short. I'm not at all convinced that consorting with Dr. King at your tender age is altogether wise."

"Because he's a politician?"

"Because he's a Liberal politician. In my position I can ill afford to express an opinion either way, but I hope you won't get caught up in the inevitable partisanship of an election campaign and defend the indefensible. The Liberals have blotted their copybooks with this customs scandal and its likely to cost them the election – including our own Dr. King."

"A lot of people seem to think so," Frank said. "Anyway, I'll just be his driver, not his conscience and I need a job. I don't know too much about it anyway. Some Quebec cabinet minister is supposed to have taken a bribe. That's kind of par for the course with those guys. As far as I can tell Doc King didn't have anything to do with it."

"But as a cabinet minister he must have known something. Surely he ought to be held accountable."

"Well, you know, I turn twenty-one this August and get to vote," returned Frank, "so I can hold him accountable at the ballot box. I'll probably vote for Mr. Sims."

"The socialist! Frank, I may have to take that letter back."

"Where I grew up most of my neighbours were union folk – or trying to be."

"The unions are one thing, Frank, but the Labour Party is quite another. It's simply a tangle of ill-thought-out good – and not so good – intentions. You know where they can lead. "

"At least it'll keep the rest of them honest," observed Jimmy who had recently joined the Cranbrook Courier's editorial staff and felt that he could speak with authority on matters of integrity.

"In any case," the minister remarked as he rose leave, "I hope you will be as forthright with Dr. King as you were with me. He's no fool and cannot abide a dissembler. Despite my reservations I wish you luck with the interview, Frank. Thank you again for the tea, Mrs. McKinnon. Mrs. McKay asked me to tell you the flowers were particularly lovely this morning. No doubt I'll see you in church this evening which is more than we can expect of these two."

Next morning Frank arrived at Dr. King's office a half hour early just as Harry Bennett was unlocking the front door. Once inside he handed Frank a broom and told him to make himself useful. "We had a committee meeting here Saturday," he said.

The constituency office had been converted from a shoe repair shop in 1916 when Dr. King won election to the British Columbia legislature. Little had changed since, apart from the cardboard notice in the window which now read

James Horace King MD
Member of Parliament

Ancient wooden chairs lined both walls, and the original counter still formed a barrier between the front room and an inner office behind an opaque glass door. On the wall to the left was a framed print of King George V in the uniform of an Admiral of the Fleet.

While hard at work sweeping up an impressive pile of cigarette butts and crumpled paper, Frank decided to ask the question many people in Cranbrook were wondering. "So, what's this customs scandal all about, Mr. Bennett? As far as I can make out it's either the worst thing to ever happen or just a terrible misunderstanding – depending on which newspaper you read." Harry laughed. "Why don't you ask the boss. You might even get a straight answer."

Frank was searching for a dustpan at that moment when a loud "Hah!" came from the office behind, causing him to suddenly straighten up and bang his head on the solid underside of the counter. The sound, which had been impressive and possibly amplified by the counter's hollow interior, brought the author of the exclamation quickly through the door. He looked down at the motionless Frank. "By God, I've killed him!"

"Call the doctor," Harry remarked dryly, "You're going to have to hire him now – if he can see straight enough to drive."

So there you have it – pure Frank. First there's The Fight – which gets him fired, which puts him in need of a job right away or Jenny will never speak to him again. Which takes him next morning to The Victoria for flapjacks with his friend Bob (where he first hears about the circus). The order comes just as Pinky turns the corner off Garden Avenue, sending Bob scurrying out the back door. Now Frank has two orders of flapjacks to dispose of, which keeps him in the café an extra twenty minutes – long enough for Sean Gourley to take delivery of the two McLaughlin-Buicks and drive them from the CPR station to Hansen's Garage. Meantime Frank finishes his flapjacks, decides he better head up to the Cranbrook Brewery to put his name down for brewers' apprentice. But first he tries that trick of flipping his hat which takes him into the arms of Mrs. Mayor Roberts. So, instead of heading directly north via Cranbrook St., he decides to go west on Baker to tell Bob this funny and embarrassing thing that just happened to him. Which takes him, a block and a half later, past Hanson's where he spies the McLaughlin-Buicks and learns about a job driving former cabinet minister and local big shot, Doctor Horace King. And then, to top it all off, Doc King hears Harry take a dig at him about straight answers and yells "Hah!" causing Frank to bang his head on the underside of that counter. So of course Frank got the job.

The Boss

After Doc King had examined Frank's skull, pronouncing it as solid as a rock, he ushered him into his office and sat him in the worn red leather chair in front of his desk. Frank took to him right away. He could see there was none of the 'big man' about him even though he was far and away the biggest there was in the East Kootenay in those days. One thing he didn't much care for though was the way he marked everyone down as a vote for or against. Although, if he lost the election, he'd go back to being a country doctor again, and he knew it.

When I try to picture Doc King I have very little to go on but here's what I come up with. Slightly intimidating veteran of a hundred political battles slowly stuffing tobacco into his pipe, striking a match on the underside of his desk, then puffing thoughtfully while giving Frank the once over. I have no idea if Doc King smoked a pipe. There's no sign of one in any of the pictures – certainly not in the painting of him done in the nineteen fifties. You could tell that his eyes, sharp and piercing, were his most commanding feature because the artist framed them with a fine pair of bushy black eyebrows. He had a strong jaw with a cleft chin but, being in his late seventies, his face sagged a bit. Overall, you'd say even-tempered, sense of humour, grandfatherly. In a newspaper photo taken twenty-five years earlier the eyebrows were considerably less bushy, but the eyes were definitely sharper, the mouth a bit meaner. He had the look of a moderately powerful corporate executive. He'd be a tough negotiator but, in the end, you'd get a fair shake. He was handsome too, like most politicians.

"Tell me, Frank," he said pouring him a glass of water. He had a slow, measured speaking style and a deep bass voice. "Does your accepting this position depend on my convincing you the customs business is all a misunderstanding?"

Frank blushed and examined the contents of his glass. Doc King laughed. "Unfair question," he said, "especially so soon after a blow to the head. Take your time."

"Well, sir, I guess my *vote* might depend on that but not my taking the job. I mean, nobody thinks *you* took a bribe."

"Hah!" Doc King barked for a second time.

"I'm not sure I'd vote for you anyway. I was thinking of voting for Mr. Sims." He had looked up 'dissembler' in Mrs. McKinnon's dictionary the night before.

"Fair enough," said the doctor with an appreciative smile. "Looks like I've got my work cut out for me." He frowned. "This one's going to be a squeaker and I'll need all the votes I can get. But first things first. Can you drive?"

Frank assured him that he could, as well as change a tire in five minutes, and began explaining the inner workings of a McLaughlin-Buick, particularly the significance of the new-fangled oil filter coupled with the vacuum ventilator. Doc King threw up his hands. "Okay, fine! Not my department. I have a meeting in Wardner this afternoon with their campaign committee. Get me there and back in one piece and I'll take you on for a week. If I'm still alive next Monday, you're on for the duration. Fair enough?"

"Sure thing!" said Frank, then, after a sudden thought, "Will you be needing me Friday night?"

"Friday? Oh, the circus. As a matter of fact, I was thinking of attending. Never too soon to start kissing babies. So yes, I will. Showing up in that car will get me some attention too. But that shouldn't get in your way." Noticing Frank's drooping shoulders he continued, "Ah, there's a young lady in the equation."

"Yes, sir,"

"Is she pretty?…. Of course she is. Well bring her along as my guest. Mrs. King would enjoy the company, I'm sure. A new car *and* a pretty girl – I'll be the belle of the ball! Who's the lucky girl?"

"Jenny MacPherson."

"Old Mac's granddaughter! Now there's a strong personality. I'm sure he voted for me last time but he cut me dead yesterday on Baker. She's only eighteen, I believe. My boy, you've got your work cut out for you and no mistake!"

A tinkle of the doorbell alerted him to the arrival of the other chauffeur candidates. "Now there's four votes I just lost," he observed dryly. "Not a good morning so far – four no's and a maybe – I'm still counting you as a maybe. You better make your departure through the alley. Be back at one and make sure the car is in good order. A quick run up Gold Creek Road might be a good idea."

This made Frank stop and look back. Doc King had turned away and was already busy rummaging through a stack of papers. Frank decided it was not the time to disturb him by pointing out that Mr. Mac's farm was up Gold Creek Rd. then realized he would almost certainly know that. It seemed that everybody was conspiring in his favour.

It was a quarter after ten when Frank, a definite spring in his step, walked into the showroom of Hansen's Garage and told Sean that the shiny new McLaughlin-Buick had been transferred to his care. "My congratulations, boyo," Sean said with a mock bow, "and I'll be happy to accommodate you the moment I see that badge." Frank slapped the metal disc onto the counter. "Where do I gas up?"

Squirming with impatience, he endured a second, less theoretical lecture on the care and maintenance of his new charge. "Here are the keys," Sean began, holding up each one separately, "door, transmission, ignition. The transmission lock is down at the base of the gear stick. That's number one. Then choke halfway out, switch on the ignition, stick the ignition key in here, turn it and step on that button to the right of the accelerator with your heel while giving her a touch of gas with your toe. It's a bit tricky at first but you'll get the hang of it. Once she catches, slide the choke in and there you have it. Easy as pie."

"Right!" said Frank, "now where's the......

"Good question – the battery is under the floorboards just in front of your seat. Now, going left to right on the dashboard you have the choke of course, and that vertical lever below it works the fuel vacuum pump. It's connected to one of the cylinders, don't ask me which. But you only need to worry about that when she's cold – otherwise leave it alone. These two levers on the steering wheel - the ignition circuit spark control for advancing or retarding the firing mechanism depending on your load and engine heat, and the light switch – up for bright, down for dim. You work the dash lights with this button here."

"Got it!" Frank said. "Gas?"

"Getting there. Finally, on the far right, we have the battery charge indicator, the clock and the mileage counter. Now she gets twenty miles to the gallon on the open road so you need to watch the gauge if you don't want to get caught short. I'd advise you to get into the habit of checking the gas gauge every time you stop. It's at the back of the car on top of the fuel tank. She's full up right now so you can stop fretting.

"Now see that bonnet ornament up front with the wings on it like a flying donut? If you look closely you can see a thermometer across the hole which lets you keep an eye on the engine temperature. I'd keep some water in the boot if I was you on these hot days. Which reminds me, that crank up there above the windshield opens it up at the bottom for ventilation. Take it for a quick spin. I'll be here if you have any more questions."

Frank told him he was thinking of stopping by Jenny's but wasn't sure how she'd take it. "Who knows how the ladies take anything," Sean grinned. "But I'd give her a call on the telephone first. If a woman has a bone to pick she generally wants to look her best while she's doing it."

Minutes later, this sage advice taken, Frank was turning onto Gold Creek Road, his heart racing in time with the engine. "I was as nervous as a long-tailed cat in a room full of rocking chairs," he'd say. It wasn't the driving, though. Steering it genteelly onto Baker St. and noting with pleasure the admiring glances of several pedestrians – unfortunately nobody he knew – he zipped around the government building and headed past Baker Park and the Auto Camp. It was the prospect of encountering Mr. Mac that had him worried.

Callum MacPherson was every inch a railroad man – all

seventy-five and a half of them. When Mike Wilson had first pointed out 'that old buzzard', Mr. Mac had been sitting down, head bent over a prayer book. It was only when he had come to take his granddaughter home after the first meeting of the Social and Literary Club, standing in the dark street towering over his rust-eaten, mud-spattered 1915 Chevy pickup, that Frank realized Mr. Mac was not one of the wee Harry Lauder Scotsmen but more the Rob Roy caber-tossing type, ruddy-faced, broad shouldered, and altogether grim and menacing.

On that occasion, he had faded into the background and walked timidly home but inevitably Frank had to show his hand, a hand Mr Mac nearly crushed in his calloused grip the following week. "This is Frank, Grampa" Jenny said brightly. "He was brought up Anglican." She laughed nervously. "But we're working on him!"

"I thought you had more sense," was his reply, apparently to Jenny but with eyes, fierce and black above a hawk-like nose, still fixed on Frank.

Mr. Mac was born in 1860 in Fort Garry which became Winnipeg in the province of Manitoba after Confederation. He was nine when Louis Riel began the Red River Resistance and twenty-three when the CPR hired him as a fireman. For the next three years he shovelled coal into locomotive furnaces between Toronto and Winnipeg before moving up to engineer and following the tracks west to Calgary where he married and started a family.

Years later, Mr. Mac's son opened a hardware store in Cranbrook. He had a daughter in 1908, the only one of three to survive infancy and then, in 1915, went off to war. When he and his wife died of the Spanish Influenza in 1919, leaving behind the eleven-year-old Jenny, Mr. Mac, now a widower, bought a small farm on Gold Creek Rd and took her in.

Despite seven months of courtship, this was the first time Frank had ventured alone to Mr. Mac's lair. On his three previous visits he had been driven by Bob in company with his girlfriend Eileen and found Jenny waiting for him at the garden gate. On all other occasions he had been happy to meet her in town. Now, despite being armoured in his shining McLaughlin-Buick and bucking along between rows of sunlit pines, the thought of himself as knight errant on route to his lady love was only faintly comforting. Nor was it long lived.

His nerves caused him to misjudge the tricky left turn into the farm entrance requiring a quick downshift to climb a short, steep rise. He almost stalled, then managed to recover – but not without a loud backfire just as he reached the front gate. With no one in sight, he was foolish enough to sound his horn, a robust claxon, before catching sight of Mr. Mac himself, not ten feet away, bent frozen over a row of cabbages. He slowly straightened up, a wicked-looking hoe in his fist.

"Now what the devil…? Oh, it's you. Why don't you get out of that thing and come to the door like a civilized person. What have you been up to anyway…robbing banks?"

"Hello sir…." Frank began, getting out just as the screen door swung open and Jenny stepped through, letting it slap behind her.

"Jennifer," said Mr. Mac without turning. "It's one of your young men. Looks like he's been robbing banks. Of course, if he can't keep a steady job that may be the only course open to him."

Frank coloured. "Was Mike Wilson here?"

"Sure he was. The gate's open, Frank. We can't seem to keep them out. It's a steady stream all day long."

Frank looked up at Jenny standing at the top of the porch steps, enjoying his discomfort. She was wearing one of her blue town dresses and carried a small, beaded handbag. She certainly looked her best, he thought anxiously. "Well, I was wondering if Jenny…."

"Says he wants to give you a ride into town, Jennifer. Joy riding in a stolen car more likely. Where'd you get that thing anyway – looks like a hearse."

Frank was glad of the opening. "Doc King got it for his election campaign. I'm his new driver."

"Doc King!" Mr. Mac exclaimed, viciously hacking some

lamb's quarter. "I might have known you'd hook up with that old pirate. Now look here, Frank Burton, McKenzie King's nothing but a smuggler and a crook and Horace King's no better. Constitution crisis, my sweet fanny! He's just trying to worm his way out of that customs scandal."

Figuring that Frank had suffered enough, at least at the hands of her grandfather, Jenny stepped off the porch and marched down the path. Before Frank could react, she brushed past, wrenched open the front door and climbed in, sitting with folded arms and tight lips while staring fixedly out the passenger side window.

"Now Jennifer, you be home in time to cook supper. Hear me?" commanded Mr. Mac. When Jenny gave no indication that she had, he turned back to Frank. "Better if you had robbed a bank," he said. Then, calling after them as Frank drove away, "Look at it! A hearse! A blessed Grit hearse!"

The Election

Driving into town with Jenny fuming beside him, Frank was hoping the new car, complete with its luxurious smell of new leather, would work its magic, earn him a little respect and maybe an appreciative remark. But the grim silence continued all the way back to Lumsden Ave. before he ventured a timid, "I thought your grampa always voted Liberal…Oh, before I forget, circus is coming to town. Lions, tigers, elephants. Bob and Eileen thought we could make it a double…."

"What makes you think I'd go out on a date with a… a hooligan like you, Frank Burton? Brawling in the street and getting yourself fired!"

Frank had prepared for this. "Ah, come on, Jen. Mike just pushed me too far, that's all. Besides, I got a new job right away, didn't I? Who knows? If Doc King wins it might even lead to something. He was a cabinet minister before and sure to be again…. So, what do you say? Coming to the circus with me?" No mention of Jenny sitting in the back, squeezed between Doc and Mrs. K, while Frank sat up front.

At this point I imagine Frank slowed down and pulled over, possibly in the shade of the big cottonwoods beside Baker Park, or maybe into the roundabout at the entrance to the Auto Camp. Then he turned off the ignition and placed his palm against the small of Jenny's back and slid it gently up and across her shoulders as she resolutely stared out the side window. Her breathing increased slightly and - here's where my imagination gets hazy - either she sighed and slowly leaned back towards him or, more likely, she lurched forward, wrenched the door open and jumped out, slamming it behind her.

Now, I happen to know that there was an occasion, never specified, when Jenny, in anger, slammed a car door on Frank's outstretched hand. This may have been that occasion and if so, the ensuing contrition the reason she ended up agreeing to go to the circus with him. At any rate, the only two certainties are that Frank got the date and, fortunately, the door had not been slammed hard enough to cause serious injury.

However it came about, with or without damage, Frank arrived back at the office punctually at one just as his new boss stepped out onto the street.

"You cut it close, son. Here, put this on." He handed Frank a red and white rosette with King for King in gold letters. "You don't have to vote for me but by God at least you can look like you mean to." He waved away Frank's attempt to open the rear door, got in and extracted a book from his briefcase. As he carefully removed the dust jacket, Frank saw that it was Stephen Leacock's latest collection of humorous essays, Winnowed Wisdom.

With a sigh of pleasure Doc King cracked the spine and settled back. "No short cuts," he directed, "Straight up Baker. Might as well let the public see their parliamentary representative hard at work on their behalf. And try to miss the potholes."

It was a perfect August afternoon with a sharp blue sky overhead, the seventy-eight degrees tempered by a cool breeze. He turned onto Van Horne St. beside the CPR tracks. Beyond was Slaterville, or Scotchtown as they used to call it, with the Sash and Door Company yards. Off to the right were the exhibition grounds where the circus would be setting up next Friday.

The McLaughlin-Buick was running like a top and the freshly-graded gravel road stretched out ahead smooth and straight. He felt a surge of happiness and confidence, a swelling in his chest and a tingling of his scalp underneath his new chauffeur's cap. He bought it for luck the previous Saturday afternoon but hadn't dared to put on until today. He glanced back at Doc King in the rear-view mirror quietly chuckling to himself. He felt like he had taken a giant step forward out of the dirty dead-end jobs in lumber yards and freight depots. Who knew where it would lead?

Happy daydreams of government patronage carried him to the junction of the Fort Steele-Wardner highway. Up ahead the Steeples rose out of the pine forest. It was a grand sight and yet, for some reason, the thought that came to him was that neither Doc King, nor Harry Bennett, had mentioned anything about the terms of his employment or even how much he would get paid. It was a sobering thought.

Frank glanced back at Doc King again. Now he was slumped into the corner of his seat, eyes closed, mouth open, the neglected Leacock tipped open at his side. Maybe this was supposed to be a volunteer job on behalf of the party with his reward coming after they'd won. If they won. He tried to remember the details of his interview with Harry and later with Doc King. Neither of them had mentioned money, he was sure of that. Harry called it a job but that didn't mean it was a paying job. Doc King called it a position which didn't help and sounded worse. Those chauffeurs would have been looking for real jobs, wouldn't they? Or maybe they were counting on patronage after the election – driving for the post office was supposed to be a good one. He'd heard you needed connections to get in there.

Well, he was stuck now after making a big deal out of it with Mr. Mac and Jenny. He'd look a damn fool if he backed out – a damned fool with no job. He could ask, of course, but he wasn't so sure he wanted to know. He'd just have to stick it out and do whatever he could to help his boss win. "Sure," Frank thought, "him a cabinet minister and I'm the guy who's going to make all the difference!"

He thought back to what he'd read about the customs scandal when he and Bob had been studying the papers at the Victoria. There had been stories, mostly in The Herald, about customs officers accused of taking bribes to turn a blind eye to liquor smuggling. First Prime Minister King had been forced to fire his Customs Minister. Then in June a report had come out confirming the whole department was rotten with corruption, most of the guilty being Liberal appointees. That brought down the government and now they were trying to get back in with half the country thinking they were all crooks.

Behind him, Doc King gave a loud snort, opened his eyes, closed them again and slumped further down into his seat. A small drop of spit had formed in the corner of his mouth, and he began to snore. He had said the election was going to be a squeaker and looked worried when he'd said it. Well, he didn't look worried now.

Suddenly a white tail jumped out of some bushes and Frank hit the brakes. Doc King lurched forward but caught himself in time. Pretty quick for an old guy. "That'll be the turn off by those ponderosas," he said. "Try to find a gentler way to wake me next time, will you son?"

Nowadays Wardner is a sign beside the highway indicating a grassed-over hillside on the west bank of the Kootenay River. Like Fort Steele and, despite having a smelter and extensive lumber operations as well as rail and road crossings, it missed out on that all-important terminus. In the mid-twenties though, it was still a cosy little town with one main street, two hotels, two general stores, an ice cream parlor, barber shop and drug store. Clustered around it were two schools, three churches, a cemetery, post office, and police station. Beside the river were two acres of land taken up by train tracks and the Crowsnest Pass Lumber Company. Most of the workers lived alongside in small company houses while the grander residences bordered a pretty decent golf club on a bench higher up. Its members and their wives were the citizens most likely to vote for Doc King.

"Drop me in front of the International, Frank," he said. "Park and come in through the parlour. You might as well start your education right away."

The parlour was dark, empty, and smelled of stale beer. A small chalk board on the counter announced that the Orange Lodge would be meeting at 7pm sharp. Beside it a large cat, also orange, was peering into a gallon jar of pickled eggs. He reached up and batted the top egg down, watched it wobble around in the cloudy brine and bob back up.

Frank found the meeting room and went in. Six men sat at a table with Doc King. "Pull up a chair," he said with a wave of his hand. "Gentlemen, this is Frank Burton, my driver. He's our problem in a nutshell."

Frank froze briefly on his way down, then sat. Doc King laughed, joined to varying degrees by the others. "Sorry, son, but you asked for it. Frank here told me this morning…. Let's see, how did you put it? 'I'm not sure I'll vote for you anyway. I was thinking of voting for Mr. Sims.'"

Ten pairs of eyes narrowed as Frank pretended to examine the grain of the tabletop. "Now last year," Doc King continued, "it was just me and Rutledge, the results as expected. Even with Sims running this time I'd be reasonably confident of winning, except this damned customs nonsense has turned it into a real horse race. A certain number of our traditional supporters are going to register their disapproval by taking a holiday and another unknown number are going to sidle up to Rutledge, making the outcome uncomfortably close. Then there's young idealists like Frank here. Normally, we could let him have his fun knowing that in time he'll come over to our way of thinking. But this time around, gentlemen, I'm damned sure we are going to need at least some of the firebrands like Frank here to realize that Rome wasn't built in a day, slow and steady wins the race, and you can't make a silk purse out of a sow's ear. I'm not sure that last one fits but you know what I mean."

The men examined Frank. "Why'd you hire him then?" one of them asked.

"Because he can drive." Doc King said. "How many men at your mill are going to vote for me, Howard?"

"That's different."

"On the other hand, I happen to know you spend an awful lot of time arguing politics with that foreman of yours. As for me, I'm going to be spending quite a few days cooped up in that car out there with my young friend here. Maybe if I can talk him round, I'll figure out how to get his comrades on board too."

Frank, his face reddening, looked up. Then he grinned. "Well, sir," he said, "if it's all the same to you, I'll do my best to get your vote for Mr. Sims."

The Job

The idea of a twenty-year-old chauffeur holding his own in a political debate with Doc King got a pretty good laugh and everybody relaxed. After that they more or less ignored him. When the meeting broke up, they shook hands all round. A couple of them even wished him luck.

The beer parlour was filled with men just off work from the lumber yard when Doc King came through with Frank. There was a brief pause in the flow of talk as he entered. Several of the older men greeted him with friendly smiles and some got up to shake his hand. The younger ones gave him no more than a glance before resuming their conversations. As he crossed the room Doc King smiled broadly, calling out to a few by name while moving steadily forward and ushering Frank ahead of him.

They had almost reached the exit when a large man wearing oil-stained dungarees rose unsteadily from his table, lurched forward and blocked their path. "Give us a speech!" he demanded. "Speech!"

Frank heard his boss utter a muffled curse as he made a half-hearted attempt to squeeze past. "Speech!" the man repeated, his tone vaguely hostile. A couple of his friends began to clap, and another said, "Come on Doc. Just a few words, no harm done." He pushed a chair towards him and called out. "Boys! Doc King here has something to say."

"Speech!" his companion echoed.

Doc King stepped up onto the chair. "Gentlemen! I have been asked to say a word or two about the upcoming election." He had a resonant and pleasant voice that filled the room without effort. "But first, on behalf of my leader the Honourable Mackenzie King, I want to congratulate you on your contribution to the development of British Columbia and the entire country. Your diligent labour and the rich bounty of our great Dominion will increase our prosperity throughout the decades ahead and in doing so will bring an ever-growing standard of living to your families."

Another voice, as resonant and pleasant in its own way with a strong Yorkshire accent, came from the back of the room "While the bosses skim off all the cream!"

Doc King went on over the laughter as though he had not heard. "And when your working days are over, let me remind you that a Liberal government is committed to providing an Old Age Pension that will secure the needs of your sunset years."

"You lot have been promising that since the end of the war," came the rejoinder from a short, wiry man in a worn black suit. "I'd say a vote for Labour is more like to get it done."

"All a vote for Labour will accomplish, my friend," Doc King retorted, "is getting Mr. Rutledge elected and he's no friend to the working man."

" At least he's no bribe-taking crook which is more than we know about you and your bunch!"

Some of the men laughed and nodded their approval, but most seemed to think this was going too far. One of them, a man in his fifties, spoke up. "Doc's been taking care of our families long before you showed up. We'd all be dead of typhoid if it wasn't for him."

"I'm not so sure anything would kill you, Sam," Doc King replied, drawing a laugh. "That was a long time ago now. Hard times for sure. But good times are here, I hope. Thank you for your patience, gentlemen."

"I'm getting rusty, Frank," Doc King observed, as he settled into the back seat. "First, I give a speech worthy of a slow day in the House and then I almost lost my temper. I'll need you to earn your pay as my sparring partner." Much to Frank's relief, he leaned back, closed his eyes and fell asleep, leaving him to ponder the exact amount of the pay he was supposed to earn.

On Tuesday they drove to Moyie Lake in company with Mrs. King who had been invited to an Eagles Ladies Auxiliary tea. "I'm along as my wife's special guest," Doc King explained. On the way down, his wife was full of ideas about redecorating the dining room of their house in Ottawa while he tried to divert her attention to the scenery. Finally, he threw up his hands as if warding off evil spirits. "Aren't you counting our chickens before they've hatched, Nellie? Things are bad enough without you riling up the election gods."

"Oh you always say that. You haven't lost an election in fifteen years."

"Sixteen years and this time I mean it. We're more likely to be moving out than buying a new sideboard. Still," he added, not wanting to abandon all hope, "the men are a toss-up between me and Rutledge, a few going to Sims. But the women are a different story. They put me over the top last year, bless 'em."

An hour later, on their way home, Doc King's blessings had changed to curses. "That damned woman should have been wearing war paint! Then I'd have seen it coming."

"I thought you handled it quite well, dear," countered his wife in a soothing tone. "It was your own fault, you know. You shouldn't have asked how Murdo was."

"How was I to know he was dead, damn it?"

"Because it's your job to know such things and please don't swear in front of Frank. He'll begin to feel sorry for me."

"I was in Ottawa, for…. heaven's sake."

"Which was precisely her point, I believe. You were his doctor, you went away to Ottawa, and he died."

"I don't believe for a minute it was because I didn't know Murdo was dead. She was lying in wait for me. They all think I'm mixed up in the customs scandal and I'll be goddamned if I know what to do about it!"

"Horace!"

On Wednesday, Frank was put to work cleaning the constituency office, washing the front window, painting the door a bright Liberal red and washing the car. On Thursday he spent a hot and dusty day ferrying families of the Cranbrook Board of Trade the four miles to a picnic at Jimsmith Lake.

About two in the afternoon he pulled in for another pick up in front of the constituency office. Leaning against a lamp post with a smirk on his face and wearing a candy-striped jacket, white trousers, and a straw boater, was Mike Wilson. Beside him stood Jenny looking lovely in a blue polka dot dress, a cloche hat pulled down to her eyebrows.

Mike quickly opened the rear door, handed Jenny inside and slid in beside her, telling Frank, "Take your time, my good man, we're in no hurry."

"Frank!" Jenny exclaimed as she caught sight of him, "I didn't know…. Mike, you told me…. Frank, he told me his car was in for repairs and we'd be getting a ride with a friend."

"Every word of it true," Mike declared, his hand on his heart. "At least I hope Frank is your friend. I know he's mine, despite our differences."

By this time Frank had recovered and stifled an impulse to renew acquaintances with Mike's jaw. "Hello Mike," he said as he calmly steered out onto Baker. "Glad to see your old man gave you a day off for once. It's tough being stuck in that dirty lumber yard six days a week. Which reminds me, Jen, it's all fixed for the circus tomorrow night. We can watch them unloading tomorrow morning too if you want. The boss won't need me until about nine thirty, so we'll have time for breakfast too. That is if the elephants don't stampede."

He laughed at the thought – and again at the expression on Mike's face. "I hear one got away in Edmonton last week, two more in Calgary. Should be quite a show. Too bad you'll be hauling lumber, Mike."

Frank kept up his needling chatter all the way to the lake, dwelling on the pleasures to be anticipated at the show the next night, once again neglecting to tell Jenny about their double date with the Kings.

"Well, here we are. See you tomorrow morning, Jen. Seven fifteen sharp. Bob and Eileen are coming too – don't be late!" He stood watching them walk away, waving when Jenny looked back. She laughed and said something to Mike who didn't appear to find it all that funny.

Next morning Frank was up at five thirty, helped Mrs.

McKinnon make the first pot of coffee, grabbed a slice of toast for himself and ran all the way down to Hanson's Garage. He got out the hose and sprayed off yesterday's dust, gassed up, wiped down the seats and headed out to Jenny's.

He wondered how he was going to break the news about her being stuck in the back while he chauffeured up front. He supposed he'd casually mention it sometime in the morning and hope with all the excitement she'd not think too much about it. Maybe he could persuade her it was an honour, but he doubted it.

As the farmhouse came into view, he remembered the sight of Jenny and Mike the day before, looking like they belonged together, a pair of movie stars, the perfect couple. How was he supposed to compete with that? With a surprising burst of homesickness, he heard his mother voice – "Well, Frankie," she'd say with a small sigh, "That's a bridge we'll have to cross a little further down the road." He remembered her sitting at the kitchen table waiting for her lost husband and suddenly the world seemed too big for him, his dreams impossible and his ambitions downright foolish.

Jenny was standing by the front gate, her chin cupped in her hands, elbows resting on the No Salesmen Allowed sign. She was dressed in old riding boots, jodhpurs, a bright yellow blouse and a leather vest. She had one of her grandfather's red handkerchiefs tied around her neck and a battered bowler hat on her head.

"You're going to stampede the elephants in that outfit!" he said as she slid into the seat beside him. Then he saw the look on her face, heard the edge in his voice and the phoney laugh that came after it and realized it was coming from the bottom of a very deep hole he had just dug for himself.

"Aw Jen," he said, "I was only joking. You look great."

A few minutes later, Jenny staring grimly ahead, it hit him that the last time they'd been alone together, they had driven into town in the same painful silence. At least then he'd known how to get out of it. But now, without understanding how it had happened, he had burned up all the credit he'd earned the day before. Here he was right back to being a jackass again. He'd hurt her feelings with his big mouth and had no idea how to take it back. What a heel. She'd be better off with Mike. As if reading his mind, Jenny said quietly, "Mike told me he might be there." And Frank was left to work out the train of thought that had brought her to that remark.

To make matters worse, the first thing Eileen said as she climbed into the back seat was, "Nice outfit, Circus Girl. Wish I'd thought of that." Jenny gave a wan smile and darted a quick look at Frank then turned back to the window. Eileen and Bob exchanged glances and joined the uncomfortable silence.

To break it Eileen said, "I hear you're going to the circus with Dr. and Mrs. King." Bob groaned. Frank had told him they'd have to cancel their double date but had sworn him to secrecy until he'd told Jenny.

Frank kept his eyes on the road. Jenny looked at Frank. "Am I?"

"I have to work," Frank said. "Doc King thought…."

"Nice to know," she cut in.

The circus train would be unloading on a spur as close to the exhibition grounds as possible. That would be where the tracks ran between the highway and the lumber yards. The circus had already taken the unprecedented step of cancelling the street parade, obviously worried about more elephant trouble. Still, the grounds were another half mile away, so there had to be some kind of parade, like it or not.

As they got closer, they could see a row of cars parked beside the road. Word had spread about the stampedes in Calgary and Edmonton and there was already a good-sized crowd with more hurrying up. Occasional cheers could be heard further up, dogs barking, and horns honking. Across the road was the circus train, thirty-two cars long, stretched out a quarter mile behind the engines.

Usually, Jenny let Frank go around to open her door because it was an innocent way of taking his hand and holding it for a step or two. This time she was out as soon as he braked and began walking briskly towards the train. Frank jumped out trying to catch up but stopped short at the sight of Mike Wilson's Studebaker near the head of the line. None too silently, he cursed.

When she reached Mike's car, Jenny stopped too and looked back at Frank. As he came up he saw that the wan smile was back. He opened his mouth to say something about Mike, probably the wrong thing, when Bob did it for him. "Looks like your other boyfriend is lurking about the premises – uninvited. When are you going to flip a coin on those two boys?"

"Bob!" exclaimed Eileen, pushing between them and taking Jenny's arm. "You just cut that out! Come on, sister, let's go see the tigers." They hurried off and disappeared into the crowd.

The Stampede

There are quite a few versions of the Cranbrook Elephant Stampede – about as many as there were elephants in fact – although even that number varies from eleven to seventeen. By the time I got to hear Frank's it was thirty years later and he had it down pat. When people started writing about it in local histories, he'd poopoo them, saying, "What do they know? I was there!" This is Frank's version.

About three hundred people came out to watch the unloading, kids playing hooky with a fair sprinkling of grown-ups, most of them hoping for a stampede, to heck with the consequences. They were trying their best to make it happen too, jammed right up against the tracks, peering into the stock cars until the roustabouts shooed everybody back so they could set up the ramps. You could see the circus people on the other side of the train having their breakfast on long trestle tables. There must have been over five hundred all together. Most looked like ordinary folks, what you could see of them, which makes sense when you think about it. Everybody was dressed in overalls, even the women – although some of them looked mighty pretty and you could tell they'd look even prettier dressed up in their pink tights.

The train had a big CPR locomotive and coal tender up front. Pete Dallas, the engineer, was leaning out of the cab window hoping a bit of the glamour would rub off on him. They always brought the horses out first to pull the wagons down off a whole string of flat cars. Everything that couldn't walk had to be on wheels, all the freight trucks loaded with tent canvas, ropes, poles, the fancy carved side-show wagons and wild animal cages. The elephants were in the next three, then sleeper cars and the caboose. It was a regular city they'd set up and take down practically every day.

Somebody blew a whistle and a flood of men, big fellas, their sleeves rolled up, came through between the cars and started opening them up. It was a heck of a noise what with the crashing of the doors and the stamping of feet, the cars swaying with the animals inside pushing, jostling against one another, trying to be first down to get at the water tubs.

They ran the horses over and hitched them to the equipment wagons and the cages with the lions and tigers inside. The shutters were closed but you could hear them roaring. When they pulled them off the flat cars the crowd started cheering, car horns honking, dogs barking. You'd think the circus men wouldn't like it, but they didn't seem to mind a bit. They were used to it – all part of the show. But that was nothing to what happened next.

They brought some camels out first and after they'd been led off, the seventeen elephants started coming out, stepping gingerly onto the ramps. They'd pause, like actors making an entrance and waiting for the applause, which they got.

Frank had seen circus elephants lots of times before and always got a kick out of how big they were. There were three men at each ramp, two in front and one behind carrying long thin sticks that they tapped against their sides to keep them moving. The one closest to him was a big female. She came down real slow and graceful and then stopped and he could have sworn she looked him straight in the eye. She was wearing a piece of red cloth across her back like a saddle with "Myrtle" written on it in blue letters.

It must have been less than a minute that they looked at each other but it felt longer. Then the circus hand prodded her to move on, but she stayed put, still looking at him. A hard whack on the rump started her down the ramp, still watching Frank. It gave him the funny feeling she wanted him to do something, like help her to escape. He tried to edge through the crowd to follow after her but just then he got distracted, everybody did, by a big ruckus that started up right in front of him.

A pack of stray dogs was hanging around the edge of the crowd and Eddie Stroble the city dogcatcher had driven up in his truck. He had a big iron cage in the back with a couple of dogs already inside, barking away fit to kill. Eddie always showed up at parades and picnics looking for easy pickings. That's how he made his money, from the fines people had to pay to get their dogs back.

This started the other strays going and what with the crowd cheering and the car horns blaring every time an elephant came down, it was quite a racket. The older boys and a pair of girls who might as well have been boys, Frank thought, the way they were carrying on, had edged in closer while the roustabouts were busy with the elephants. So naturally some of the dogs went in with them.

There was this one dog, Ralph –big haystack of a dog, that belonged to Frank Stevenson who was a big fellow himself, foreman down at the city works yard. The two men were pals so Eddy would leave Ralph alone which, along with his size, made him top dog and full of himself. Ralph was a smart dog too and never bothered people, but for some reason he decided he could take on an elephant. Naturally he picked the biggest one, named Tommy. The elephants weren't shackled. The keepers just counted on them being used to crowds and doing the same thing day after day without thinking.

They got Tommy down the ramp and onto the road where he came face to face with Ralph. The closest roustabout had been walking backwards in front and didn't see Ralph until he almost tripped over him. He whipped around with his stick in the air and yelled at Ralph to get the hell out of there and took a swipe at him which didn't go over too well. Ralph started barking and jumping stiff-legged, side to side, the hair along his back standing straight up. It was a sight.

Tommy stood there for a second, looking dumbfounded. He even started to go backwards up the ramp until his hind leg slipped off. That must have scared him because all of a sudden, he lunged forward and reared up, letting out one of those trumpeting elephant yells like in the jungle movies. For a second everything stopped dead while people were making up their minds whether or not to be scared. Asking themselves, was it all part of the show or were they about to get killed?

The circus men answered that soon enough. Tommy came crashing back down, landing on the foot of the fellow swatting at Ralph. He let out a terrific scream. Tommy swung around and slammed the second fellow against the side of the box car. He let out a scream too. Then just about everybody started screaming and trying to get out of the way. Except Ralph who stood his ground like a trooper, barking his head off.

Frank started to look around for Jenny...

Frank always used to say that – "I started to look around for Jenny" – and it wasn't until Granny J explained to me what had happened between her and Frank, how she and Eileen had gone on ahead and were nowhere in sight, that it became clear Frank looking around for Jenny wasn't about which side of him was she standing on but "Where the hell did that crazy dame get to and is she about to get trampled by an elephant"? So Frank had to slide around that part.

Frank started to look around for Jenny but just then all the other elephants came rushing down the ramps, bellowing like, well, like elephants, and charging madly off in all directions like in that Stephen Leacock story. One came straight at him, eyes blazing, his tusks looking about ten feet long. It was the first but not the last time that happened to him and it was never a pleasant experience. He jumped out of the way and ended up in the middle of a pack of kids – the ones who had been up front with the dogs. They were looking pretty scared, but then Frank was too.

He yelled at them to follow him and they all, Bob included, scrambled behind Eddy Stroble's truck. Eddy was in the back holding a dog by the collar and trying to jam him into the cage. Once the elephants started going by, though, Eddy let go of the collar and jumped down behind the truck. The next thing they knew, the other strays were flying out of the cage and going every which way and Eddy taught those kids a few words they had not heard before.

Once he'd caught his breath Frank started to worry about

what had happened to Jenny and ran out from behind the truck. The last three or four elephants were only then coming out of the boxcars and, with no one to round them up, headed over to the water tubs. In the end, only six of them really took off – Tommy, Tilly, Trilby, Freida, Myrtle, and the baby, Charlie Ed. Nobody knew for sure which way they'd gone but a couple of minutes later a bunch of circus men on horseback came riding up, a regular wild west posse, and galloped away in the direction most people were pointing, along the tracks and through the cemetery.

Meanwhile Frank had lost all interest in the elephants and was practically in tears. People were coming out from cover, including Bob who'd ducked behind a tree. But there was no sign of Jenny. By a miracle it looked like nobody had been hurt except the two circus men. It was hard to move because after the posse had taken off, they started to corral the remaining elephants, the horses, and camels to get them back to work. The circus still had two shows that day and they weren't about to let a little thing like a stampede stand in their way. All the spectators were pushed out of the way and Bob and Frank ended up pinned against a fence.

It took them a while to squeeze their way along to where they guessed Jenny and Eileen had gone. The crowd was buzzing with excitement and relief and the realization that they had a great story to tell. That came later for Frank. He still needed to find Jenny and there was no sign of her. Then it occurred to Bob they might have gone back to the car looking for them, so they turned around and made their way back.

It turned out that when the stampede started the girls were a little way ahead by the second boxcar beyond the spot where Ralph started in on Tommy. They were watching a different bull elephant coming down a ramp, probably the one named Trilby. When Tommy reared up and took off, Trilby followed him. It seems likely he was the one that nearly ran over Frank and those kids.

Jenny and Eileen made their escape in the opposite

direction and almost immediately ran into Mike Wilson. He always claimed he'd just happened to be there but Frank believed he'd been hovering around looking for a chance to horn in. To be fair, Frank would have done the same. Once the elephants had scattered, the two girls wanted to find out what had happened to their boyfriends. With the circus men rounding up animals and starting to unload the rest of the cars, that was easier said than done so they decided to cut down an alley and around to where the cars were parked. They came to Mike's Studebaker first and he suggested they wait there while he went back to search. That was how come Eileen was sitting in the rumble seat and Mike was handing Jenny into the front when Frank and Bob came running up.

Frank always glossed over what happened next and concentrated on the main story - the roundup of the less adventurous elephants and the desperate hunt for the six escapees. And we'll get to that, don't worry, but while we're here I might as well tidy things up with help from Granny J. who told me her side of the story years later.

"When the boys appeared with their hackles up, looking exactly like that dog Ralph, Frank and I were already out of tune with each other. After his fight with Mike we'd managed to patch it up – I told them they were both a pair of hooligans – and in a moment of weakness I agreed to go to the circus with him. But I was beginning to think having two strings to my bow, or two beaus on a string as Eileen liked to say, was all very well but the time had come to make up my mind.

"It seemed Frank and I were always at cross purposes. I knew my indecision was at the back of it and there always seemed to be something to set us off. I had put a lot of thought into my circus outfit that morning, a lot more than the old polka dot thing I was wearing the day before at the picnic - if he'd only known it. But being a man, he hadn't. Eileen spotted it right away, of course.

"Now I know everybody loved Frank so this may come as a surprise but sometimes he could be extremely annoying. We all are at times but Frank's way of being annoying, and entirely unconscious of it at the same time, was particularly maddening. If something was bothering him he wouldn't put an ounce of effort into thinking about what it might be or what he could do about it. Not on your life. He'd feel sorry for himself, get depressed, then take it out on me. Nothing terrible, he never raised a hand to me in all the years we were married, which is more than I can say for some men around here. I wouldn't have put up with it, but anyway that wasn't Frank.

"Instead, he'd poke at you, little jabs that were supposed to be good natured teasing and if you didn't like it that's when the 'I was just' came out. "Ah, come on Jen, I was just joking. Where's your sense of humour?" Then I knew something was bothering him and it usually took hours and a big argument to pry it out of him. Sound familiar? As far as I can tell it's the basis of most marriages since Adam and Eve. Men!

"When Frank made fun of my outfit, he hurt my feeling and I knew him well enough to see something was bothering him, and of course it was. He was jealous of me and Mike and who could blame him? If he was making up his mind between me and some other girl, I'd have been jealous too. But there wasn't any other girl. There was only me, Jenny MacPherson, and he was asking me to turn myself over to him, to have his children and to feed them whatever he could put on the table. He didn't see it that way naturally. It was all hearts and flowers to him. Men are the romantic ones when you come down to it. Biology makes us practical.

"I was in love with Frank even then. He was the sweetest man I'd ever met and very nice to look at - which they used to tell us didn't matter much to us girls. A lot of hooey made up by homely men for their own comfort if you ask me. How many ugly movie stars are there, for heaven's sake? But to tell the truth I was just as much in love with Mike who was equally handsome and nice and one of the most eligible bachelors in town. And don't forget, I was only an eighteen-year-old small-town girl. Not a very sophisticated one at that – even by Cranbrook standards.

"I was the only one in my set who took Frank at all seriously as a prospect and beginning to think I was making a darn fool of myself. It was certainly taken as gospel among my friends that I was a flirt. Nobody minded that too much, we were all flirts to some extent, having our bit of fun before settling down. But nobody doubted for a minute that I'd wind up marrying Mike.

"If we had gone to see them unloading the circus by ourselves that morning we might never have gotten out of the car. It makes me laugh to think of the pair of us squabbling in the front seat of Doc King's sedan until that herd of elephants came charging past. But Bob and Eileen coming with us made that impossible. Bob, in a rare moment of insight, managed to press his finger right on my sore spot.

"We'd been driving in deathly silence from downtown when Eileen broke the news that Frank had arranged for me to go to the circus with the Kings. Then Bob told me I should flip a coin between Frank and Mike! That was the last straw so when we arrived at the train I jumped out of the car and started off with Eileen before I could rearrange that pointy nose of his. Away we scurried, right into the middle of that famous stampede."

The Show

Eileen, who could never stay mad at Bob for long, climbed down from the rumble seat and ran over to throw herself into his arms. Jenny resisted the temptation to do the same to Frank, a choice made easier by the expression on his face. Unfortunately, she couldn't see the smirk on Mike's or she might have realized his glower was not directed at her. As it was, she decided to call it a day and got into Mike's car. Frank took a step towards them and then stopped. "Ah to hell with it," he said, "I need some breakfast," and walked back to his own car.

At the Victoria Café they were already talking about the stampede, one of the elephants having put in a brief appearance on Baker St. Frank took a stool at the far end of the lunch counter. Mavis saw the look on his face and said, "Let me guess, Jenny ran away with an elephant…. ah, honey," she added when he brushed away a tear from the corner of his eye. "What happened?"

"She might as well have," he said. "She dumped me. We had a fight, I guess. I mean, I don't really know what happened. I was just joking around about the outfit she was wearing and she got mad at me and then we got separated when those damn elephants went crazy. She ended up with that son of a bitch Mike Wilson….and she went home with him."

"So, what was she wearing?" Mavis asked, getting straight to the point.

"Some dumb circus outfit, jodhpurs and a red scarf, a bowler hat and God knows what else. I mean yesterday at the picnic – did I tell you I had to drive them out there? – yesterday with Mike she looked like a movie star and then today she was dressed up like some damn clown."

Mavis laughed. "Boy, you sure don't know girls. She's so pretty she could look like a movie star any day of the week. I bet she didn't think twice about what she wore with Mike. But with you she really thought about it. She wanted to be *in* the movie with you, you dumb cluck. Let me get you a coffee and doughnut.

"Well, it doesn't matter now. Looks like she's made up her mind. I should have known I couldn't compete with all that money."

"Oh boohoo, what a cry-baby! Drink your coffee and tell me about the stampede...."

An hour later, feeling better for having poured his troubles into Mavis' sympathetic ear, Frank was driving to Kimberley with Doc King. Harry had arranged for him to shake hands with the men coming off shift at the Sullivan Mine.

On the way Frank announced that Jenny wouldn't be coming to the circus with them. He had to shout because the Wycliffe Road was awful. It had been a wet spring and a mass of ruts had been gouged into the mud. Now, well into August without rain for a couple of weeks, it was like concrete. Frank was beginning to wonder if the wooden wheel-spokes would hold out.

"Can't come!" Doc King yelled. "She sick? She looked fine yesterday with Chuck Wilson's boy – what's his name? He's old enough to vote, isn't he."

"Mike."

"Mike. Mike. I always say it twice and mostly I remember although it's not as easy as it used to be. Damn these elections! What happened? Had a falling out?"

Frank didn't answer.

"None of my beeswax, eh? Fair enough. Too bad though. I was looking forward to our double date tonight."

Eager to change the subject, Frank said, "I'm not so sure there'll be a show." And at the top of his voice, for the second time that day, he told his stampede story, ending with, "Who knows if it'll go ahead, or they'll all be out hunting elephants."

"Oh sure there'll be a show! I remember when I was a kid back in New Brunswick they were setting up in a thunderstorm and the tent pole got struck by lightning. Killed a man and set fire to the tent. Show still started, right on time."

Kimberley was a jumble of small shingle-sided company

houses and flat roofed commercial buildings. The mine was just beyond, surrounded by a maze of railroad tracks. You wouldn't know to look at it, but the Sullivan was on its way to being one of the world's greatest mines. They shipped twenty billion dollars' worth of galena – ore full of lead, zinc, and silver - to the Trail smelter starting a few years before Frank was born and kept on until three years before he died.

The road brought them onto a wide ledge carved across the base of Sullivan Mountain with a row of workshops and sheds along its length. Down the slope the powerhouse was pumping coal smoke out of twin stacks accompanied by the steady thump, thump, and clang of the Pelton wheels. A streak of sunlight shimmered across the tailings pond, the light breeze stirring rainbow-coloured swirls onto the oily surface.

They pulled up close to a low, clapboard building. As they walked towards it, a tall man in a brown suit came out and stood on the steps waiting for them. "Howdy, Doc. What's this I hear about an elephant stampede?"

Doc King laughed. "You should ask my driver. He was there."

"Hello, Mr Ironsides," Frank said, sheepishly. "Remember me?"

"Frank, is it?" Then to Doc King, "I took him on as a yard man a year or so back. Did a pretty good job but always late. Not good in the train business."

J. A. Ironsides was the CPR train master. He had come up to the mine on business that morning by the early train and had just received a telegram asking him to return right away on account of a stampede of circus elephants. "Damnation, I miss all the fun. What happened? Anybody hurt? Damage?"

For the third time in three hours, Frank told his story – a shortened version this time. It was then he realized that he would be telling it for the rest of his life. When he finished, his boss said. "Unless there's a train in the next hour, you'll be quickest to come back with us - after I've shaken a few hands."

It was well after four by the time they dropped Ironsides

at the Cranbrook station. As they drove away, Doc King said, "That reminds me. Nellie ordered me to invite you and Jennifer to supper." Before Frank could answer he went on, "You're coming and that's that. It's been a depressing enough day as it is and I'll be damned if I'm going to spend supper trying to satisfy my wife's curiosity about your love life. You can tell her to mind her own business if you like – although I wouldn't advise it. Just look pale and interesting and keep working on your pork chop."

Mrs. King decided to take Frank's declaration that Jenny was under the weather at face value and instead had him tell the story of the elephant stampede for the fourth time. "I was in Fink's this afternoon and the shop girls knew all about it. It seems to have been a well-attended event. I got the latest from Ruth just now. She got it from the ice man. Ruth's our cook whose Chicken Marengo you're devouring."

Ruth's story, via the ice man, which from then on became part of Frank's, was that most of the elephants were found milling about among the stacks of finished boards at Burns Lumber and rounded up with little difficulty. The truant six on the other hand had scattered far and wide leaving a trail of destruction through the back yards of Slaterville and the tombstones of Westlawn Cemetery. At least one was sighted on Baker St. by a number of people, a number which, to Frank's annoyance, increased with each passing year. The rest disappeared into the maze of ravines and dense bush south of The Slough, heading in the direction of Jap Lake.

The Slough was a marsh south of town and is now a bird sanctuary called Elizabeth Lake. As for Jap Lake, it was so-called when Rikuzo Futa, known as Harry, set up a sawmill there around 1900 and hired some fellow countrymen. It's now called Hidden Valley Lake.

"You'd think six elephants crashing through the underbrush would be easy enough to track," Mrs. King remarked later as Frank was driving them to the circus. "But perhaps they had to get to work, setting up their tents and what not. I imagine the elephants haven't gone very far in any case, but I don't suppose we'll be seeing any tonight. And we'll just have to postpone our double date."

That's when Frank, always ready to spill any beans handy, confessed that he and Jenny were no longer a couple and that he'd rather skip the circus, mind the car and "think things over."

"Oh, you poor boy," Mrs. King said as her husband snorted. "The course of true love never did run smooth, the poet said. And please, call me Nellie." Then, because she was certain, like everyone else in town, that Miss Macpherson was destined to become Mrs. Wilson, she added, "Remember, there's more fish in the sea than ever came out of it?"

"There may be a lot of fish," Doc King said, "but damned if there's many that taste very good."

"Horace!" his wife declared, "I believe the strain of this election is making you vulgar."

"That may very well be, my dear," he replied, helping her out of the car. "So long, Frank. Come along, my tasty wife. Let us add a touch of glamour to these tawdry proceedings. Why hello, Mrs. Hicks. My, what a beautiful baby!"

Frank parked the car within sight of the entrance, pulled his cap down and slumped into his seat. He watched Doc and Nellie make their way slowly through the crowd towards the ticket booth, Doc slapping men on the back and shaking ladies' hands. Most of them seemed glad to see him although some turned away at their approach.

A few minutes later, after they had gone inside, Frank noticed Dr. Rutledge, the Conservative candidate enter the scene as if he had been awaiting their departure. He was a homely man, stocky, broad shouldered, of average height with a pudgy face, a few strands of hair plastered across the top of his high forehead, a wide nose, and a Charlie Chaplin moustache. But for all that, he looked as reliable and honest as the day is long. Since he was a vet, Doc King used to say the Tories had asked him to run so he could take care of all the jackasses in the government.

Dr. Rutledge was also accompanied by his wife, a motherly woman wearing a flowery print dress and a jaunty red hat perched atop a mass of curly grey hair. Their reception was about the same. After they had gone inside, three older boys arrived, probably high school students, and started handing out flyers. As they passed his car, Frank reached out and snagged one.

VOTERS of
EAST KOOTENAY

ARE you satisfied in your own mind that the CUSTOMS SCANDAL of the late Liberal administra tion is an ESTABLISHED FACT, proved by a Committee of 4 Liberal, 4 Conservative and 1 Progressiv members of the House of Commons?

DO you realize the extent to which the Public Purse of our Dominion has been robbed during the pas few years by the maladministration of LIBERAL MINISTERS?

IN the face of this public exposure of rottenness and corruption do you believe that LIBERAL EX MINISTERS and LIBERAL POLITICIANS are honest when they would tell the public that there no such thing as the Customs Scandal?

DON'T LET THE CONSTITUTIONAL QUESTION AND OLD AGE PENSION TALK BLIND YOU.

VOTE FOR RUTLEDGE
AND CLEAN GOVERNMENT

Frank read the flyer twice. Then he carefully folded and tucked it into his pocket, got out of the car, locked it, and started walking. He had a couple of hours before the circus let out and decided to head across to Chinatown. Along with a number of restaurants, laundries and the homes of the families that ran them, the three blocks east of the train station also had the remnants of the old red-light district - not that Frank was looking for chop suey, a clean shirt, or paid female companionship but it was usually the liveliest part of town on a Friday night.

Frank's destination was frequented by the town's few coloured people, mostly CPR porters and the men working the sleeping and dining cars. Known to Frank and his friends as the Green Door because of its otherwise unmarked entrance at the rear of a house, it was the nearest thing to a jazz joint that Cranbrook could boast and a lot better than the gloomy beer parlours on Baker. The alcohol sold there came out from under the counter and was served in small glasses. The tables all contained a bottle of soda to be poured out if a cop came in looking for trouble. Opium was sold there too. They were raided two or three times a year mostly for appearances sake. Sometimes, especially in the summer, there was a real jazz band passing through from Calgary or Vancouver. The rest of the time somebody was trying his luck on a battered old upright piano.

Frank and Bob had taken girls there a few times in the early days of their friendship, when they were still unattached, but he hadn't been there since taking up with Jenny. She and Eileen weren't the kind of girls you took to a place like that. Bob's uncle had a Victor phonograph and they listened to the latest tunes on his front porch instead – Louis Armstrong playing with Fletcher Henderson, Paul Whiteman, and even Fats Waller – the kind respectable citizens disapproved of and called nigger music.

He walked quickly, head down, deep in thought. The words on the flyer had brought home to him that Doc King was probably going to lose the election. Which meant he was stuck in a dead-end job of very short duration with absolutely nothing to show for it, no connections, no patronage job in the post office, no future. In fact, as Doc's driver, he would be branded a Liberal and unlikely to get any kind of a government job, ever. Doc King was the only elected Liberal in the province, for God's sake, so it was going to be Tory blue right across the board for years to come.

"Ah, to hell with it," Frank said for the second time that day.

Clark St. was quieter than usual, probably because of the circus but as he got close he could hear what sounded like a pretty good band and someone singing the last few bars of Sweet Georgia Brown. There was applause and whistles and just as he reached up and grabbed the doorknob they started in on How Come You Do Me Like You Do. He recognized the tune from the

Marion Harris record Mavis had brought over one evening last June. The singer sounded familiar too and as he stepped inside and looked toward the stage at the far end of the room, there she was. The band had a guitar, cornet, trombone, and a stand-up bass and Mavis Weeks was leaning against the piano, her hip up against the keyboard, her arm across the top propping up her head as she looked down with smiling eyes at the young, handsome, and very black pianist. He was grinning up at her while she sang.

"When soon this morning, I come rapping at your door
You kept me waiting like you never did before
That's a sure sign brown skin
I'll never rap no more, no more
How come you do me like you do do do?
How come you do me like you do?
Why do you try to make me feel so blue?
I ain't done nothing to you
You might be the meanest man in town
But I'm just mean enough to turn your damper down
How come you do me like you do"

Frank was flabbergasted. Apart from himself, she was the only white person in the place. He sat down at the back and listened. He thought she was terrific. When she finished, the band put down their instruments while the piano player stood up and he and Mavis sang Swing Low, Sweet Chariot. You could tell they'd practiced it.

Just before they finished Frank got up and left. He'd almost reached the end of the alley when he heard his name. Mavis came running up. "I saw you leave, Frank." She smiled nervously. "Didn't you like my singing?"

He blushed. "I...No, I thought you were terrific. It's just... I'm working tonight. I got to get back to pick up Doc and Mrs. King - at the circus."

"Not because of Reuben?"

Frank played dumb. "Reuben?"

"The piano player, the guy I was singing with. The guy you think is my lover."

"Isn't he?"

"Not all wishes come true, Frank. I just met him this afternoon. That was his wife on guitar. They'll be gone tomorrow."

"Oh."

"I figured everybody would be at the circus tonight, so I took a chance. Let's make it our secret, ok? My dad would kill me if he found out."

"Sure."

She stood in front of him for a minute in silence, looking down at her shoes. Then she said, "I got to get out of this town, Frank. It'll kill me even if my dad don't. You ever think about....? No, I guess you got a reason to stay. Well, let me know if things change. A girl could use a little company out there in the wide world....",

He watched her walk back towards the club. Her dress had a fringe across it, about eight inches below the waist. He watched it swing back and forth as she walked away. He thought maybe he'd fallen in love. Again.

The Hunt

Frank's head was still spinning an hour later when he picked up the Kings outside the circus. They were among the last to leave and came out surrounded by a crowd of well-wishers, all sharing the good feelings generated by clowns, bareback riders, trapeze girls, and lion tamers. As Doc King helped his wife into the back seat, Frank noticed he was holding one of Rutledge's flyers.

"This is what the opposition calls playing hard ball. That son of a…"

"Horace!"

"Sea cook, my dear, sea cook. But he made a mistake with this little poison pen letter. Hershmer - that's his agent, Frank – always had a nasty streak. Invective may go down well with juries but people don't like seeing a neighbour urinated on in public, especially when he's enjoying a night out with his wife."

"For heaven's sake Horace, any more of that and I swear I'll walk home!"

"An idle threat, my dear. It's such a lovely evening, Frank can drop us off at Garden Avenue and we'll stroll home from there. Besides, urinating is a perfectly natural act which I do believe we all commit from time to time."

"Pity me, Frank," his wife said, laughing, as she exited the car and slipped her arm through her husband's. "It's a terrible life he leads me."

"I'm up to my eyebrows in paperwork tomorrow, Frank," Doc King said, "so you can take the day off. But I've a hankering to go to church in Fernie on Sunday. We'll set off at nine and stop for lunch in Elko on the way back. Make sure you have a good breakfast."

It had been quite a day, starting at 5:30 am. There had been his quarrel with Jenny, an elephant stampede, campaigning in Kimberley, supper with the Kings, a drive to the circus, and maybe falling in love with Mavis Weeks. He found himself yawning through mostly empty streets as he drove to Hanson's Garage.

Negotiating the turn off Baker toward the alley entrance, he thought he caught sight of something large moving in the shadows and twisted around to get a better look. A sudden jolt and the crash of his lunch pail as it hit the floor told him he'd caught the curb with his rear tire. He swore, got out and crouched down on one knee to peer under the body. Fortunately, the tire hadn't burst and the axle seemed intact. As he began to stand up again, he heard what sounded like the scuffle of a foot and felt a waft of warm breath on the back of his neck.

Frank froze. It wasn't uncommon for bears to come into town, looking for garbage. He began to inch around towards the tire iron strapped to the spare when he felt a hand gripping his right shoulder. A mugger, he thought. Reaching across his body he made a grab with his left hand and jerked quickly down, simultaneously springing up and turning to face his attacker, right fist cocked.

The shock of coming face to face with an elephant while holding on to its trunk caused Frank to throw himself violently backward, banging his head hard against the metal landau ornament on the side of the car. The elephant disappeared in a burst of stars and the night went black.

When he came to, the elephant was gone. But in the split second of eye contact, he had recognized Myrtle. She had the sweetest, gentlest face, he thought.

Frank had no idea how long he'd been out although judging by how cold he felt and the condition of the blood on the back of his head, it had been a while. He made only a brief search for the elephant. After circling the block and encountering neither man nor beast, he steered the car into Hansen's yard, locked it and set out for home on foot.

That should have been the last twenty minutes of a very long, hard day, but it wasn't. On the corner next to Mrs. McKinnon's boarding house he saw Bob leaning against his uncle's Ford, engine running. Beside him were Harvey

McDougall and fellow boarder Jimmy Wainwright. Harvey was a member of the baseball team they'd put together for the Dominion Day tournament.

"Hurry up," Bob called, "We're out hunting elephants. There's still six of them running around somewhere. Harv says one was spotted near downtown." And as Frank got closer, "Is that blood? What happened?"

Frank told them about his encounter with the mugger turned elephant which got barks of laughter from the boys and an excited "Come on!" from Jimmy. "He can't have gone too far. Did you see which way he went?"

Frank guided them to the alley behind Hanson's, explaining that he hadn't seen anything after the back of his head had made contact with his car. They looked around for tracks but couldn't find any on the hard-packed dirt although Frank did manage to locate a large pile of dung. As he scraped it off his shoe with a stick, it occurred to him that the elephant must have stood there for a while, looking down at him.

They began to drive slowly back and forth along the streets close to the southern city limits figuring the elephant would likely have headed towards open country. When they reached the corner of Dennis and Fenwick they were rewarded by the sight of a small crowd standing beside a broken fence. Jimmy jumped out and extracted a notebook and pencil from his jacket pocket. "Cranbrook Courier," he declared, "What happened?"

An elderly man wearing pyjamas and a threadbare dressing gown stood at the centre of a ring of spectators, lantern in one hand and a leash, with dog attached, in the other. A large woman in a pale-yellow nightgown watched from an upper window. The dog, a cheerful and alert hound of indeterminate breed, wagged his tail and sniffed each of the newcomers in turn.

"An elephant's what happened!" the man said and waved his lantern towards the dog. "Hector here spotted him. Broke open the gate and just waltzed in and went after my beets. I was upstairs about to get into bed when Hector started barking fit to bust. I stuck my head out and there he was. Biggest thing I ever saw. Enough to make a man swear off drink -except I don't," he added with a quick glance up at the window.

"Enough to make a man start, I should think," Frank said.

"I yelled at him to quit eating my beets but he didn't and so I ran downstairs, lit my lantern here and grabbed a pot and spoon - with the idea of beating on it to scare him off. But what with me charging out onto the porch and Hector's barking, he spun around like a top right up on his hind legs, came thumping down again on all fours and made off. He did it just like we seen at the circus last year except he was bigger than any of them. Instead of leaving by the way he came, the damned thing went straight through my fence! The name's Alfred Whitmore – w-h-i-t-m-o-r-e - if you're going to write it up."

"Which way did he go?" Harv asked.

"Didn't I just finish telling you? Straight through…."

"He means after he went through your fence," Jimmy explained. "And are you sure it was a he? I mean just how big was he - it? There were a bunch of females who escaped too." He consulted his notes. "Tilly, Freida and Myrtle. If you throw in the baby, Charlie Ed, that's most of them."

Alfred held up his lantern and peered into their faces. "You fellas sure ask a lot of damn fool questions. Are you sure you're from the paper? First off, I have no idea which way he went and I have no idea if it was a he either, because I wasn't inspecting his undercarriage at the time. It was damned big! Now is this going in the paper or not?"

"Sorry, Mr. Whitmore," Jimmy said. "This will be old news by the time the paper comes out next Thursday. But thanks for the help. We'll let you know if we catch him – or her…" With that the four boys jumped into their car and raced off.

"Hey, come back here, you damned fool!" Alfred Whitmore yelled after them, but they didn't hear him above their own whoops of excitement. He wasn't yelling at them anyway.

Taking a line from the beet patch, extending outward from the hole in the fence, they continued south down Fenwick.

The smooth gravel road soon turned into a rough wagon track which led towards a field containing about a dozen quietly grazing cows. It looked like a dead end.

By now it was close to midnight and since there was no moon, they couldn't see much beyond the circle of the car's headlamps. As they turned around to head back to town the lights shone briefly along a track skirting the fence. It dipped to a ford across a small creek where the water had spread out forming small puddles and a wide patch of mud.

"Hold on a second," Frank said, "there might be some tracks down there."

Sure enough, after manoeuvring the car to illuminate the soft ground on both sides of the creek, they saw a line of six shallow depressions a little over a foot across, a couple of inches deep, with scalloped edges like giant lily pads. "Big all right," Frank observed, "It's gotta be Tommy, "He pointed west toward the Slough, "Looks like he went thataway."

Past the creek, the road turned off into a small gravel pit, too shallow to hide an elephant. While they were looking about for more tracks they heard heavy panting behind them and Hector appeared out of the darkness, tail wagging, leash trailing behind.

"Maybe he's part bloodhound," Frank said, releasing him. "Hey, Hector, go get 'em!"

"Hold on, Frank," Bob objected. "I'm not driving down there in Uncle Walter's car."

Frank began to protest but Hector cut him off with an excited explosion of barks as he bounded forward and vanished into the night. "Come on, fellows!" Frank cried and plunged after him. His three companions hesitated for a moment, then stood and watched him go.

Frank didn't realize he was alone until he had run past the gravel pit and well outside the car's circle of light. Once his eyes got used to the dark, however, he found it was not quite pitch. The hills to the southwest were still outlined by the faintest glow, the sky thick with stars and the branches of the trees outlined by the lights of the town. In the gloom he saw a dark shape sitting on the path ahead, breathing hard.

"Well, Hector, looks like you and me are the last men standing." Hector wagged his tail, watching him expectantly. Frank pointed into the darkness "Okay, fella, go find him!"

The dog stuck his nose in the air, sniffed, thought about it for a few seconds, whined softly, huffed, then sat down and began to scratch himself. Frank was about to remonstrate when he leapt up again, produced a series of low growls and padded away towards a line of firs about a hundred yards off. Frank trotted cautiously after.

When he reached the end of the field, Hector lay down, paws forward like a sphynx, and regarded the deeper darkness of the trees. Frank came up behind. As his eyes adjusted, he gradually made out the object of Hector's attention, a large black shape a short way into the woods. Whatever it was emitted a whooshing sound as if air was being expelled from a funnel which, Frank suddenly realized, described it perfectly.

Peering intently, he saw the faint gleam of two large, wide-set eyes staring back. With a gulp of fear, he remembered what Ironsides had told him that afternoon. "They say there's fewer animals more dangerous than an elephant on the run. They're not afraid of you and they know you're trying to catch them." Frank slowly raised his hands, palms forward, and took a step back. Tommy – it couldn't be anyone else – whooshed again, turned ponderously away and disappeared into the trees.

An elephant pushing his way through a forest of fir and pine interspersed with alder, clumps of thimbleberry and devil's club is easy enough to follow, even in the dark. Frank kept well behind and Hector even farther, whining his reluctance and stopping every few yards to look hopefully back the way they had come.

Even though Frank managed to keep within the swath of crushed bushes and broken saplings that marked Tommy's passage, it was a miracle he avoided serious injury while enduring the slashes of face-high branches and bangs to his shins from tumbles over fallen trees. After about half an hour he realized his folly. His shoes, suitable for a chauffeur, were wholly inadequate for bushwhacking down a forested slope, first damp, then sodden, as it reached the margins of a swamp. Twice he stepped into mud well above his ankles. His suit - his only suit - needed for the Sunday drive to Fernie - fared even worse, by the sound of it.

Stopping to wipe a trickle of blood from his face with his tie, he looked down at Hector. "I don't know how good your eyes are, old fella," he said, "but I can't see a goddamned thing."

He couldn't hear anything either. Tommy must have stopped, found a piece of open clearing, or possibly, he thought with a giggle of exhaustion, quietly tip-toed away. Either way he was lost. Feeling around for a relatively dry patch of ground, he sat down, leaned back against what he hoped was a solid tree trunk, put an arm across Hector's shoulders and tried to think what to do next.

A couple of hours later he awoke from a dream that had something to do with Jenny and, alarmingly, just as much to do with Mavis. Hector was still beside him but was now sitting rigid, quivering, whining softly and staring off into the trees. The dog had brought Frank up out of his dream but it was the elephant, looming out of the mist just fifty feet away, who dashed it clear out of his mind.

What he saw then would come back to him every now and then at the tail end of a dream. There was something downright primeval about it - the first light of dawn, dew dripping from giant ferns, the smell of the skunk cabbage – it could have been a dinosaur standing there. Herbivore, of course.

By his size it was Tommy for sure and from Frank's perspective, seated on the ground almost at his feet, he seemed twice as big as Myrtle. They regarded one another, Frank with trepidation, Tommy, who may have been doing it for some time, with a wary tilt of his massive head and a slightly puzzled look.

Frank decided it was probably up to him to make the first move but there was something hypnotic in Tommy's calm gaze that kept him rooted to the spot. A circus elephant, of course, was used to humans. We must be a confusing mix, Frank thought - the bane of his existence, the source of his food, the crowds who cheered when he danced.

By now he was seeing elephants as individuals. Stampeding, they had been identical and terrifying, but Myrtle's sweet face seemed to reflect her own distinct personality and he could see there was something altogether different about Tommy too. It took him a while to realize what it was.

He had a high forehead that sloped up to a huge skull. The bones beneath his grey, wrinkled skin formed hollows over his eyes and so up to a dome rising above his large ears. Every now and then he flapped them gently as though with the rhythm of his thoughts. His tusks were about a foot and a half long, sawn short where they curved upward, blunted at the ends with round knobs. He curled his trunk around a tuft of grass, pulled it up and tucked it into the side of his mouth. His whisk of a tail flicked back and forth.

The difference, Frank realized, was that Tommy was no longer a circus elephant. At least not in his own mind. Standing alone in the forest, Tommy considered himself a wild animal now, his own boss. It was a nice thought, and with that Frank once more closed his eyes.

It took Hector's barking to awaken him a second time. Sitting up with a jerk he was blinded by the sun shining straight into his face. Shading his eyes, he looked around for Tommy. But he was gone. Only then did he notice that Hector's barking was being echoed several times over, somewhere away to his right. He pulled himself up and peered through the trees. Not far off was the western edge of the Slough and running across it at top speed was a pack of dogs followed by four men.

It looked like Tommy had made his way around the swamp and gone farther south towards Jap Lake. The dogs must have picked up his scent and were going full tilt. The men were falling farther and farther behind, stumbling through the clumps of marsh grass and yelling encouragement to the dogs.

Frank watched them go. He could hear their barks growing fainter. As he listened, it seemed that their sound had changed tone, become shriller and more intense. After a while he could hear that it had not faded away.

"Ah shit, Hector," he said, "they've cornered him."

The Scandal

While Frank was engaged in his wild goose chase, all sorts of sightings were being reported all over town and considerably beyond. But one thing is certain. No elephant travelled the forty miles to Yahk despite numerous assertions by any number of eyewitnesses. The most likely explanation for this phenomenon is that once news of the stampede became widely known, via passengers on the west bound trains, more than one elk got transformed into an elephant. So when Frank, still in company with Hector, limped back into town along the train tracks, he arrived at the CPR station just in time for the transmission of Cranbrook's most famous, and least necessary, telegram.

The Cranbrook station had a garden on the west side with a path bordered by zinnias, snap dragons, marigolds, and hollyhocks leading to the side entrance. The station itself was a Crowsnest Style A: two three-story office blocks flanking a gabled hall containing the main entrance, waiting and baggage rooms, telegraph office and ticket counters. CRANBROOK was painted in white at each end.

Frank went in the side door and along the corridor where he made quite an impression on passengers arriving from Fernie as well as those about to embark south to Idaho and Washington. As a particularly good-looking young man, he was used to being noticed, especially by women, but there was something in their glances, downright stares in this case, that seemed different. His first thought was that it was because of Hector who had followed him in, nails clicking on the hardwood floor, tail wagging. Frank grabbed his collar to guide him out but then his own reflection in the etched glass of the pendulum clock beside the baggage room set him straight. He was a mess, a scratch across his cheek, unshaven, blood smearing his tie, shirt tail hanging out, the sleeve of his suit torn in two places, mud splattered above his trouser cuffs, bleary-eyed with lack of sleep. He looked like the town drunk.

"Hey mister, you'll have to take your dog.... Frank! What the hell happened to you? You better come in here. That's Hector isn't it – Al Whitmore's dog?"

"Oh hello, Francis,' Frank said, grinning sheepishly. "That's Hector all right. We've been elephant hunting."

"Me too!"

J. Francis Guimont was the daytime telegraphist, only a few years older than Frank. He had been kept busy the day before exchanging telegrams with circus headquarters in Peru, Indiana trying to get hold of Lewis Reed, their elephant trainer. Failing that he had managed to reach 'Cheerful' Charlie Gardener and Jim Dooley. Dooley was the tour manager in charge of elephants, and Gardener was his boss. They had been in Chicago opening the Hagenbeck-Wallace Show. As it happened, though, they had just left for the training facility in Wichita, Kansas. Finally tracked down there, Cheerful rounded up a crew of elephant wranglers and hired a plane to take them to Cranbrook.

Meanwhile, the circus boss Zack Terrell was supervising the hunt locally. He cancelled the shows scheduled for Fernie that night, sent the rest of the circus on its way south, recruited Ironsides as assistant and arranged for any recaptured elephants to be housed in the local arena.

"Take the load off your feet," Francis said, indicating a swivel chair in the corner. "On second thought, stay where you are, you're tracking mud on my rug. Hector, sit! What gives, Frank?"

Frank gave him a quick sketch of his last thirty hours, leaving out the personal stuff – the break-up with Jenny (if that's what it was), hearing Mavis singing at The Green Door, his last sight of her lodged in a guilty corner of his mind.

"You seem to have a knack for finding pachyderms," laughed Francis, "or them finding you. I've been getting reports from all over. There's even talk of elephants in Yahk which is ridiculous. Look at this damned thing." He handed Frank a yellow telegraph form.

Train Order: 465　　　　August 7, 1926
To: All trains west　　At: Cranbrook
Keep lookout for elephants on track
advise if sighted from first telegraph office
giving location.　J.F.G

"They'll think you've been drinking," Frank said.

"Don't tempt me. I'm heading home for lunch - one of the joys of married life. Speaking of which, how's your pursuit of the lovely Miss MacPherson?"

Frank shrugged and smiled faintly. He watched enviously as his friend tapped out the message, hung his Gone To Lunch sign on the office door and locked up, all with the air of a man who believed the world was treating him right. Falling in behind, Frank wished he had a skill like that and the steady job to go with it.

After the two weary hunters had been dropped off at their respective abodes, Mrs. McKinnon greeted Frank with the same question Francis had, although phrased with greater decorum. He went through it all again, again leaving out the personal stuff.

"You poor foolish boy," she said. "If you're taking Dr. King to church in Fernie tomorrow I sincerely hope you have a second suit. And while I appreciate you taking your shoes off at the door, I believe those socks are making matters worse." Frank had to confess that he possessed no second suit, nor second tie for that matter.

"What do you spend your money on? Not savings I'll be bound." remarked Mrs. McKinnon. "Don't tell me, I can guess. She's a nice young woman and you don't deserve her – no more does young Wilson. Off you go. Take a bath, leave everything outside your door and I'll see what I can do. Get some sleep and I'll wake you in time."

Mrs. McKinnon, who should have had children of her own, was as good as her word. At 6:30 next morning, she knocked on Frank's door, opened it just enough to thrust in a dried, brushed and mended suit followed by a pile of clean laundry and topped by one of her late husband's ties.

"There's coffee, toast, eggs and shoe polish on the dining room table," she said. "The rest is up to you. Don't thank me, I'm charging three dollars extra."

The road to Fernie took Frank and Doc King past Wardner and across the Kootenay River, the main route into the coal mines of the Elk Valley and so east to Alberta. It was the reverse of the way Frank had come by train three years before. He was about to remark on this modest fact when the scowl on his boss' face made him hesitate. "Don't talk," Doc King commanded. "Just drive."

They travelled in silence as far as Elko, Frank concentrating on his driving and managing to cover the forty miles in a very respectable hour and five minutes. The more he concentrated the better he was able to extract some sense out of the chaos that had been swirling around in his brain since the morning of the stampede. Had Jenny really broken up with him? Had she ever been his girlfriend in the first place? What about Mike? What about Mavis! Had she really invited him to run away with her? Whatever he felt about her, if it wasn't love it sure was something. She was a peach. It made him happy just to think about her. A lot easier than thinking about Jenny – getting married, raising a family, tied down....

The road narrowed into a blind curve, with high rock walls scraped out on both sides. Then a nice straight stretch, the valley opening out, a bridge over a creek, the August sun sparkling on the water, some cows in a field, a herd of big horns. He began again. Had Jenny....? What did being in love mean anyway?

He thought about their first time together at the Social Club, sharing the songbook, her warm smell, lavender soap and the trace of mint on her breath. How he'd had to slide away from her a few inches on the bench so she wouldn't feel him shaking, her turning to him with that impish smile.

That time outside the Star Theatre, standing in the dark street, waiting for Bob and Eileen to bring the car around.

"Take your time, Bob."

"Sure thing, buddy…."

"Can I kiss you, Jenny?"

"Sure thing, buddy"

"Jenny…."

"I heard what you said!"

"Well, can I?"

"I already said so, didn't I?"

Then later in the back seat, her body pressed against him, arm around her, head tucked under his chin, fine strands of hair tickling his nose, and the tips of his fingers feeling the swell of her breast under her coat, Jenny letting it rest there maybe half a minute before straightening up, kissing him briskly on the cheek and announcing, "Ronald Coleman sure is handsome!"

Did she do that with Mike? Or more? No Bob and Eileen there to keep him honest…. And what exactly did Mavis have in mind? Boy, she sure was a peach! Not exactly a Presbyterian either by all accounts.

Every once in a while he glanced back to check on Doc King. If anything, the scowl on his face had deepened. That started another train of thought. Monday was the day his probation was over. Was he getting the job or was that scowl because he'd shown up this morning with a scratched face and a sewn-up suit? And what made him think hitching himself to the Liberal bandwagon was such a great idea anyway? Both Bob and Jimmy said Rutledge was a sure winner – a banker and a newspaper man, so they should know. Jimmy said some people were always looking for ways to put a big man down.

If the Liberals lost the election, he'd be out of a job with nothing to show for it. The last nail in his coffin as far as Jenny was concerned. Even supposing she was still concerned at all after what had happened. What exactly *had* happened, anyway?

After they'd gassed up in Elko, Doc King threw down the papers he hadn't been reading. "Say something for Christ's sake! What happened to your face? You look like you were in a knife fight."

With an inward sigh, Frank once again narrated his adventures, starting at his inglorious encounter with Myrtle. By the time he'd got to the telegram, the scowl was gone and they were both laughing. "Thank you, Frank. I needed that. It's been a rough week."

A minute later the scowl was back. "These damn things," he said waving the sheaf of papers and slapping them down on the seat. "They're telling me my goose is cooked – every one of them as gloomy as a graveyard in November. This blasted customs foolishness is sinking us just when the country needs us most. If the Tories get in it'll be big business, high tariffs, and union busting from here to Christmas. It'll tear the country apart.

"Meighan's got a silver tongue all right," he went on, as much to himself as to Frank. "He could convince his granny she's a hippopotamus, but he has no idea how to run a government. All rectitude and fatuity! Mackenzie thinks this business with Byng will pull us through but I'm not so sure. The whole thing's as phony as a three-dollar bill. The simple truth is our beloved leader tried to pull a fast one and Byng called his bluff. Lucky for us Meighan dropped the ball."

Frank nodded sagely. "It sure looks bad," he said with no idea what Doc King was talking about. Me neither - so I looked it up.

At the end of the First World War, the Union government broke up leaving two parties – the Tories and the Liberals - led by Arthur Meighan and William Lyon Mackenzie King respectively. But times were changing and two new political movements came marching over the horizon, the socialists and the Progressives.

The socialists had been around for a while, of course, but they were a fractured bunch and not very effective although they could still determine the outcome of an election by syphoning off votes from the Liberals.

The Progressives were a marriage between farm organizations and anti-tariff, free trade Liberals. In the 1921 election they won sixty-four seats, reducing the Tories to third place. With their support Mackenzie King was able to form Canada's first-ever minority government.

One of the few Liberals seats in BC was Kootenay East. In 1922, they needed a western heavyweight in the cabinet and recruited Doc King, then a provincial cabinet minister. After the incumbent had been persuaded to step down, he was appointed Minister of Public Works. MacKenzie King spent the next three years keeping the Progressives happy with promises of lower tariffs. In the summer of 1925, however, he faced a serious threat which came, not from his political enemies but right inside his own government.

By the mid-twenties, prohibition was still going strong in the States but was either gone or on its way out in most of Canada and had never existed at all in Quebec. This meant that liquor smuggling and the corruption of customs officials that went along with it, was in full swing, especially in La Belle Province. Customs jobs often being patronage appointments, most of the corrupt officers had Liberal connections and the money trail went straight to the top.

The Minister of Customs and Excise was a powerful Quebec politician named Jacque Bureau who had appointed some decidedly shady characters as customs inspectors. The Liberals depended on Quebec for over half their seats in parliament, so King was in a bind. On the one hand he didn't want to upset the francophone apple cart and on the other, he couldn't expect the Progressives, not to mention his own supporters in the rest of the country, to stay on board once they found out Bureau was in bed with bootleggers.

King realized he couldn't keep the lid on too much longer so in September he called an election, hoping to win a majority that would enable him to sweep everything under some convenient rug. Unfortunately, Meighan's Tories were just as big in Ontario as King was in Quebec and when the dust had settled, it was Tories 116, Liberals 99, and the Progressives 24 with a couple for Labour and 4 independents.

As leader of the party with the most seats, Meighan expected to take over. King, however, refused to resign and went to the Governor General, British war hero Viscount Sir Julian Byng, and claimed the right to maintain his government with the continued support of the Progressives - which he got by promising them an old age pension scheme and lower taxes.

Sir Julian was somewhat reluctant to go along with King but felt he had no choice but to follow the advice of his Prime Minister. He also warned King that if he was unable to keep the support of parliament, he (Byng) would let Meighan have a go. By all accounts, King accepted the bargain, no doubt hoping he could ride out the storm.

Alas, the customs scandal just wouldn't go away. In February, parliament set up a committee to investigate. The report came out in June and revealed some top-notch corruption implicating Bureau directly and suggesting that King had known about it all along.

The Tories added an amendment to the report censuring King which, if passed, would have brought down the government. After some back and forth motions and just before he had been backed into an inescapable corner, King slid over to Rideau Hall once again and advised Byng that he should dissolve parliament and call another election.

Byng said, "Not so fast! We had a deal. I'm going to ask Mr. Meighan to form a government."

King went away in a huff, drew up an order-in-council dissolving parliament and brought it to Byng to sign.

Byng still said, "No!"

King returned home, made a few political and mathematical calculations, smiled, rubbed his hands, and resigned. Byng then called on Meighan to try his luck. Meighan could smell a rat, of course, but also felt obliged to accept.

Now here's where things get funny. With only 116 seats, the Tories were shy of a majority and needed to keep the Progressives on board. To make matters worse, Meighan had to appoint cabinet ministers to run the government. Nowadays that would not be a problem but back then newly appointed ministers had to resign their seats and get them back again in by-elections. This was usually a formality but not this time around because if those new ministers resigned, the math told Meighan (as it had already told King) that he might not have enough votes to continue. He should have accepted the inevitable and called an election then and there but instead he foolishly ploughed on.

If you're wondering about the resignation/by-election rule, it originated in England in the 17th century as a way of establishing the sovereignty of parliament in the days when king and parliament didn't get along. Thus, any member accepting a paid position as an officer of the crown had to resign. This was later amended to allow him to accept office and regain his seat via a by-election. Ironically the English parliament abolished this rule in that very year but in Canada they didn't get around to it until 1931.

After accepting the job as Prime Minister, Meighan tried to keep his ministers in place by appointing them without portfolio, arguing that because such positions were unpaid, they were therefore not required to resign. King, conveniently forgetting his bargain with the Governor General and claiming to be outraged by these "illegal" ministers and Byng's "unconstitutional" refusal to heed his advice, called for a non-confidence vote. After only three days in office, the Tories came up one aye short and the race was on.

"Well, that's Mackenzie's problem," Doc King said. "All I have to do is convince the voters of Kootenay East I'm a good fellow and it's in their best interests to overlook the bad company I've been keeping." He laughed bitterly and returned to a scowling perusal of his notes.

The Curse

From Elko, the road to Fernie follows the Elk River for twenty-two miles. It's serpentine now and tortuous then, with blind corners and steep drops to the valley bottom. Frank stopped thinking about his troubles, or Doc King's, and kept his eyes on the road. About halfway there he noticed the temperature gauge on the hood ornament was creeping up and realized he'd forgotten to check the radiator that morning. In fact he hadn't checked it all week.

It was a toss-up whether he'd make it without stopping to cool down the engine or adding more water. He'd meant to bring some along but had forgotten that too. All he had was an empty can in the boot. If the road dipped down close to the river, he could make a dash for some. That would be bad enough but a lot better than being stuck by the side of the road with steam pouring out of the hood.

Frank began looking for a place to pull over, wondering what to tell his boss. That was taken out of his hands a mile later when Doc King looked up from his reading and saw Frank's nervous glances. "What's up, Frank?"

There was nothing for it but to confess. Doc King pulled out his watch. "I can't be late for church, damn it, Frank. People will think I did it on purpose to make an entrance. Better press on and cross our.... God damn it, Frank!" This explosion followed the sudden rush of steam swirling up through the vents at the side of the hood. "Pull over!"

Doc King yanked open his door, stalked out and slammed it behind him. "This is what comes of hiring a goddamned socialist!" he roared. "You're...." No doubt the next word would have been "fired!" but at that moment an ancient Ford came chugging around the corner behind them.

Doc King waved his arms and moved further out into the road. The car stopped and the driver reached over and rolled down the passenger side window. Frank saw Doc King lean in, say a few words, suddenly pull back and then turn towards him with a look that suggested a second calamity, also his fault. After hesitating a moment he got into the car. As it swept past, he called out, "Christ Church. Be there or else!" Frank caught a quick glimpse of the driver who was laughing uproariously. He was wearing a black suit that looked older than his car, a plaid bow tie and a crumpled hat. His gaping mouth revealed tobacco-stained teeth.

A half hour later, after bushwhacking up and down a steep embankment and pouring a couple of gallons of the Elk River into his radiator, Frank was on his way. His troubles, general and particular, now included imminent unemployment. It reminded him what a cursed town Fernie was supposed to be, having endured a couple of the worst mine disasters in Canadian history, been wiped out by fires twice, and washed away in a flood.

But the last couple of miles into town Frank, ever optimistic, began to feel better. It was very beautiful. The road hugged the river and the valley had opened up to reveal a panorama of mountains, all of them snow-capped even at the height of summer. He crossed the Elk River bridge, and immediately spotted a large church up Howland St. It turned out to be Catholic but right next to it, like a younger sister, was the Anglican Christ Church. It was a small, comfortable looking brown brick building with a slate roof and a large stained-glass gothic window. He could hear the choir inside and decided he had time to take a quick tour of the town.

Victoria St. had the usual shops, restaurants and hotels housed in fine stone and brick buildings, legacy of the fires. He had turned onto Railway St. beside the tracks, lined with a row of coke ovens on the far side, when his own Fernie curse struck. It came in the shape of a pack of dogs, one in possession of a bone and the rest wanting it, which streamed out of an alley and fused into a snarling tangle directly in front of his car. The squeal of his brakes alerted them to their danger and suddenly there were dogs everywhere. With two desperate swerves he managed

90

to carve a passage through the fleeing canines that brought the right wheel of the McLaughlin-Buick hard into a corner of the fine stone building housing the N. E. Suddeby Drug and Book Store.

Frank never said so, but I expect he cried. Unless he swore loudly and threw whatever came to hand at the dogs. Although they may have disappeared by then. An inspection of the axel showed that the car at least was not going anywhere further that day. He managed to back away and park but the sound it made in the process confirmed his fears. It was Sunday too – everything closed.

He sat for a while, numb, telling himself it was all over. No job. No Jenny. A ticket out of town with Mavis, maybe, if she'd still have him. He got out and walked down towards the train station. The thought of showing up at the church and telling Doc King what had happened seemed too much to handle. There was a train heading to Cranbrook in a couple of hours. He bought a ticket and sat outside on the platform. After about ten minutes he swore, got to his feet and headed up to the church.

When Frank arrived, both congregations had already come out of their respective churches and were mingling on the grounds between. Doc King's mood had lightened considerably, and he was laughing and shaking hands all round. He had joined a group of attractive young women who were enjoying the attentions of the great man. He waved and smiled at Frank and motioned him over.

If this was a movie, they'd shoot the next scene from a distance. Doc King, with a gesture of friendly impatience, would walk over to Frank intending to overcome his shyness and drag him across to meet the young ladies. Frank would resist and say something. Doc King would let go of his arm and step back. Frank would point back towards town. Doc King would flap his arms and say something to Frank who would hang his head and then look away. Doc King would walk a few paces away and come back and say something else. People would start to notice. Frank would reach into his pocket and offer Doc King his train ticket. Doc King would take it, look at it and hand it back – you could hear his faint bark of a laugh with a touch of bitterness in it - and then the camera would begin to pull away, up and up, showing the pair of them together, then Doc King walking back to his friends, Frank alone, the congregations slowly dispersing, the two churches, the town, and finally the circle of snow-capped mountains stretching for miles and miles all around – thereby demonstrating the insignificance of man's petty troubles against the vastness of the world.

It was decided that Frank would stay behind, try to get his money back on the train ticket and get the car fixed next day.

"I have a luncheon engagement in Elko," Doc King said. "I'll catch a ride and take the train home from there. Here's another ten for the repairs."

Frank hesitated and, anxious to get it over, said "I guess this is it."

"We'll talk about that later. Banging up the car may not have been your fault. I'll give you the benefit of the doubt on that. As for the radiator business, my conversation with our Good Samaritan turned out to be worth it." He laughed. "That gentleman was your hero, Sims. He's speaking at the Miner's Hall tonight. The son of a bitch actually thinks he can beat me!"

Frank spent the day hanging around the train station where he could keep an eye on the car. He got his money back on the ticket and used it to get some lunch at a nearby café, the only place open in town, it seemed. He decided he'd sleep in the car that night both to save money and to keep it safe. It was a long day with nothing to do but fret.

He spent most of it sitting outside the train station, with a couple of excursions down the empty main street. He didn't feel like going further afield. He was sitting outside the station around six when the night crew came up, four men carrying hefty lunch pails. They eyed him and walked by. Five minutes later the day crew came out and as they passed, one of them stopped.

"You been here all day, mister," he said. "No law against it, don't get me wrong. The name's Vernon. What's up?"

Frank explained, leaving out who his employer was. Vernon commiserated. "You're wise to sleep here. There's bad characters hang around after dark. I'll tell the boys to keep an eye out. Mr. Sims is at the hall tonight. Come along home with me, we'll get some supper and head over." Frank noticed that he took their shared political affiliation for granted.

Vernon was in his late thirties, bald, with a fringe of close-cropped hair and a worried look on his homely face. His nose had been broken some time and been set slightly to the right. He was about Frank's height, a bit heavier and looked tough. His house, a single-story cabin, was at the end of Railroad St. among a couple of dozen others clustered along both sides of the tracks.

After a supper of a small amount of stew over a large amount of potatoes and a steady supply of strong tea, they walked to The Miner's Hall at the north end of town. As they approached, they could see a crowd of men standing outside smoking and talking. There was a handful of women too, standing together on one side.

When Vernon introduced him to some of the men, he mumbled his hello and kept quiet. They heard the banging of a gavel inside and filed through a narrow passage with small offices on each side. The rows of benches were already half full and they found themselves a place near the centre facing a raised platform. Five men and a woman sat behind a table while another man stood beside it and banged his gavel again.

"Brothers and sisters," he said. "I guess you didn't come for our regular business but too bad. Now we've got you, you're just going to have to put up with it." Over the groans he continued, "Sister Hallaran will read the agenda." Forty-five minutes later there were cheers when he said, "Now it's my pleasure to call upon Fernie's legislative representative, Mr. Tom Uphill."

"Buy me a beer, Tom!" someone called out to general laughter and cheers in recognition of his famous fight against prohibition. He was a short stocky man with a pleasant bulldog face and a wide politician's grin. "Tell you what," he shouted, motioning the audience to be quiet. "When we send my good friend Jim Sims here to Ottawa next month, I'll join you all in buying *him* a beer! You've heard enough jawing from me over the years so here he is, the man of the hour, a working man through and through, Jim Sims!"

When a tall gaunt man in a shabby black suit unfolded himself from his chair and stepped forward to shake Uphill's hand, Frank saw at once that it was the Good Samaritan. He acknowledged the crowd with a wave and a shy smile.

"Good to be in Fernie, the home of the working man. I drove here today through your beautiful Elk Valley and a funny thing happened. Now, I drive an old Ford that's seen better days. A lot of miles on her. A little way south of town I come across a shiny new McLaughlin-Buick by the side of the road and there's a cloud of steam coming out from under the hood. An older gentleman steps out onto the road to flag me down and lo and behold it's my opponent, the Honourable Dr. James Horace King!

"Hold on, now," he said as the crowd began to jeer and boo. "Dr. King has done fine service for the East Kootenay. He's been a good doctor and if he'd only stuck to doctoring we'd all be better off today. Trouble is, he didn't stick to it. He fell in with the wrong crowd and now he drives around in fancy cars with fancy chauffeurs."

He pronounced this last word with a bit of a sneer and a country accent that got a laugh. Frank squirmed as Vernon gave him a look.

"He drives around with a fancy chauffeur," Sims continued, again drawing out the word, "who doesn't even know enough to keep water in his radiator!" This time he allowed the jeers to rain down while Vernon, keeping a straight face, quietly nudged Frank. "My point being," he went on after the laughter had subsided, "here's a fine piece of machinery, made by Canadian workers, on its way to ruination from the lack of proper care and attention, just like this great country of ours. Isn't it time we had a working man representing this riding in Ottawa, a man who knows what he's doing, who knows what other working men need? A man who won't lose his way among the rich and powerful and all the corruption that goes with it!"

He spoke for another half hour, outlining the evils of the Liberals in particular and capitalism in general and what he and his colleagues were going to do about them – all of which Frank would have heartily agreed with had he been listening. He longed to get out of there, go back to his car and curl up in the back seat. He was only held back by the thought that suddenly standing up in the middle of the hall would surely reveal him as the incompetent chauffeur and subject him to even more cat calls and ridicule.

It was over at last. They all stood up and sang For He's a Jolly Good Fellow, slowly filed back down the passage and out into a surprising shower of rain. Frank was probably the only one not glad of it as he could foresee a night huddled in damp discomfort. They walked quickly back to the car and parted with an invitation from Vernon to an early breakfast. "Don't take it to heart," he said. "Mr. Sims didn't know you. Nobody knew you was there. You got to admit, it was a good way to start a speech." They shook hands and Frank continued down Railway St., hunched up against the warm rain. At least the worst is over, he thought, but of course, this being Fernie, it wasn't.

At first Frank thought the dogs had come back. He saw a dark shape trying to get into the boot but when he yelled, a man stood up and faced him. Another man stepped out from the shadows. Frank ran towards them yelling to get the hell out of there, but they didn't, and before he knew it the nearest had him twisted around, his arms locked behind and the second was punching him in the stomach, expertly, high up, knocking the wind out of him. Then he passed out.

"He's waking up," he heard his brother Ted say. Then a young man was peering down at him while another propped him up against the front wheel. He held a vacuum flask and offered him a mug of sweet tea. "I guess we didn't do a very good job of watching your car, mister," he said. "You, okay? Vern'll have my scalp in the morning. They dropped these."

95

He held up Frank's lunch pail and Doc King's satchel stuffed with papers. "And we found this on the back seat. I guess they used it to pick the lock." It was a lady's nail file. "Don't suppose you saw their faces."

Frank shook his head and winced. He felt a sharp stab in his ribs as he shakily stood up and felt for his keys. They were still chained to his belt.

"We got here before they could rob you. You can spend the night in the station if you want."

Frank said he'd stay with the car. They helped him to stretch out in the back and he quickly fell asleep. A few minutes later he woke with a start, but it was someone handing him a worn grey blanket and an old chair cushion. "Don't worry," he said. "We'll keep an eye out this time."

He woke up several times in the night as the trains came and went. After a while the sky cleared and he saw stars, still no moon. His ribs ached and he had to keep changing sides. Each time he woke up he thought about finding Tommy watching over him. Somehow it made him feel better about things.

By morning he had stopped worrying. He reminded himself he had come west three years ago with no clear destination in mind. Maybe Cranbrook was just a stop. He thought about Mavis and snuggled down deeper under the blanket for warmth. Boy, what a peach...

As the day came, cars started to drive by. He got out and looked at the front end again. Maybe it wasn't so bad. The fender looked all right except for a large dent. He was glad he hadn't walked away. Vernon would help him find a good garage. Then he'd head back to Cranbrook, maybe pick up a week's pay and move on. "To hell with it," he said out loud.

It turned out Vernon was the yard foreman. He told him the boys would fix the car in the machine shop. "I'm doing it for you, not your boss," he said. On their way back to the yard he said, "If things don't work out, you could come back here. There's always work either here in town or at the mines."

The car was done by noon. They hoisted it up and levered

the axel straight, made up a couple of spokes on a lathe and replaced the broken ones. One of the men mixed some paint and touched up the fender so it hardly showed. It made him want to vote for Mr. Sims even more.

The Hunter

The car ran fine. Taking no chances, he fuelled up in Elko and again at Wardner where the gas jockey had been quizzing customers from Cranbrook for the latest news.

While Frank slept through Saturday afternoon and night, the circus had packed up and gone south to Spokane, leaving some of the camels behind. It turned out that two of the runaways, Tilly and Charlie Ed, were the stars of the show, the former trained to dance the Charleston and the latter an indispensable part of the clown show.

"Some Indians tracked down a pair yesterday. Cornered them at Gordon's ranch up Wycliffe Road. There's a reward, so those boys should be in for a good payday."

Frank hurried on, wondering if he could intercept the elephants as they came into town. After his encounters with Myrtle and Tommy he had begun to take a personal interest in them. He wanted to add all six to his collection, like baseball cards.

At the corner of Van Horne and Marpole, a boy of about eight told him they'd already passed by on their way to the arena, adding in disgust that his Ma wouldn't let him go with them. Not similarly constrained, Frank decided to make a quick detour. He knew he should report to the office but wanted to postpone the unpleasantness as long as possible. An hour wouldn't make any difference one way or the other.

There was a faint animal smell coming through the arena windows, but the doors were locked. He climbed up on some crates to peer in. A man stepped out of a side entrance and Frank flattened himself against the wall. He looked the other way, lit a cigarette and strolled off, leaving the door propped open. Frank jumped down and slipped inside.

The sweet odour of hay and sawdust mixed with dung got stronger as he moved down the passage between the stands and out into the centre of the arena. At the far end, where the big gates opened to the outside, he could see the captives by the dim light, corralled into a makeshift pen. He spotted Tommy right away, towering above the two new arrivals. At the far end, three camels regarded him with haughty stares.

A deep silence hung over them, the elephants occasionally flicking their tails and slowly flapping their ears, heads down, lost in thought. He felt a tingling in his scalp as if he'd stepped through into another world. He stood entranced for a couple of minutes until a voice came out of the stands behind him. "Who let you in?" It was Mr. Mac.

Still in his what-the-hell mood, Frank said, "I might ask you the same question," leaving out the sir for the first time ever.

Mr. Mac smiled and grunted. "Same as you, I imagine. Paid the man a dollar."

Frank let that go, walked up and sat down beside him. They contemplated the elephants in silence. One of the camels, slowly chewing his cud, began to urinate loudly. After a while Mr Mac said, "Looks like the mountain's finally come to Mohamed after all these years."

Frank gave him a questioning look and Mr. Mac told his story.

Callum MacPherson's dream began in a Toronto bookstore in the late winter of 1886. He was twenty-six years old, still a CPR fireman, working the overnight to Winnipeg. It was a long run and could get boring between shifts. He could usually get through an average-sized novel on a single round trip and was in the habit of purchasing one at a store just north of Front St. This time he knew what he was looking for because he'd read about it the week before in the Free Press. And there it was in the window, dressed in a lurid yellow dust jacket and propped up against a wire stand. A placard proclaimed it "The Most Amazing Book Ever Written!" Two men in khaki shirts and pith helmets, a third, bare-headed, standing beside a mysterious native in a red hat and one large silver earring were gazing at a sinister witch-like creature beckoning them forward. King Solomon's Mines, H. Rider Haggard, Raiders of the Lost Mines.

That night, off shift as the train steamed through the endless scrub of Northern Ontario, Callum MacPherson was tramping through the African veldt in search of lost treasure. He fell asleep just after the thrilling events at the edge of the desert and for the first of many times over the years, dreamt of putting a bullet between the eyes of a massive, charging elephant.

It was a dream he was determined to fulfil, although life almost immediately took him in the opposite direction, to Calgary, where he became, in rapid succession, an engineer, a married man and a father. In the meantime, he read everything H. Rider Haggard wrote, and anything else he could find about the depths of the Dark Continent.

Twenty-three years later his chance came. His son had married and moved to Cranbrook to become, with his father's backing, the junior partner in a hardware store. The birth and early death of a grandson took his wife there for an extended visit. He announced that the time had come to spend the small 'Africa Fund' he had been putting aside over the years. "Well, be careful," his wife had said.

Next day, Callum boarded the transcontinental for Toronto. On a limited budget, he used his connections to reach New York, then took a room near the docks on Water St. near Rutgers Slip. After a couple of day's search, he used his railroad experience to secure a position in the engine room of the S.S. Guelph of the Union Castle Line which would be sailing for Cape Town in two days' time. Lastly, he went looking for the biggest damn gun he could find

In the hunting department of Abercrombie and Fitch, he found, the salesman assured him, exactly what he was looking for. "President Roosevelt has several of them," he said and handed him a Holland and Holland, double-barrelled, .577 Nitro Express. "There's talk of him going on safari once his term is over so you'd better hurry while there's still some game left." He also sold him a gun case, ammunition belt, and fifty, three inch long, half inch diameter brass cartridges. Looking him over, he added, "Wait until you get to Cape Town for the rest. They'll be cheaper there. And may I wish you the best of luck."

"The bastard jinxed me. I went to bed feeling fine. I woke up in the middle of the night all in a sweat and aching from head to foot. Had a fever for a week, could hardly get out of bed and came out of it as weak as a kitten. It was a miracle I wasn't robbed of everything but the woman who ran the place was honest and took care of me. I talked to a doctor about it later and he said sounded like glandular fever.

"Took me two weeks to recover. Used up all my money. Just enough left to crawl back home." Then, looking towards the elephants he said, "Still got my gun, though."

It took Frank a moment to pick up his meaning, even then not quite catching it. "What are you saying? You're not thinking of....," He laughed, disbelieving. "Those are circus elephants! They're worth twenty thousand dollars apiece. They'd put you in jail!"

"I'm not talking about them!" Mr. Mac said contemptuously. "What do you take me for? But those other three... They're out in the bush now. That makes them 'returned to the wild' in my book."

Frank continued to stare. Mr. Mac stood up and looked down at him. "Anyway, who are you to tell me what I can or can't do, you young puppy? Hanging around with crooked politicians, trying to land some soft government job." He snapped his fingers in Franks face and laughed when he flinched. As he turned and walked away, he muttered, "Can't for the life of me understand what Jennifer sees in him."

It was a low moment for Frank. The old man had just about summed it up. The only comfort was his use of the present tense in that last sentence. But then there was no reason to suppose Jenny had kept him up to date on the latest developments.

He walked down to the elephants. They were used to men and didn't stir. The camels eyed him knowingly, as if they understood everything about him, better than he did, and they couldn't have cared less. Tommy had his head down, remote, eyes blank, a prisoner waiting on events.

The two newcomers were rocking from side to side in unison. He wondered where the other three were and whether they were enjoying their freedom. He thought about Mr. Mac and his gun and if he should tell Jenny her grandpa was off his rocker.

As he drove away from the arena, still in no hurry to get fired, he turned back towards the CPR station, thinking to check in with Francis and get the latest news. Outside in the car park there was a group of people with a pair of horses, standing in a circle, talking. By their gestures and the sharp growl of their voices, they sounded angry about something. When he got closer Frank saw that they were Ktunaxa, six men and a woman.

They stopped talking and turned to watch as he steered the McLaughlin-Buick up beside the station. He got out and stood a moment, looking across at them. He thought they were probably the trackers who had brought in the elephants. He wanted to ask them how it had gone but hesitated. They looked tough and none too friendly. They were dressed in rough, worn work clothes and cloth caps. The woman wore a brown ankle length dress and soft leather laced-up boots. Her black hair hung down in two braids beside her face. She was bare headed and had sharp dark eyes which she fixed on Frank.

The woman said something to the men which Frank couldn't understand. It sounded like a foreign language which, when he thought about it, made him laugh. He raised his hand to them and he thought the woman acknowledged it with a slight upward nod of her head.

The Ktunaxa

The station was quiet and empty. He could hear the mutter of voices coming from the telegraph office. Inside two men were talking to Francis - Ironsides and a tall, energetic man in a tweed suit introduced as Zack Terrell, the circus boss.

"Anyway, it's all I'm paying," he was saying. "Jesus Christ, two hundred bucks and they want four?"

"You did offer two hundred a head," Ironsides said.

"I got carried away. They'd have my scalp, my bosses not them Indians, if they heard I was giving away that much alfalfa. Two hundred's twice too much. It's more than generous for a night's work from a bunch of Indians. And I'm paying in American dollars!"

They were expecting four hundred and getting about one fifty Canadian, Frank calculated. No wonder they looked mad.

"You may need them again, you know," Francis said.

"If I do, they'll be back. Anyway, my boys can take it from here. I don't doubt we would have found them without any help from our red friends. The other three were spotted close to - what do you call it, Jap Lake? We'll stake out some camels up there tonight. That'll bring 'em in. Who knows that country? Besides the Indians, I mean." They all looked at Frank.

"Not especially," he said, "but it's easy to get to. There's a road that takes you up to an abandoned lumber mill. Me and my friend Jim can show you." He didn't mention that Jim was a newspaper reporter, not knowing what Terrell might think about that. Looking ahead to his coming interview with Doc King, he added, "I should be free in a couple of hours."

They arranged to meet back at the station. Returning to his car, Frank saw that the Ktunaxa had left. He felt vaguely guilty about offering to guide the circus men. Whatever the pay, it was probably better than they would earn anywhere else. And they were likely to know the country better too. It was theirs after all.

Frank drove the few blocks along a nearly deserted Baker

St., a quiet Monday afternoon, the sun hitting the upper windows on the north side and the air starting to cool in the shade. Almost supper time for most folks. When he pulled up in front of the campaign office he saw that the cardboard sign in the centre of the door was flipped to Closed. In the window was a poster that said Seven Reasons To Vote Liberal with the rest in print too small to read. Frank figured he knew most of them by now and wasn't much interested anyway. He was about to drive away when he spotted a light blue envelope tucked into the edge of the frame beside the knob. It was addressed to him.

Frank

Hope you got here safe and sound. The car too. Report for duty eight thirty o'clock tomorrow. All is forgiven (more or less).

Harry.

PS: Miss MacPherson dropped by this afternoon looking for you.

Frank read the note three times. He'd spent the last two days getting himself ready to leave Cranbrook, to leave Jenny. He thought of the expression Mr. Mac had used – returned to the wild. Now it looked like life had suddenly and unexpectedly clicked back to normal. He didn't know what to think. But that was normal too.

It took him five precious minutes to give Mrs. McKinnon the barest sketch of the last two days with a promise of details later. No time for supper though, sorry for the late notice, going elephant hunting with the circus men. "Is Jimmy around?"

It was a quarter to six by the time he got to the Courier offices, still working on the sandwich his landlady handed him on his way out. Inside was a dimly lit hallway leading to the rear of the building where the printing machines were. To the right was a door with Advertising painted on the glass panel in an artistic curve and below that, Your Printing Needs. Another door to the left said Editorial. Opening it, Frank stepped into a beehive.

There was a long counter blocking off the room. On the other side were four desks strewn with paper, one unoccupied, each of the others containing a reporter hunched over an Underwood, banging away with varying degrees of speed and skill. Farther in were three more, containing female typists, fingers flying. The copy boy trotted between them distributing sheets of imperfectly typed foolscap and placing corrected copy into a tray marked Dispatches.

At the back was an office behind a large window. Frank could see Jimmy inside talking to Betts, the editor. When he came out, he spotted Frank and walked over. "Can't talk. Wires coming in from all over asking about the elephants. Everybody wants a different angle." Pointing to Frank's old work clothes, "Not driving tonight? Where were you anyway? We missed you at breakfast."

"Long story," Frank said. "Listen, if you want a good angle ask Betts if you can come out with me tonight." A quick explanation had Jimmy back in with the editor, returning with a grin and a thumbs up. "Keep at it boys and girls," Jimmy called out as they left.

They dropped the McLaughlin-Buick off at Hansen's and ran all the way to the station arriving to find a trio of trucks out front. The front two had wooden slats eight feet high up each side with a dark green canvas top. Each had two camels inside, their heads poking out, looking about them with the supercilious self-confidence of their kind. The third truck, an open flatbed, was piled with ropes, chains, bulky canvas bags and three bales of hay. Zack Terrell and four circus hands stood beside it.

Pointing to Jimmy, he said, "Hop on with these guys. Frank, come up with me. Let's go."

They drove south along the Moyie road and turned off towards Jap Lake, kicking up a lot of dust. Frank didn't envy Jimmy and the others bringing up the rear. They reached a clearing on the south side of the lake containing a few abandoned sheds with corrugated iron roofs and some rusted machinery. The trees circling the lake were small, second growth, just starting to hide the big stumps dotting the slopes.

Between them were masses of huckleberry and thimbleberry, good food for bears. Maybe for elephants too.

"Told you they'd be back," Terrell said, pointing up at two men on horseback where a rock outcropping stuck out from a fringe of trees. Frank guessed he had seen them before, back at the station.

"The idea's this," Terrell explained. "We tether the camels here for the night. If they're anywhere close the elephants should pick up their scent and come to bed down with them like they're used to.

"We'll clear out down the road half a mile or so and spend the night. You're welcome to stay – or we could drive you back to the main road once we're set up. You can hoof it into town from there. At first light we'll tiptoe back here and catch the buggers napping. They'll think it's just a normal day and won't give us any trouble. That's the plan anyway."

They set about unloading the trucks. Frank figured he'd stay despite having to report for work next morning. If he did report. He hadn't altogether made up his mind. It got light early so there'd be plenty of time to make it back.

The two men on horseback had dismounted and were staying put, watching. Terrell kept glancing up at them. Finally, he said to one of his men, "Go tell those fellows to clear off. They'll spook the elephants. Start by being polite."

The man looked up at the two watchers. "Unless you've got a gun handy, I intend to stay polite right through." He started to work his way slowly up the slope, scrambling over a crisscross of old waste logs and scrub. Every once in a while he'd stop and look back at the trucks, then up at the two men who had dismounted and were squatting beside their horses. After he'd gone about halfway, he shouted and gestured at them to move off. When they didn't respond, he continued on for a few yards, then stopped and did it again.

"What the hell's that idiot doing?" Terrell said. "If the elephants are up there…. God damn it, why doesn't he just set off an alarm!"

As the circus man got closer, the two Ktunaxa stood up and slowly mounted their horses. One of them began to ride down towards the circus man but the other called out and gestured at him to come away. They rode around a section of the outcropping and started along the lower edge of the trees. Suddenly a large grey shape appeared out of the shadows and charged towards them.

The elephant slammed into the side of one of the horses which gave a scream of terror and swerved away, throwing its rider. The other rider barely controlled his rearing horse but managed to force it into the gap between the elephant and his fallen companion. After striding a few paces up the hill, the elephant turned back and stopped. It stood watching, swaying from side to side. Then it seemed to make up its mind and trotted back down towards them. The man who had been knocked down limped to his horse and pulled a rifle from a sling behind the saddle.

"Oh Christ!" Terrell yelled.

The Ktunaxa stepped towards the elephant and pointed his gun into the air and fired. The beast turned away, ran along the edge of the rocks for about fifty yards then plunged back into the trees. The man with the rifle got back onto his horse and shouted contemptuously at the circus men. Then they both wheeled around and disappeared after the elephant.

"Get the fucking camels back into the trucks," Terrell said. "We're done here."

On the return trip to town, Frank sat beside Jimmy, sharing dust at the back of the last truck. "I got you a good story, anyway," he said.

"Don't know if Betts will let me use it," Jimmy said. "They're advertisers. He won't want to show them up."

"It was like something out of Zane Grey," he added.

"Or Rider Haggard," Frank said with a worried frown.

Mrs. McKinnon was still up when he got home. She made him sit down at the kitchen table with a bowl of left-over soup. He told her about his adventures in Fernie, and the failed stakeout at Jap Lake. "It was the wild west. That one fellow could handle his horse like Tom Mix."

"The poor souls," Mrs. McKinnon said, shaking her head. "Pushed off their land and turned into Catholics. Well, at least they're getting an education up at the mission school, little good it seems to do them."

Growing up back in Ontario, Frank never saw any Indians, as far as he knew. There was a small Mississauga reserve further north on Scugog Lake. In school he was taught about Tecumseh fighting the Americans in the War of 1812 and then they made a big deal about the ones who joined up during the war. 'Best job they're ever likely to get,' his mother had said.

The Decision

Frank was sitting on a grassy slope beside the smaller of the two Norbury Lakes. He was naked, as were his companions who were horsing around, laughing and splashing each other in the icy water. Bob was one of them, and Jimmy, but oddly enough, so were Mike Wilson and the pianist from The Green Door who stood out because of his black skin. He was the only one not completely naked, wearing tight trunks like the boxer Jack Johnson.

He suddenly became aware of Mavis sitting on a blanket a few feet away. She was wearing the dress with the fringes that she had worn the last time he'd seen her. She smiled at him and patted the blanket beside her. Frank got up and walked towards her, painfully aware of his nakedness. As he sat down beside her and she reached out to him, he saw something moving in the bushes across the lake. At first he thought it was an elephant but then he saw it was Jenny who called out to him....

"Frank.... Frank!" said Jimmy. "You've missed breakfast already and you're gonna miss work too if you don't get the lead out."

Frank sat up quickly. "Okay, okay!" he said, pulling the sheets up around him.

Going to bed the night before he had been far from certain about going to work next morning. He had fallen asleep wondering how much a train ticket to Vancouver cost and whether he'd leave a note for Jenny or ask Mavis if she'd care to come along. Now it just seemed too complicated. He thought he might as well find out what Harry and Doc King had to say. And why Jenny had dropped by the office yesterday.

Harry's note hadn't said anything about bringing the car, so he walked. His route took him past the Victoria where he could see Mavis pouring coffee for a pair of early lady shoppers. She looked up and waved. He waved back and hurried on. His dream was still with him and he didn't feel like looking her in the eye.

"You lead a full life, Frank," Harry greeted him. "This ought to slow you down a bit." He was standing behind the counter sorting through stacks of paper. "Voters lists this week. I don't know how they manage it – last election was only a year ago - but you'd be surprised how many get left off. We match last year's against the new list. Then there's the newcomers and the first timers. We try to figure out which way they'll vote and then make sure they get on - or leave it up to them - depending. We've got until Saturday, after which they go before Judge Thompson. We've got canvassers here in town but you can take care of these on the outskirts." He handed Frank a manila envelope. "The boss won't be needing you today - a speech at the Board of Trade luncheon."

"I thought he'd fire me after what happened in Fernie."

Harry grinned. "I probably would have. But he says you're his lucky charm. Said you were a bit of a – well it starts with f and ends with up. You crashing the car meant he had to catch a ride with one of the church wardens who was heading into Cranbrook. Turned out to be old Charlie Hobden, part owner of the Crowsnest Pass Coal Company. Doc took him to lunch with his Elko campaign committee. Got his vote and a fat contribution to boot."

Frank ran his finger down the list and stopped at an address near the bottom with a puzzled look. "You got it right," Harry said. "Macpherson's hired hand came over from Ontario last summer. We're guessing he'll vote Liberal. Say hello to your girlfriend for me."

"Did she say what she wanted?"

"Nope. Just wondered if you were back. I told her about your adventures."

"Who told you?"

"Oh, we have our ways. One of our Fernie people was at the Labour meeting Sunday night. Sat right behind you as a matter of fact. Funny story."

After Harry had given him some forms and a list of questions, Frank picked up the car and headed out. He could have gone straight up Gold Creek Rd. but decided he needed some practice before tackling Mr. Mac's hired hand – or Jenny – or Mr. Mac for that matter.

As instructed, he collected a couple of voters who seemed friendly and left forms with four more who didn't. After about three hours work and a half hour's meditation beside Joseph's Creek, he drove to Jenny's.

His knock elicited a yell from Mr. Mac. "I'm in the kitchen. Don't let the flies in."

Frank walked down the hall and stood in the kitchen doorway. Mr. Mac was at the sink holding an oily rag. Frank saw, but pretended not to, a very large double-barreled shotgun, its breech open, lying along the kitchen counter. There were some shells beside it with a couple cut open, grains of gunpowder spilled out onto the oilcloth.
"I'm looking for Mr. Hines," he said.

"What do you want with Albert? Oh, the voters list. I used to do that – more fool me. You think he's dumb enough to vote Liberal? Come to think of it, he probably is. Anyway, he's working. Come back some other time. And Jennifer's in town. She's got something to say to you."

"It'll only take a few minutes," Frank said and, in response to Mr. Mac's look, "As a candidate's agent...."

Mr. Mac threw down his rag which made Frank jump. "All right, Mr. Candidate's Agent. Albert's in the barn shoveling manure. You'll feel right at home. And be sure to look up my granddaughter when you get back to town. She's helping the Knox ladies set up their booth for the band concert. You were going to escort her there I'm told."

"Thank you, sir," Frank answered with as much dignity as he could muster.

Albert Hines proved to be a worried looking, middle aged man with a formal manner and a more cooperative attitude than his boss. He told Frank that in the absence of a United Farmer's candidate, he'd probably exercise his franchise in Dr. King's favour. He signed the affidavit, flicking a piece of cow manure off it and they shook hands. As he left, Frank noticed the barnyard smell had followed him out. He decided to knock off for lunch and clean his shoes.

After a quick stop home and a sandwich at Fink's lunch counter he whizzed through the rest of his list, giving everyone the benefit of the doubt, and drove over to Knox Church. About a month ago the newspapers had announced with much fanfare the upcoming visit of the world-famous Coldstream Guards Band, the oldest band in the empire. They were the ones who wore the big bear skin hats outside Buckingham Palace. He'd asked Jenny to go with him, more to cut out Mike Wilson than any love for their kind of music. Now he thought the concert might give him a chance to patch things up although Mr. Mac's use of the past tense in referring to it had him worried.

The two concerts, matinee and evening, were to be held next Monday at the arena which meant the elephants would have to be moved out and the whole place sweetened and gussied up. Inside the Knox Hall he found the church ladies busy sewing a banner for their booth, deep in an animated discussion about whose recipe to use for the shortbread.

On seeing Frank, Jenny excused herself and walked out into the narrow garden squeezed between the hall and the minister's residence. There was an arched trestle covered with climbing roses at the centre and Jenny sat down on a bench inside. Frank thought it looked like the perfect place for a romantic rendezvous until he saw the tears welling up in her eyes and realized he had some work to do before that was going to happen. He stepped towards her but hesitated when he saw her shoulders stiffen.

"Grampa…." She began and stopped.

"I was just there. On election business. He said you had something to tell me." He heard his voice sounding cold and angry and he tried to think of something softer to say but couldn't.

After a long silence Jenny said, "I've decided I need to stop seeing you and Mike until…." She hesitated.

"Until you've made up your mind? Hell, that suits me."

"Frank!"

"Sorry, but it does. And if a fellow can't swear at a time like this I don't know when he can. Seems to me you should be able to choose between us pretty quick. You've got all the information you're ever going to need. Was this your grampa's idea?"

"No it wasn't, and I was thinking until after the election as a matter of fact."

"The election! What the hell's the election...."

"If you'd stop swearing long enough for me to get a word in! Now that you're driving for Doc King, maybe you can get a real job out of it like you said and make something of yourself."

"So why are you cutting Mike out? He's got a steady job. Hell, he'll be taking over the whole works from his old man one of these days. You'll be in the lap of luxury! Why don't you just say who you want and get it over with. I can stand it."

Jenny looked down at her shoes and picked at a loose thread on the front of her dress. As he waited for her answer, Frank found himself thinking of Mavis. He tried to banish her from his mind without success.

"Oh, I'd probably pick you, if that was all there was to it," Jenny said at last, looking up with a distressed smile. "But, Frank, I've seen too many girls stuck with the wrong man and trying to give their children a decent life with little or no help..."

"Is that what you think?"

"It's not what I think, Frank. It's what I don't know. And you don't either so don't tell me you do. You're all hopes and dreams and better luck next time – which is okay in a boyfriend, I guess but it's not much use in a husband."

"Sounds like there's only one use you've got in mind." Frank said with a hard laugh. "A stud bull!"

Jenny jumped up quicker than Frank had ever seen her move, slapped him hard across the face and ran back into the church hall. Even in his shock, clutching his stinging jaw, he couldn't help admiring her lithe figure as she flew away across the grass.

"Ah come on Jen. I was only joking!" he called after her.

He turned away and saw the Reverand Mackay regarding him from his doorway, shaking his head. "You'd better make your escape this way, son," he called, adding, as Frank approached, "Never tell a woman you're only joking. They think they do, but most of them don't have much of a sense of humour. Not when it comes to matters of the heart."

Frank was about to say that the heart was not the part in question but thought better of it. He hoped to get through the parsonage with just a smile and a thank you but when they were within a few feet of the front door, the minister took a firm grip on his arm and steered him into the front parlour. It was stuffed with heavy, nineteenth century furniture. A large clock ticked loudly below a portrait of a fierce gent with a shapeless velvet hat and a long silken beard. John Knox.

"Sit down, Frank. As your minister, not to mention one of the references for that chauffeur's license of yours, I think I'm entitled to a progress report."

"Oh, it's going great," Frank answered brightly. "It's a great car and Doc King..."

"I'm sure it is, and Dr. King is a fine man, certainly, but that's beside the point. Please, sit down. I won't keep you long." He quietly closed the door and looked down at him.

"Miss MacPherson is worried about you Frank," he began at last. "She came to see me yesterday – in my capacity as her spiritual advisor – and she told me that she cares about you, as a friend and possibly as more than a friend, but she feels that you are a lost soul. Morally adrift."

"Morally adrift? Jeez!"

"She also said you curse. Now 'Jeez' seems to have entered common parlance of late as a mild explicative but it is really an abbreviation of our Lord's name and as such....

"I'm sorry Reverend, I wasn't thinking. But J... I mean heck, morally adrift? Did she really say that?"

Mr. Mackay ignored the question. "I understand you have suggested marriage on more than one occasion. Were you serious?"

"Yes, sir, as serious as I've been about anything in my life," Frank said, once again trying to banish Mavis from his thoughts and so bringing her squarely in.

"I'm not sure how far that takes us, Frank, but leaving aside that slight equivocation, you must realize that marriage carries a weight of responsibility and while Jennifer has a strong faith in our Lord, she is not about to take anyone else on the same terms.

"And furthermore...." he continued, gesturing Frank to silence, "she has a fierce dragon guarding the gates. A dragon, I might add, with a guardian's power to prohibit her from marrying anyone at all for the next two and a half years."

"Oh, Mike and I know all about that," Frank said, getting to his feet and taking a half step towards the door. "But... well, I don't know what he thinks about it, and I don't much care, but I figure once Jenny makes up her mind, she'll get the old man to come round. In the meantime, she's put the kybosh on either of us seeing her 'til after the election - which is fine by me. I've got some thinking to do myself and who knows? Maybe by the time she does decide to pick me, she'll discover she's not the only one around here with an interest in yours truly.

"Anyhow," he finished, edging around the astonished minister and reaching for the doorknob, "as my mother used to say, and Mrs. King too, there's more fish in the sea than ever came out of it. I have to get back to work now. We've got an election to win."

As he closed the front door behind him, Frank thought over what he had just said, not entirely sure what he *had* said and, if it was what he remembered saying, a bit surprised that he had, in fact, said it. Over the course of the day he had been getting increasingly fed up, first with Mr. Mac who was obviously toying with him and enjoying it, then with Jenny who had more or less said she loved him but didn't trust him as far as she could throw him and finally with Reverend Mackay, who ought to mind his own goddamned business. Anyway, if it got back to Jenny that he was scouting out other possibilities so much the better. He hoped.

At the constituency office, Harry was still behind the counter stacking papers. He added Frank's offerings to its pile. "Good work. You can knock off now. You're driving up to Golden tomorrow. It'll be a couple of overnights, maybe more if you get held up, so get the car ready – don't forget the water this time, take an extra jerry can for gas too – and pack a bag. Put in a clean shirt. Christ, I sound like your mother!"

As Frank was leaving, Harry reached out and took his arm. "Listen, Frank," needlessly lowering his voice, "The boss isn't quite himself these days. He's getting discouraged. His speech today at the Board of Trade... he was rambling, incoherent, muffed the punchline of a joke he's been telling for the past ten years. See what you can do to cheer him up. Like I said, he likes you."

The next morning was Wednesday, August 11th, five days after the elephant stampede. He picked up his boss at his house at six thirty. Mrs. King, wearing an elegant kimono dressing gown, stood on the porch ready to wave them off. Doc King walked around the car like a general inspecting his troops, pausing at the slight dent still visible on the fender. Glancing reproachfully at Frank, he shook his head. "Let's go."

Neither spoke for the next hour and a half as they drove north, crossing the Kootenay River at Fort Steele and so along its east bank past Wasa and Skookumchuck. Doc King dozed over a sheaf of notes and occasionally looked out the window. From time to time Frank glanced at him through the rear-view mirror and wondered if this was what they called the silent treatment.

They had just passed a wooden signpost announcing 'Canal Flats - Three Miles' when Frank's glance into the mirror met his passenger's piercing stare, startling him into a sudden swerve towards the opposite ditch.

"Easy now," Doc King said. "You're as skittish as a horse. Ever been to Canal Flats?" Without waiting for an answer he went on, "It's a funny story. About forty years ago when this was still empty country, except for the Indians, a fella named Adolf Baillie-Grohman came up with a hair-brained scheme. He was an Englishman, more or less, big game hunter, collected trophy heads and all that. His mother was related to the Duke of Wellington and his father some sort of Austrian nobleman. He took it in mind to drain the swamp at the south end of Kootenay Lake where the river flows in, turn it into farmland for retired military types. Up here, that same river runs a few miles east of Columbia Lake, the headwaters of the Columbia River which sits just a wee bit lower in elevation. His idea was to connect the two so the spring run-off from the Kootenay would flow north into the Columbia, thereby lowering the level of Kootenay Lake and draining the swamp. He raised a fair bit of capital and went so far as to put in a canal. The CPR finally put a stop to it, concerned about their Columbia River crossings and all their preempted acreage getting flooded. A lot of work for nothing. You can still see the ditch."

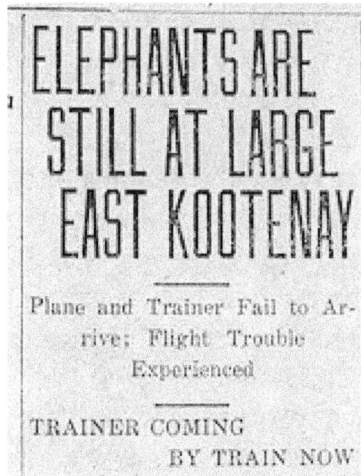

ELEPHANTS ARE STILL AT LARGE EAST KOOTENAY

Plane and Trainer Fail to Arrive; Flight Trouble Experienced

TRAINER COMING BY TRAIN NOW

The Idea

"Tell me, Frank," Doc King said a while later, "You're a smart young fellow with your ear to the ground, what are they saying about me in the city?" When Frank hesitated, he added, "Out with it now. This is back-room stuff."

Frank gripped the steering wheel a little tighter. What the hell, he thought. "Well, it's pretty bad, sir. Yesterday when I was doing the voters lists, some people said they thought you were a crook. Or if you weren't," he added quickly, "your friends were. Even Mr. Mac. And Jenny says he's always voted Liberal."

Doc King laughed bitterly. "Calling a politician crooked is like calling a cow Bossie. But you're right, it's pretty bad. Don't tell Nellie because she's got her heart set on another few years in Ottawa, God knows why, but the way I read it, I'm going to fall short by maybe a hundred and fifty votes. Just about the worst way to lose…. Mr. Mac too, eh?"

"Well, sir, I think he just likes getting steamed up over something. I don't think he cares all that much who wins when you get right down to it. I mean, he probably cares more about shooting one of those elephants."

"He told you that?"

"Yes, sir. Crazy, isn't it. Seems he's always wanted to bag an elephant and now he says his chance has come. Maybe it's just talk but what I mean to say, people make a big deal out of politics but there's usually a whole bunch of things they care a lot more about. Why the heck does it really matter to him? Apart from the old age pension, I guess."

They drove on in silence. Frank watched Doc King brooding in the back seat. "It's not all bad, sir," he said with a mischievous grin, "My friend Bob says he'll vote for you – cause I'm your driver."

Doc King hooted and slapped Frank on the back. "Hah! There you go. You have stumbled on one of the great political truths. Find a way to connect yourself to a man personally, convince him you're a good fellow, one of the boys, and chances are he'll vote for you no matter what you stand for – within reason, of course. I started out around here as a simple country doctor, did a lot of good work fighting the typhoid epidemic, helped found the hospital. That got me elected in the first place. But since then it seems I've turned myself into a stuffed shirt. Everybody wants to take pot shots at a big target, the bigger the better – like Mr. Mac and his elephants – and I guess I'm just about the biggest there is in these parts, even if I do say so myself.

"What I need is to take myself down a peg or two. Get back the personal touch." With that he resumed his inspection of the scenery while Frank chewed over what his boss had just said.

Their northward journey down the Columbia took them the best part of the day, Frank trying to catch hold of an idea just over the horizon of his mind and Doc King staring gloomily out the window. He'd rouse himself every so often, telling Frank to turn off at this or that country store, lumber operation or farmhouse. Then he'd jump out, hollering somebody's name, hand extended, greeting whoever appeared like a long-lost cousin. Five minutes of some variation on 'how have you been, you old son of a gun, how's your back holding up, did that reference I wrote for your daughter do the trick?' with no mention of the election – no need, they all knew what he was there for. Then, 'well, as much as I'd like to stand here jawing all day....' and so back in the car bumping down the road as glum as ever.

They were passing through Parsons when Frank finally got it straight in his mind and blurted out, "About those elephants, sir, I've been thinking...."

After a minute's silence, Doc King said, "Are you going to tell me where those thoughts have taken you, Frank?"

"Well, it's kinda dumb."

"If you mean dumb as in you not talking, I'll have to agree," He laughed. "Spit it out, son. So far we've got elephants and a dumb idea. I'm all ears."

"Well, sir, everybody's talking about them, the elephants I mean, and wanting to know the latest. I've lost count of how many times I've told it. And there's something new happening practically every day. With all due respect, sir, people find it a whole lot more interesting than the election campaign. It makes them laugh too.

"I was thinking.... well, if you could work it into your speeches - show them you're as excited about it as they are, tell jokes about it and keep everybody up to date.... After all, the paper only comes out once a week. Folks would like you for it and maybe they'd see you as more of a regular fellow."

Doc King thought a moment and then said, "You're right, Frank, it is a dumb idea. But I've been in this business long enough to know that sometimes the dumb ideas are the best. I'll think about it. As for me being a regular fellow, well...."

They drove on in silence except for the occasional chuckle emanating from the back seat which Frank found encouraging. The road took them down into the Kicking Horse Valley, across the river and into Golden. They were spending the night as guests of the Regional Postmaster, Chas. Harding, an ardent Liberal. The short main street ran behind a sprawling sawmill with a tall beehive burner and a pair of even taller smokestacks. Near the end of the last block Frank was surprised to see a file of six men crossing the road a few yards in front - all wearing orange or blue turbans and sporting bushy black beards.

"Who the heck are those fellows?" he asked, slowing down to gawk.

Doc King looked up and smiled. "A good omen, I'd say. They're Sikhs - from India, you know, like our elephants. Supposed to be some of the best soldiers in the empire. They started coming here about twenty-five years ago to work for Columbia River Lumber. They have their own temple somewhere hereabouts. Good workers, I'm told, model citizens – except they aren't, of course – citizens, I mean. Too bad – I could use their votes."

Always back to the votes, Frank thought. It conjured up a

picture of Mrs. King at the altar promising to love, honour and vote for him 'til death do them part.

"What are you laughing at?"

"The way you think about everybody voting for or against you. Or is it just at election time?"

"Good question. I'll have to ask myself that next month."

"Do you really expect to lose?"

Doc King didn't answer. "That's the house," pointing towards a large, three-story residence with a handsome wrap-around porch. As Frank opened the car door, he said, "Not quite *expect*, I guess. You never know in this business. I might pull a rabbit out of my homburg. Or maybe an elephant."

The meeting was set for seven o'clock at the Lyric Theatre. Frank dropped off Doc King and Mr. and Mrs. Harding at the rear entrance about ten minutes early. Not liking the look of the alley, he drove around to the front. The street was packed with cars and it took him a while to find a parking spot. By the time he got inside, the speeches were in high gear. He leaned against a pillar at the back and folded his arms. A young man with a notebook sat in the seat closest to him, a reporter, Frank guessed. He looked bored and the page in front of him was blank.

The rows of red upholstered seats, all occupied, sloped down towards a low stage framed by an ornate gold arch decorated with blue and scarlet flowers. The movie screen had been removed and replaced by a row of chairs containing Doc King's party and two other couples. The ladies wore coats with fur collars and feathered hats. A man behind a podium was speaking earnestly about tariffs, freight rates and Alberta wheat. Doc King sat, legs crossed, his arm draped across the back of his wife's chair, listening with careful attention and giving benevolent nods of approval. It's going to be a long night, Frank thought. It occurred to him that he would not be needed for some time so he went outside and settled into the car. Since the long night had been preceded by a long day, he promptly fell asleep.

He was awakened a little over an hour later by the

sound of footsteps running towards him. It was the reporter, obviously in a hurry and looking considerably more excited. Behind him people were streaming out of the theatre, laughing and chattering away as if they'd just seen a Harold Lloyd movie instead of a campaign speech. He nosed the car out into the street and drove slowly through the crowd of jay walkers towards the rear entrance. They were definitely charged up about something. Doc King emerged surrounded by his friends. They were all laughing too. Must have been a hell of a speech, he thought.

"Frank!" Doc King cried, throwing an arm across his shoulder and spinning him around. "Come and meet my friends. Ladies and gentlemen, this is the budding political genius I was telling you about. How about it, Frank? Was that what you had in mind?"

Of course Frank had no idea what he was talking about. Once it was explained that Doc King had taken his advice and spent most of his speech talking about the elephant stampede, he had to confess the truth. To do him credit, Doc King took it well. "You were tired after all that driving. Long day," he muttered, looking deflated. "I guess you'll have to read about it in the paper."

"Too bad you missed it, son," Mr. Harding said before steering the conversation towards Prime Minister Meighan's upcoming visit to Golden and the chances of getting their own leader to do the same. Their discussion continued on into the house and all he got was "Good night, Frank. Breakfast at six" from Mrs. Harding.

As he steered the car out of the driveway next morning, expecting to retrace their route south, Doc King pointed him west toward Donald instead.

"Can't be helped, Frank. Forget about tariffs, freight rates and the damned constitution crisis. When you get right down to it, politics is personal. There are twenty-nine electors in Donald. I'll bet half of them haven't made up their minds yet. It's bad enough Meighan is speaking here on his way out to the coast.

He'll be coming back through Donald too. That's two visits against Mackenzie's passing by at night both times. He's just about written off the west and his one trip out here is mostly for show. I'm supposed to hold the fort in Kootenay East all on my lonesome. If I don't show up, we can kiss most of those undecided votes goodbye. A couple of hours on a rough road is worth six or eight, wouldn't you say?"

Doc King's tour of Donald's main street took him in and out of stores shaking as many hands as he could grasp. Once or twice he told a joke but Frank was too far away to tell if it involved elephants. While he waited, a truck pulled up and dumped a pile of newspapers outside the drug store. The headline read: DR. KING'S ELEPHANT BULLETIN DELIGHTS CROWD.

His boss came up behind him and peered over his shoulder. "That's promising," he said. "Let's go. You drive, I'll read.

"'The audience at the Lyric Theatre might have been excused for supposing that the famous American humourist Will Rogers had stepped out from the movie screen yesterday evening and joined the assembled politicians on stage. The occasion was a public meeting in support of Dr. James Horace King, late cabinet minister in the recent Liberal government who is again standing for election as member of parliament for Kootenay East.

"Dr. King was introduced by Mr. Archibald Havershaw, QC, chairman of the Golden Liberal Association. Mr. Havershaw stated that Dr. King's character and accomplishments were so well known as to require no further exposition. He then proceeded to enumerate them at some length.'

"Ha! Just what I was thinking."

"'Mr. Havershaw then continued with a comprehensive statement of the policy platform of the Liberal Party which was also so well-known as to require no further elucidation.'

"The man's a comedian!"

"'At this point the floor was surrendered to Dr. King who

had clearly come to the same conclusion.'

"A mind reader as well!"

"'After thanking Mr. Havershaw for his kind words, Dr. King announced himself puzzled as to how best to proceed. 'Mr Havershaw has assured us that I am already well known to you all,' he remarked, 'and had I not been so before I am certain that I am now.'

"Received with mild laughter and a smattering of applause. Enough at least to embolden me."

"'As for the record and policies of our government under the leadership of Prime Minister Mackenzie King before it was usurped by the collusion of Mr. Meighan and Viscount Byng,' Dr. King declared, 'I will make so bold as to aver that you have heard quite enough about that too. On the other hand, I am confident that there is one subject upon which your curiosity has not been sufficiently satisfied. I refer to recent events in Cranbrook concerning the escape of six elephants from the Sells Floto Circus.'

"'This remark was met with cheers from the crowd. Shouts of 'Tell us, tell us!' rang out. Thus encouraged, Dr. King launched into a series of increasingly fantastical anecdotes beginning with the stampede itself, a terrific affair in which the screams of spectators were blended with the wild trumpeting of the escaping pachyderms and culminating in a hair-raising description of one of their number vanishing into thin air at the top of a cliff. Between these two terrifying events, the audience was treated to comic visions of an occupied outhouse swept from its moorings and Mrs. O'Grady's bloomers plucked from her clothesline and carried off upon a raised tusk like a banner charging into the fray.'

"Whoa! Jesus, Frank! Would you stop doing that!"

Listening at first with amusement and then with rising disbelief and indignation, Frank had so forgotten himself as to fix his eyes on the rearview mirror. This caused him to steer toward the opposite ditch. Fortunately he was able to swerve back in time and lurch to a stop.

"Sorry," he said, somewhat insincerely. "But…. but…"

"I know, I know. I told a few stretchers. No dumped outhouse and no Mrs. O'Grady. At least I hope not."

"And no elephant vanishing into thin air either!" Frank added indignantly.

"But we all had a heck of a good time. Best speech I ever made. Thank you, Frank. Sorry you missed it. But if it makes you feel any better, here's how I finished up. I can't remember it word for word but let's believe what we read in the newspaper just this once."

"'In conclusion, Dr. King declared, 'My fellow Canadians. As I look back over the past six weeks of the Meighan administration, I cannot help but think of those poor elephants out there in the wilderness, completely out of their element, lost, blundering about in the underbrush, injuring themselves and everything about them. Indeed, we can only hope that the day is not far distant when they will be restored to the arena best suited to their abilities, namely the benches reserved for members of the opposition.'"

"A mixed metaphor, I suppose but they got my drift. I'll tell Harry to give you a raise."

Caught by surprise, Frank blurted out, "How much?"

"Straight to the point. Ten dollars sound about right?"

"No… I mean, yes. But I don't know how much I'm getting to start with. Nobody told me."

"And you didn't ask? You're an odd duck for a socialist, Frank. You've been driving me around for what, a week and a half not knowing how much you're getting paid? Mighty trusting, son. Forty a week I think so you'll be getting fifty now. Well, starting next Monday if you don't kill us first."

As a former minister in both provincial and federal governments, Doc King had obtained permission to drive up the new, unopened highway to Field, Lake Louise and Castle Junction. They would then turn south along the Banff-Windermere Highway down to Radium Hot Springs. Frank didn't like the sound of 'unopened' and was even less thrilled to see the big DANGER! HIGHWAY CLOSED sign outside Golden. "Don't mind that," Doc King said. "They assured me the road's perfectly passable. Just some rough spots and a few sections without barriers."

Frank wondered who 'they' were and hoped it wasn't some bureaucrat in Vancouver. At least it took his mind off what had been bothering him ever since he'd heard the account of Doc King's speech. Something didn't sit right with making up stuff about the elephants and comparing them to blundering politicians. He supposed it was his fault, being his idea. Still, knocking over outhouses and charging around with lady's underwear felt like carrying things too far. They deserved more respect than that. It seemed to him there was something special, momentous even, about them breaking free and heading for the hills.

That was as far as his thoughts took him for the rest of the day. He and Doc King were probably the first to travel over that section and Frank found it the most hair-raising experience he'd ever had – although he wouldn't have said so a couple of weeks later. Around Cranbrook the mountains hold up the sides of some wide valleys but the Kicking Horse Canyon was a horse of a different colour. At one point the river dropped down six hundred feet over the edge with nothing but air. It's a superhighway nowadays, which in a way is a shame.

They stopped in at Leanchoil, a CPR lumber camp that voted eight to one Doc's way the year before but with a Labour candidate running, he wasn't taking any chances. Field, where it had gone 102 to 59 in his favour, he spent two hours working the main street and then checked them into the Mount Stephen for the night. It was a fancy hotel for such an out of the way place although Frank's room was more like a broom closet compared to his boss'.

Supper was a meeting of the local Board of Trade and this time Frank, starved since breakfast, stayed awake all through. Doc King started out with his standard stump speech but after about ten minutes someone called out asking about the elephants. This got a laugh and a round of applause. Apparently the Golden Star had preceded them via the rail line.

With a grin towards Frank, Doc King launched into his latest version of events. This time one of the elephants charged through Chinatown in and out of a laundry, soap suds flying, before being cornered in Mrs. O'Grady's back yard, once again tangled up in her bloomer-festooned clothesline. Like the night before, he ended with, "My fellow Canadians. As I look back over the past six weeks of the Meighan administration......"

When he'd finished Frank went off to bed, leaving Doc King basking in applause and heading off to the bar.

The Carnival

Wearing his glove, flannel pyjama tops and nothing else, Frank was standing in centre field at Sportsman Park in St. Louis, Missouri, although it looked a lot like the ballpark in Whitby. It was the bottom of the ninth and the Cards had men on second and third. The Cubs were up by a run on the strength of Hack Wilson's homer in the top of the inning. Grover Cleveland Alexander was pitching, so everything was well in hand despite the two bloop singles he'd given up after striking out the first two men he'd faced. Sure enough, Tommy Thevenow, the Cards' light-hitting shortstop, hit a lazy fly ball for the third out straight at Frank. It curved slowly up into the sky towards a bank of silky grey clouds and then suddenly disappeared. A second later it came down with a thud at Frank's feet. The crowd roared as Rogers Hornsby crossed home plate with Les Bell chugging round third right behind him. Up in the stands Jenny and Mavis were deep in conversation and didn't appear to notice.

Frank woke at 5:30 on the morning of Friday, August 13th, exactly one week from the day the elephants stampeded. The terrible feeling in his stomach as the ball hit the ground was slowly dissipating. Doc King had said they were leaving early so he figured he'd better get up and find out exactly what that meant. All was quiet in the dining room except for the murmur of voices from the kitchen. At the desk they told him his boss had left strict instructions to be woken at six. "Tell Frank to knock loud and keep knocking." The desk clerk laughed. "I hear they made quite a night of it."

After obeying instructions and being sworn at for it, Frank went back downstairs and started in on a hearty breakfast. A few minutes later Doc King sat down opposite and sourly nursed a tomato juice. "Don't look so damned smug. You haven't got your raise yet."

That day was a carbon copy of the drive north with Frank

once again lost in thought and the old man scowling, although for a different reason. They went east across the Alberta border to Castle Junction, then south and back into B.C. By the time they reached Vermillion Crossing, Doc King was recovered enough to hop out at the Kootenay Park Lodge and shake a few more hands. Then on to Radium for lunch with the ladies of the I.O.D.E. a quick tour of the new hot spring facilities, a few elephant anecdotes and more handshakes.

By dusk they were in Invermere, having departed the main road to take in Wilmer and Athalmer. Frank noticed that the more hands Doc King shook the sprightlier he became. As he shook his way through the lobby of the Invermere Inn, he was beaming and back slapping with maximum gusto. That evening he was attending a private dinner with Robert Randolf Bruce, chairman of Columbia Valley Irrigated Fruit Lands Inc. He had just been appointed Lieutenant Governor of British Columbia and had political ambitions of his own. "Prying a kind word out of R.R.," Doc King explained, "is all the campaigning I'll need around here."

Frank walked down to the shore of Lake Windermere where the slowly revolving silhouette of a Ferris wheel told him some sort of summer carnival was going on. He bought his dinner from a stall selling hot dogs and corn on the cob then wandered among booths offering cheap trinkets and stuffed animals as prizes for hitting targets with balls or popping balloons with darts. He tried his luck at knocking over a pyramid of milk cans, missed and gave up.

As the day faded, strings of lights flickered on overhead. Parents with children swirling around them and younger couples, their lives drifting in the same direction, strolled up and down. Everybody seemed to know everybody else and Frank began to feel alone and out of place. He was heading back to the hotel when he heard music coming from beyond the booths.

The picnic grounds above the lake had been converted into an outdoor music hall, lanterns hanging from tree branches, chairs and tables surrounding a dance floor laid out beside a small bandstand. The orchestra was playing a slow-tempo foxtrot, a sandwich board announcing Bill Hankey's Smooth Seven. Several couples glided across the floor.

Frank wasn't much of a dancer but was always willing to give it a try. Before he'd taken up with Jenny a fair number of young ladies had been happy to put up with his two left feet to have his arms around them. He sat down at a table and looked about for a partner, but all the numbers came up even.

Some of the dancers were impressively graceful, others more in his league. One was a soldier in uniform. Suddenly he was back to an August evening ten years before. He and Ted were watching their parents dancing at the Canadian National Exhibition in Toronto. It was the last time he would see his father until he came back from the war a broken man.

They had been taken to the C.N.E. every summer for as long as Frank could remember but this year was different. Their father had joined up that June and the exhibition grounds had been turned into an army camp. They moved most of the troops out during the fair but kept a few back for demonstrations, Corporal Burton among them. As a recruit older than the average and having been a foreman at the tire factory, he'd been promoted right away. Every morning and afternoon they were paraded down the main avenue to some demonstration trenches, slits in the ground about six and a half feet deep and half as wide. About as much like a real trench, never mind the total absence of mud, vermin and death, his father once told him, "As spit is to vomit."

Ted was fifteen and loved it all. When their father's company came roaring up out of the trenches going over the top and chasing the Hun all the way back to Berlin, Ted roared with them. That evening it had been their father's turn for a few hours leave and he had taken his wife to the dance pavilion. While they sat on the side lines and watched, Ted told his brother, "I'm joining up the first chance I get."

Two months later, a couple of the older boys from his hockey team went down to the armoury and Ted went with them. He was big for his age but not quite big enough. Later in the war, recruiting officers didn't look too closely but in 1915 this one did, called him 'Sonny' and sent him home, slightly humiliated. A little over a year later he tried again and this time got his wish. A few months after that, pieces of his body were scattered over several square yards of Flanders mud.

Frank loved his brother more than anyone, certainly more than his distant and now absent father and his harried mother. The fourteen months when Ted was 'the man of the house' were the happiest he'd known and the short goodbye note he had left him came as a terrible blow. It was the last anyone heard of him until after the war. Afraid of a second humiliation, he'd not only lied about his age but his address too. When his father came home three years later, he tracked down Ted's records. He'd taken the train to Toronto and chosen the address of a vacant lot on his way to the recruiting office.

"After he left, I spent the rest of the war being scared," Frank once told Jenny, the only time he ever talked about it. "I'd always had Ted to look out for me. For years I wondered what would happen if I had to do anything brave. I sure didn't go looking for it."

The dance over, the soldier and his girl strolled down towards the lake. As Frank enviously watched them disappear into the darkness, he caught the eye of a woman sitting alone on the far side of the floor. He quickly looked away. Looking back a minute later she was still watching him, a mocking smile on her lips. She patted the seat of the chair beside her.

"Want to dance?" she said when Frank sat down. "Want a drink?" She took a cigarette out of a beaded purse on her lap. "Got a light?"

A strong wave of perfume enveloped him. "You sure ask a lot of questions," he laughed, "Yes, yes, and no. I'm Frank by the way."

"Me too," she said. "My name's Harriet." She was in her early thirties, he guessed, wearing a lot more make-up than he was used to, a bright red cupid mouth, rouged cheeks, painted eyelids and thin pencilled brows. Her face under it was thin with prominent teeth and a sharp nose. She had a nice figure though.

"You're not from around here, are you?" Frank asked.

"I'm with the show." She jerked her thumb over her shoulder, sliding the hem of her dress up over her knee and extracting a metal flask from the garter at the top of her stocking. At his look she added, "What haven't you seen before, the flask, the garter, or the leg?"

"None of them," Frank said. "At least not all in the same place." He took a swig, it was rye, and they got up to dance. Harriet snuggled into his arms and pressed herself against him in a way that Jenny never had. His body's response made him want to pull away but she held on tight. She looked up at him. "Let's finish the dance and then we can take a walk."

Frank began to wonder what he had gotten himself into and whether he liked it, or rather whether he should like it. And what he might be called upon to do about it. This was almost virgin territory. There had been a few mild encounters back in Whitby and a bit of fumbling in the back seat of Bob's uncle's car. One or two had made it clear they were willing to go further but Frank was just wise enough, scared enough, he told himself, to keep free of that inevitable entanglement. It was tough, though, and Jenny had made it clear that anything serious before marriage was definitely not on the cards. With two boyfriends that stood to reason. If she ever made up her mind, who knew what might happen. All too soon the music stopped – they had hardly moved for most of it. Harriet took his hand and led him down towards the lake.

They walked quickly away from the lights, Frank's heart pounding. Harriet clutched his arm and propelled him further down the beach. The music faded, replaced by the sound of ducks quacking and splashing away at their approach. They passed couples sitting or lying close together on blankets. Harriet giggled. "Same idea as us. And speaking of ideas, got any?"

Frank took the plunge, his voice shaking. "I've got a hotel

room," he offered.

"Which one?" she asked quickly. He told her.

"No good," she said. "They'll never let me past the desk." While Frank was wondering how she knew that, she said, "Got a car?"

Frank had already rejected that. The idea of doing anything in the back seat of Doc King's car was out of the question. First of all, he'd know. There would be no escaping that perfume. And the thought of figuring out how to go about things in such cramped quarters felt too daunting. He'd seen pictures, of course, but none involving back seats. He was about the tell her he'd come by train when they heard a man's voice calling from the direction of the carnival.

"Haaarr-iet.... Haarr-iet....Harriet!!"

Harriet pulled him quickly in the opposite direction, away from the beach and up into a stand of trees near the edge of the park. They stopped and listened above the sound of their breathing.

"Haaarr-iet," the voice repeated, coming closer.

"Who...?" Frank began.

"Shut up!" Harriet commanded, pulling him further into the shadows and the low hanging branches of a giant cedar. The outline of a large man appeared against the faint glow of the lake.

"Your father?" Frank whispered hopefully.

"Old enough to be," she answered. "Husband."

"Is that you, Harriet?" the man said. "Who you with? Have you....?"

"Never you mind who I'm with. You go on," Harriet suddenly yelled, pulling Frank farther into the trees. "I'm with a man and he's a lot bigger and younger than you so just go on home. I left your supper on the stove."

The man hesitated, took a step towards them then stopped.

"He'll come down there and beat you black and blue," Harriet called.

"Now wait a minute," Frank said, but at the sound of his voice the man turned and walked away.

"I guess this will have to do," Harriet said. "Nice and dry. Soft," she added, crouching down and patting the ground. "Take off your jacket and spread it out."

"You didn't tell me you were married."

"And you're not, I suppose," she retorted.

"No, I'm not!"

"No best girl, neither?" Frank didn't answer. "Yeah. And I just bet you'll be telling her all about it when you get home. Now are we going to or not?"

Frank stalled. "How about another drink."

"Come and get it."

Frank took off his jacket, spread it out beside her and sat down. He couldn't remember which leg the flask was on, guessed wrong but got it right on the second try. Harriet began tugging at his belt as he gulped down too much rye.

"Haarr-iet," came plaintively out of the darkness. "Come on, honey. Come on home."

"He's not giving up," Frank moved away, relieved, taking a third swig.

"Oh hell, you're just a big chicken" Harriet said, getting up "We almost had ourselves a good time too." She snatched the flask out of his hand, shook it reproachfully, kicked him and pushed her way back through the trees. A minute later he could hear voices, one low and muttering, the other louder, high and sharp.

Feeling dizzy, Frank pulled on his jacket. He staggered through the trees, across a road and into a maze of streets lined with holiday cabins, giggling to himself and mumbling. "Lucky escape. Just like those damned elephants!"

Lost, blundering about in the underbrush. That was him all right, heavy feet plodding up the road, head down, trunk swaying. Suddenly he was stumbling across a ditch and into a tangle of poplars and alder bushes. He sat down abruptly, felt around for a tree and propped himself against it. Tracking

Tommy with Hector. One week to the hour. Getting to be a habit.

Music from the carnival drifted faintly through the dark. He thought about Harriet, a missed opportunity. Miss Opportunity. More fish in the sea.... There was Jenny....Mavis.... singing tonight at the Green Door. Or tomorrow night. He'd be home by then. What a peach.

The barking of dogs woke him at dawn. They came vaulting through the bushes, stopped to examine him with saliva slobbered muzzles, tongues slapping into his face, then bounded away. Something large crashed deeper into the woods. Not an elephant for sure, elk by the sound of it.

He retraced his steps to the hotel, using the carnival as a landmark. All was quiet. No sign of Harriet and her unfortunate husband. "Boy," Frank thought, "the joys of married life. Poor fella."

All quiet at the hotel, the night clerk dozing behind the counter. He borrowed a clothes brush, went to his room, had a quick wash, changed his shirt, brushed his jacket and pants, combed his hair and lay down on his bed to think things through.

A knock on the door woke him two hours later. He and Mr. Mac had been watching elephants mate. In the dining room Doc King was telling the waiter one of his stampede whoppers over a plate of ham and eggs. "Toast and coffee," Frank said.

They took all morning and a good chunk of the afternoon to drive the eighty miles to Cranbrook. Frank noticed the closer they got to home, the nearer his boss' stories approached the truth. The rest of the day was like all the others, handshakes and long-lost cousins.

"We're not out of the woods yet," Doc King said as they pulled up in front of his house, "but I feel a lot better than I did three days ago. I'm in your debt, Frank. Why don't you come in to supper. I'm sure Nellie has an extra plate somewhere about."

"Well, sir...."

Doc King laughed. "My company wearing a bit thin? A certain young lady might be more to your taste for a Saturday night?"

"Yes, sir," Frank grinned.

"Wise choice. Tomorrow's Sunday. We'll put our feet up. Monday too, damn it. I'm going fishing. See you Tuesday morning."

"There's the Coldstream Guards concert Monday," Frank reminded him.

"Hell, so there is. Rutledge will be there, too, handing out his damn pamphlets. No need for you to go, though – at least not in your official capacity. Give my best to Miss MacPherson."

Frank smiled and nodded. It wasn't exactly a lie.

The Singer

"A girl could use a little company out there in the wide world," Mavis had said. Somewhere between Invermere and Cranbrook, Frank had made up his mind to find out exactly what that meant, and if it was what he thought, he'd take her up on it. Such was the effect of his encounter with Harriet. He hoped to catch her at The Green Door, not liking the prospect of showing up at her house.

Mavis' father, Llewelyn Weeks, was not the friendliest of men at the best of times and by suppertime on a Saturday night was "well into it." Frank knew him from his time at Wilson Lumber, a short, broad Welshman who could toss a twelve foot two-by-ten a whole lot farther than anyone else. He was another damaged veteran who had brought the horrors of war home to his family in 1919.

When work in the mines was cut to one shift, Llewelyn joined up. Trench warfare had put a premium on mining skills and he became a sapper, part of the army of former miners, lumber jacks, and railway men preparing for the attack on Vimy Ridge. He and his mates were at work on a communication tunnel when a German shell found a seam in the earth and exploded a few yards above their heads. He was buried for three days, the only one to come out alive, cushioned from the blast by the bodies of his comrades.

"Wacky" Weeks was a valuable employee at the lumber yard and having sacrificed for king and country was considered entitled to the occasional blow-up. These took the form of tossing those two-by-tens in random directions and screaming obscenities at Mike Wilson or his father. At home he was as quiet as a lamb except on Saturday nights when he drank himself into a weeping stupor.

Evelyn Weeks was not afraid of her husband and would have stayed by him during his night terrors were it not for the children. The elder two, both young women, had left home, one married, the other living in Wasa. But Mavis was only fourteen, her brothers ten and eight. Evelyn's solution was to take them to choir practice at the Methodist church every Saturday evening and afterwards to leave them for the night at her sister's house. Evelyn then returned home to attend to her husband.

This arrangement worked well for almost three years, especially as it turned out that Mavis had an exceptional singing voice and soon became one of the choir's star soloists, along with a Chinese girl, Ling Chou who became a close friend. The Methodist church was home at that time to a Chinese mission serving a district population of two hundred families. Mrs. Chou, a widow, lived in Chinatown, just across the alley from The Green Door.

Unfortunately, as she grew older Mavis began to experience unwanted attention from her uncle which became increasingly difficult to ignore, laugh off, and finally to physically repel. Because of her friendship with Ling, Mavis had visited Mrs. Chou with her mother who found it "clean and Christian" and so it was decided that spending her Saturday nights there made sense.

The girls would walk home from choir together and if they heard music behind The Green Door, would lean a ladder against their bedroom window and, after retiring for the night, climb down and sneak in through the club's back door. They would hide in a storage room and listen to hot jazz for hours. This went undetected for about six months until they were discovered by Lennie Chung, the cook. "No problem." he said installing them on stools behind a folding screen. "You sit here. More comfortable for sure."

The two friends shared a bed every Saturday night for almost a year until Ling moved to Vancouver to live with relatives. After that Mavis had it to herself. She kept up her visits to the jazz club and eventually got to know some of the musicians as they passed through. After learning that any attempt on her virtue would have to be negotiated with Lennie's cleaver, they adopted her as their 'white doll' and began to teach her rhythm. Pretty soon, when the coast was clear, she got to sing with the band. She was very good.

The sun was down and porch lights were coming on by the time Frank got to the club, bathed, wearing his best clothes, full of Mrs. McKinnon's left-over stew. He hadn't heard any music as he approached but that wasn't surprising. They didn't usually get going until well after dark. But the door was locked and there was no answer to his knock.

"Not open," a man said as he came out onto Clark St. A shadowy figure was sitting on the porch of a derelict house opposite. "Got raided last night."

Frank walked over. He was startled to see that he was Ktunaxa. They looked at each warily.

"You're one of the fellows who brought in that elephant a couple of days ago," Frank said at last. "I saw you at the station."

"And you're the fellow with the fancy car." He said 'fellow' with a mocking drawl.

"Not mine. Wish it was. I'm Dr. King's driver. What brings you here?"

"How's that your business?" the man said, standing up on the lower step and towering over Frank.

"It isn't," he said, hurriedly. "Sorry. Just curious. You like jazz?" Dumb question, he thought.

The man sat down again without answering. He smiled and shook his head. After an uncomfortable minute, he said, "Wife's mother's sick. We came for some medicine. There's an old China woman makes good stuff. Who knows what the hell's in it, but I seen it work. Those two, they're a couple of old medicine women. Been trading back and forth for years."

"Might have opium, I guess"

"Might."

Greatly daring, Frank sat down beside him. The man shifted over to make room and looked across at him, unwavering, leaning his elbow on the next step up. He looked somewhere in his thirties, a wide mouth curved up into a slight smile, a broad nose with high cheek bones, his face framed by long braids. His hands were powerful looking, well-used, with long fingers.

"Have much trouble with those elephants?" Frank asked.

"Not much. If you know how to break horses, a tame elephant's no problem. We tracked them over to Wycliff. They started running but we drove them into the river and kept them there. Tired them out. After that they came quiet enough. Sent for the circus fella and they came and got 'em."

"Did you get the reward?"

"Half." He spat between his feet. "That man's an arsehole."

"Yeah," Frank said. "How about the one over at Jap Lake?"

"You there? We decided to hell with it, catch him yourself." They both laughed. "I took the crazy man's money though. The old coot with the big gun." Frank sat up. "Old man's been out looking for elephants. Got a gun that could kill a grizzly on the other side of a moose. Offered me fifty dollars to locate an elephant."

"Say," the man continued while Frank took that in. "The wife wanted some booze to put the medicine in. They usually sell me one but they're all jittery after the raid. It's the only place I can get decent stuff." He took some money from his shirt pocket and held it out.

Frank looked at it. "I don't turn twenty-one until next week."

The man continued to hold out the money. "Okay," Frank said. He got up and walked back across the street, still thinking about Mr. Mac and his gun. This time he pounded hard on the door. Lennie Chung opened it. "We closed," he said. Frank told him what he wanted.

"For that Indian?" Lennie asked. "Bad idea."

"He's all right. It's for his wife's medicine. I'm a friend of Mavis. Is she around? I hear you got raided. Is she okay?"

"Yeah, she okay. Wasn't here. Gimme your money, I get a small bottle." He picked out a couple of bills and went inside.

When Frank got back, the man's wife was there and saying

something to him in a restrained angry voice. He grinned at Frank. "She thinks you're an agent, gonna arrest me."

"No ma'am," Frank said. "We're friends." He handed over the bottle and the change.

"No we're not," the man said. "You just bought me a bottle that I paid for." He stood up. "Thanks," he said and started up the street, his wife walking a couple of steps behind.

"Wait a minute," Frank called. "That old man with the gun. Did you tell him where to look?"

"Might have."

"Where?"

His wife said something that Frank couldn't understand. He laughed and said, "By rights you oughta pay me but since we're 'friends'," he said it like he'd said fellow, "I told him to take the trail over the ridge to Mayook. Easy to find. There's a burnt-out farmhouse with an orchard a few miles along. An elephant's hanging around out there."

Frank thanked him and went back to the porch and sat down, cupping his chin in his hands. Another of his mother's sayings came back to him – a fine kettle of fish. No sign of Mavis and now Mr. Mac and his gun to worry about. The old bastard really was going to shoot an elephant.

"Over my dead body," Frank muttered, then swore. Not at all unlikely if he tried to stop him. That tough old bird carrying a gun – what was he supposed to do about it? After five minutes of deep thought, the best he could come up with was to sneak into his house in the dead of night and steal the gun. Or wait behind a tree on the trail, rush out and grab the gun and run like hell. Yeah, sure, Frank. Great idea. Should have bought a bottle for myself while I was at it.

A woman turned the corner of the next street. "Mavis?"

She walked across and stood in front of him, smiling down. She looked beautiful, bursting with summer in a flower dress, her black curls like a halo around her head, large dark eyes shining with excitement. "Why, Mr. Burton as I live and breathe. Just when I thought I'd have no one to tell my news to."

"News?"

"I'm running away," she said giddily. "I'm taking the overnight to Vancouver tomorrow. Going to seek my fortune. Want to come?"

Frank stood up. "Yeah." His throat tightened. "I do." He felt a rush of desire, wanted to take her in his arms, wanted to… He stuffed his hands in his pockets and took a step back.

"Really?" Mavis said. "Really and truly, Frank?" She laughed as he took another step back. "You're going in the wrong direction. I'm over here." Frank moved towards her, his hands coming out of his pockets, but she held hers up, palms out, lightly touching his chest. "What about Jenny?"

He was ready for that one. "The last time I saw her she slapped my face."

"Getting too fresh, I bet. Not convincing."

"No, I wasn't. Honest. Cross my heart." He made the sign, leaving his hand on hers. "The other way round if anything. You know Jenny. She wants steady jobs and babies. I'm not ready for either. I want…" He looked down at her taking it all in.

"Don't, Frank. Don't say it unless you mean it. Let's go for a walk and talk it over."

They started down Edwards St. toward the park along St. Joseph's Creek. Mavis let him take her hand. Second night in a row walking with a girl, this one a whole lot nicer. For something to say he asked, "Why not tonight? Why aren't you leaving, tonight?"

"I spend Saturday nights with Mrs. Chou. After choir practice - long story I'll tell you sometime…. maybe," she added, not taking anything for granted. "I don't want to get her in trouble. And there's church tomorrow. Thought I'd sing one more time."

"Lucky for me," Frank said.

"Maybe," Mavis said again. "Maybe not. I've made up my mind, Frank. I can sing. I can sing better than anybody in this whole town. It sounds corny, I know, like in those movie magazines, but I'm going to be a star." She stopped and turned to him. "I'll be on that train tomorrow night no matter what. I'd like you to come, Frank. I wouldn't feel so scared with you along. But I'm not ever giving up. You need to know that."

They crossed a low bridge over the creek. A frog plopped into the water near a patch of bullrushes. Crickets chirped. There was a sand box and a set of swings on the other side. Mavis sat and Frank stood behind her, pushing gently against her back, smelling her each time she swung up to him. After a while he grabbed the ropes and held them. She leaned back against him.

"I wish we had somewhere to go," he said, suddenly bold.

"Do you now, Mr. Valentino?" Mavis said, bending back her head and looking up at him. "You could always throw me across your horse and carry me off to your tent. Oh, I forgot. No horse. No tent." She stood up and faced him. "So...what about Jenny?"

"She's made up her mind. She's going to marry Mike." It didn't feel like much of a lie. "And that's fine by me," he continued, which was a lot more of one. "The worst man won."

"And that makes me the consolation prize, I suppose."

He smiled ruefully. "Not much chance of any consolation tonight."

"I'm not fast, Frank," she said. "I've never..."

"Me neither... at least not...." They looked at each other and burst out laughing.

"That does it," Mavis grabbed his hand. "Come on."

They walked back up Edward St while Mavis explained. "Mrs. Chou will be home by now. I'll go in. You go around the back. There's a ladder you can put up to my window."

"And climb up?"

"Are you crazy? She's not deaf. No, I'll come down. You'll see." They hurried up the street, his heart pounding, mouth dry.

When they reached Mrs. Chou's, Frank did as he was told. Twenty minutes later, true to her word, she climbed down the ladder, put her finger to her lips and led him across the alley to The Green Door. "Lenny lives over there. He's gone home by now, I hope," she said, knocking quietly.

After listening for a minute, she reached into a crack along the wall and fished out a key. "He got tired of letting me in." She pulled him into a hallway beside the kitchen. It smelled strongly of Chinese cooking, garbage and stale lard.

They felt their way along the hall and up a flight of stairs. At the top was an open space dimly lit by the moon through a pair of grimy windows. The slope of the ceiling showed patches of corrugated tin over wooden slats. It was hot and stuffy. Mavis crossed to a table and struck a match, lighting a candle. Frank could see a couple of beds, some straw mattresses on the floor and a worn jute rug.

"The bands usually sleep up here when it's not too cold," Mavis said. "They always get the worst room in the hotels. The ones with the bedbugs. Lennie swears there aren't any up here. I guess we'll find out." She walked over to a bed and pushed it close to the window, slid up a bottom frame and propped it open, letting in a breath of cooler air. She straightened the sheets and lay down, looking at him with her head held up in her hand. She tried to smile but it wobbled. "Hurry up," she said, "before one of us…"

Frank lay down, put his arms around her and pressed himself against her. He was shaking. She took his head and drew it down to her breasts. He felt her skin under his hand and then they were helping each other out of their clothes.

"Wait," Mavis said. She reached into the pocket of her dress crumpled on the floor and held something out. "You'll need this. It's…."

"I know what it is," Frank said. "Where'd you get it?"

"Estelle gave me some. Reuben's wife. She said a girl never knows when she might need it. She said boys never think about it. I guess she was right. Here let me…"

"I know how to do it," Frank said, turning away. "At least I think I do."

The Trail

After a couple of weeks driving all over the East Kootenay with Doc King, Frank was pretty sure he wasn't going to win. On the other hand, he knew the old man was getting hopeful because of the way everyone was eating up his elephant stories. But Frank found it hard to believe people were stupid enough to vote for him just because of that. Shows what he knew. He wasn't rooting for him anyway. He liked him but he was a socialist, although he knew Mr. Sims wasn't going to win either. He was also sure Jenny wasn't going to marry him so there was nothing to stay for. The sooner he left the better.

Frank woke up Sunday morning to the sound of church bells coming from the Methodist church a couple of blocks away. Mavis had told him she had to sneak back into Mrs. Chou's as soon as it started to get light. He said he'd get up with her but of course he didn't. She left him a note.

Hello Sleepy Head.

Just kissed you and you didn't wake up. Is that what I can expect from now on? Lennie will be at church but you need to get out of there before noon. And get rid of those things. I think there were three!! See you at the station. 7:15pm. Don't be late.

Love, Mavis.

Frank had a note of his own to write too. At Hanson's he spent some time cleaning the McLaughlin-Buick, topping up the oil and water and filling her with gas. It was the least he could do. Then he retrieved the extra office key from the back of the car, crossed the street and let himself in. His note read:

Dear Dr. King.

I'm sorry to walk out on you without notice but something of a personal nature has come up which requires me to be in Vancouver immediately. I assure you I am not in trouble with the law or anything like that.

The car is all set to go and I'm sure one of those fellows who applied for the job will be happy to take over. At least he won't forget to put water in the radiator or get into accidents -although he might not be as good a political genius as me. Ha ha.

If things go according to plan I should have another good elephant story for you which I will mail when I find out what it is. When you tell it, please don't make fun of the elephants. I wish you luck with your election campaign although I am still a socialist. You won't be losing a vote with me leaving anyway.

I'll send my address in Vancouver and I hope you will be generous and forgiving enough to send me my pay. I will understand if you don't.

Please give my best to Mrs. King and Harry.

Sincerely, Frank

He slipped it under the blotter on Doc King's desk, leaving a corner sticking out. Now there was only one more thing to do before leaving Cranbrook for good. He figured he had just enough time but wished he'd told Mavis about it so if something happened she wouldn't worry.

It was nearly noon when he got home. Mrs. McKinnon was at church and the house was quiet. He changed into old work clothes and packed a bag with everything he needed for Vancouver including a thin wad of bank notes he'd kept in a sock.. On his way out he stole a hunk of cheese out of the ice box and a fat square of corn bread from the counter.

He zig-zagged towards Gold Creek Rd., eating as he went. As he passed the Whitmore house he saw that the hole Tommy had made in the fence had a few boards nailed across it. Hector was sitting on the porch. Catching sight of his old hunting companion he trotted over. When Frank kept going, he fell in behind.

Frank still had no idea how he was going to stop Mr. Mac. His best hope was that both Jenny and her grandfather would be at church. He could sneak in, find the gun, and hide it somewhere in the barn. When all the elephants had been caught, he could write and tell him where.

Frank slowed up when he came in sight of the house, crouched down and began to move stealthily forward, keeping Hector behind him. Peering over the garden gate he saw Jenny alone on the porch pacing up and down, looking agitated. Hector put his paws up on the fence beside him and barked, so Frank straightened up.

Jenny swung round, cried, "Oh Frank!" and ran down the porch steps. She was halfway along the path before she controlled herself and stopped. "I'm glad you came," she said, as calmly as she could. "I may need your help,".

"Keeping your crazy grampa out of jail?" Frank said. "Has the damn fool gone after that elephant already?"

"There's no need to talk like that, Frank," Jenny retorted, but unable to keep her composure, said "Oh Frank," again, her voice trembling, "He took his big gun. I tried to reason with him but he told me to mind my own business. An Indian came by yesterday evening and told him where to find one. He wouldn't tell me where. He said he wasn't going to church and he wouldn't be home for supper. He's never missed church before, ever."

"Come on, Hector," Frank said and started to walk away. He stopped and turned around. This would probably be their last time together and it was the first time he'd ever seen her so helpless. It didn't suit her, he thought. She should always be on top of things. He realized for about the thousandth time how beautiful she was.

"I'm sorry I'm not a better man, Jenny," he said. "Mike will make you a good husband. I'll see what I can do about your grampa. Goodbye."

"Frank!" Jenny called after him. "What are you talking about?"

Walking slowly backwards away from her he almost told

her he was leaving town and would never see her again and he loved her. But instead he said, "Even if I find your grampa, I might not be able to stop him. You need to go find that circus guy – Terrell – and tell him the elephant's over at Mayook. Near some abandoned homestead. Burnt out. Tell him to hurry.

"Mr. Terell's gone. He left last week with all the other elephants. It's in the newspaper. He turned things over to Mr. Ironsides."

"Then go find him. Up at the train station." He remembered who else would be there later. And Jenny was the one person he couldn't ask to take her a message. "Go right away. Don't tell him about Mr. Mac if you can help it. If you can't find him, get Bob and Jimmy. They'll be at Gyro playing ball." He turned away and this time kept walking.

He wished he was better at telling the time by the sun because it must have been after one already. That gave him about six hours. He had no idea how far down the road the trail to Mayook was and or how many miles a Ktunaxa would call 'a few'. He picked up his pace, hoping to keep it up long enough. Hector trotted contentedly behind, stopping every now and then to sniff at something interesting and then lolloping along, ears flapping, to catch up.

He'd have to find the old homestead and hope Mr. Mac was using it as a blind. He couldn't see wandering around looking for fresh elephant scat and it made sense it would stick close to the orchard. He wondered which one it was. There were three still out there; Tilly, Myrtle, and Charlie Ed.

He found the Mayook trailhead easily enough but after that the going got a lot tougher. It was an old prospector trail traversing the lower slopes of Mt. Baker and hadn't been cleared in a long time, jammed with deadfalls, crossing several boggy ravines full of skunk cabbage and devil's club. He was glad he'd changed into work clothes although his boots had never been particularly waterproof. It also occurred to him that he was in grizzly and cougar country without a gun.

An hour later he was starting to get desperate. He'd have

to find Mr. Mac right away, talk or threaten him out of shooting that elephant and then head straight back. Soaked with sweat, he struggled up out of a particularly deep ravine and told himself, as he'd done a couple of times already, that if he couldn't see any sign of an opening up ahead, he'd quit. This time he saw one.

A bank of earth that looked man-made turned out to be a wagon road. It led to a clearing full of huge tree stumps with notches for chopping platforms cut into their sides. The Mayook logging road came in near Wardner, farther east, so any homestead had to be somewhere along it. He whistled to Hector and they began to trot.

A half mile of switchbacks took them up to a screen of cedars beside a small creek and a rail fence, still intact. Beyond that a field full of chest high grass. The road passed through an opening in the fence and proceeded diagonally across the pasture towards the burnt-out remains of a house. A well-constructed stone chimney still stood at one end. There were a dozen or so fruit trees beside it, a couple of tall cherry trees, their leaves brown with blight, another smaller one dotted with purple plums and the rest straggly apples badly in need of pruning. Frank wondered what had happened to the family and why they had not rebuilt.

Taking the road across the field would have given him away to any hunter or elephant in the neighbourhood so Frank looked for a way around. He ducked in among the cedars, Hector right behind. It occurred to him that bringing the dog might have been a mistake. He looked back and pointed down. "Stay," he said.

Hector crouched low and cocked his head to one side. When Frank moved forward, the dog followed, belly scraping the ground. As Frank turned to admonish him, he scurried ahead and looked back as if to say, "Follow me." Of course, Frank thought, he's probably better at this than I am.

They had covered about half the distance to the house when Hector stopped and sniffed at a stretch of wet sand beside the creek. Beneath his nose was the impression of a large boot, fresh as far as Frank could tell. Almost for sure it belonged to Mr. Mac. He stepped across the creek and scrambled up onto the lowest branch of a large cedar commanding a view of the house, the pasture and the orchard. With a sigh, Hector settled down at its base.

The only sound was the occasional snap and whir of grasshoppers at the edge of the pasture and the lazy waving of the grass stalks. A faint, hot breeze wafted across the field. To Frank the air was dry and sweet smelling but Hector had begun to detect other odours. He lifted his nose at a sharp angle and sniffed in earnest. Then he growled, a low rumble like a chorus of baritones.

"Quiet," Frank hissed. Hector subsided. Then he growled again, more insistently and crept to the edge of the trees. He looked up at Frank then across to his right where the road entered the field. It all looked the same to him until, as if moulded from the weathered grey of the fence beside her, a full-grown elephant appeared.

He could tell it wasn't Myrtle even at that distance, so it had to be Tilly. She walked at a leisurely, swaying pace, slowing every now and then to pull up a tuft of grass and tuck it into her mouth. As he watched, Frank felt a tingling up his spine to the back of his neck and the roots of his hair. He seemed to be floating.

Everything was slow and peaceful. He thought, "Boy, what a treat for her. All her life she's been hauled from pillar to post by that damned circus, noisy trains, noisy crowds, bright lights, leg irons. This was what she was made for." He was mesmerized and probably wouldn't have noticed Mr. Mac at all if it hadn't been for Hector.

Not able to see over the tall grass, the dog had been busy with his nose, growling quietly to himself. But now he whipped his head around in the opposite direction and gave one soft, sharp woof. Frank looked down at him and then along the line of his gaze. Only a few yards away, Mr. Mac had stepped out from the shelter of the cedars, moving stealthily along the creek to where he could see directly up the road at Tilly. He was carrying the big gun Frank had seen on his kitchen counter. He wanted to shout a warning to the elephant but it seemed just as likely he would drive her further along the road, closer to Mr. Mac.

He jumped down and hurled himself blindly through the maze of trees, his boots slipping on the wet mud, branches slapping his face. Suddenly the trees parted. Mr. Mac was down on one knee, the stock of his gun already pressed against his shoulder, his eye sighted along the barrel, focused on his target. Frank drew himself up and threw his full weight across the creek. His stride fell short of the opposite bank, front foot slipping against a submerged rock. He skittered forward, tumbled sideways and rolled helplessly along the ground, his momentum carrying him within a foot of the startled hunter.

The old man's hearing and reflexes weren't what they used to be, allowing Frank time to scramble up and snatch the gun out of his hands. He might have gotten clean away except, true to form, he snagged his foot on a protruding root and sprawled forward. He scrambled up again but Mr. Mac had recovered sufficiently to reach out and catch hold of Frank's shirt. This spun him around, sending him flying out towards the pasture. He plunged blindly ahead and came out into the open a few yards from Tilly.

Meanwhile, Hector and Mr. Mac were engaged in a shouting match as the latter attempted to catch up to Frank. Evading a kick, the dog ran forward towards Frank. Tilly had reacted calmly enough to Frank's sudden appearance and might have allowed him to get even closer had not Hector, now fully aroused, suddenly burst out of the tall grass, barking furiously. This was too much. Ten days in the wild had awakened her jungle instincts and she charged.

Frank turned to run and collided with Mr. Mac. They fell into a heap, hastily untangled themselves and fled. Hector, roaring and bouncing in front of Tilly, slowed her down just enough for all three to escape towards the dubious shelter of the orchard.

As they approached the nearest trees, Mr. Mac gave a cry of pain, clutched his knee and went down. Frank dropped the gun and hauled him to his feet. A few steps more and Frank collapsed onto his hands and knees at the base of a gnarled apple, allowing Mr. Mac to clamber onto his back and hoist himself up. From there he helped Frank up beside him, just out of reach of a charging Tilly.

But Tilly didn't stop. She ran full tilt into the trunk giving a squeal of rage as her shoulder smashed against it. With a sharp crack, the trunk, rotten with age, bent and snapped, sending Frank and Mr. Mac flying. When they landed, their former roost came down on top of them, momentarily blocking Tilly's path.

She circled around trying to get at them. They crawled out and made a limping dash for the largest of the cherry trees, scrambling up it with seconds to spare. It looked like Tilly was going to attack that one too, but she halted a few feet away, blood streaming from her wounded shoulder. Hector tried to distract her with charges and a volley of barks but she ignored him, stood her ground and watched her quarry malignantly.

Mr. Mac shifted himself onto a thicker branch and began to massage his injured knee. "Frank!" he said

"What?"

"You're a pinhead, Frank. You know that? A real pinhead."

"Look, Mr. Macpherson," Frank replied indignantly, "I'm no happier about this than you are. But I'm not sorry either. Another minute and you would have shot that elephant..."

"Don't talk any dumber than you have to, Frank. That damned gun wasn't even loaded! Where would I get bullets for a gun like that around here? Think I'm gonna use thirty-year-old ammo? Most likely get my own head blown off. I was just trying to get her in my sights. Best part of three hours I've been stalking her..... Pinhead!"

There wasn't a whole lot to say after that. About fifteen minutes later Frank began to inch his way down but Tilly, as vigilant as ever, edged closer. They were treed like cats. Mr. Mac wedged himself down into a cluster of branches and closed his eyes. Frank climbed as high up the tree as he dared and looked both ways along the narrow valley. There was no help in sight. Hector wandered off in search of rabbits.

The Misunderstanding

Jenny watched Frank and the dog walk away, wondering what he had meant about Mike and goodbye. She hurried into the house, put on her walking shoes and a hat and headed off in the opposite direction.

That should have been one of the worst days of her life. Her Grampa was off hunting elephants and might end up in jail for all she knew. She couldn't understand what had gotten into him or why anyone would want to shoot a beautiful creature like that. And Frank had just told her goodbye. Although it wasn't exactly clear what he had said. You almost always had to ask him to start over once or twice until you understood what he really meant to say but this didn't sound good. But even then, just past eighteen, she'd already had a few days a lot worse than that one.

Jenny had been an orphan since she was eleven. Her father had bought into a hardware store with money loaned to him by his father. He ended up owning it a few years later. The store was on Fenwick Avenue, and she was born in the apartment above.

Willie Macpherson was a restless man who yearned for adventure. The hardware business gave him a comfortable living, but when the war came along he turned it over to a manager and joined up. Ironically, his hardware experience denied him the adventure he craved. He spent the war in a warehouse in the south of England stocking shelves and filling out forms. In early 1919 Quartermaster Sergeant Macpherson returned home to a hero's welcome bringing with him an Iron Cross souvenir, which he had bought for a pound, and the Spanish Flu.

After her father left, Jenny and her mother felt worried about him at first, then relieved when he wrote home complaining about his job and how he would never get near the front. There were even hard feelings about it with some people in town. When he came home it was all sunshine and blue skies. He took them out to the Mt. Baker Hotel to celebrate. It felt so grand. Jenny wore her best dress and a pink ribbon in her hair that came from London with little v's for victory along both edges. Papa had a cough and Mama wanted to put it off until he felt better but he said he'd be fine and wasn't going to let it spoil their fun. The next morning he couldn't get out of bed. When Mama took to hers too, Jenny went to Mrs. McKinnon's whose husband had been killed two years before. And then they both died.

Jenny stopped believing in sunshine and blue skies for a long time after that. If it hadn't been for Mrs. McKinnon and then her Grampa, she might have curled up and died herself. She cried herself to sleep for a year.

Mr. Mac came to Cranbrook as soon as he heard what had happened but stayed away until he'd bought the farm and decorated her room. Then he came through the door one afternoon and scared the daylights out of her. He was so big and rough but like her Papa at the same time. She didn't want to go near him. So he sat down on the sofa at the far end of the parlour and started singing. He had a fine baritone voice and sang Loch Loman, sang it through twice and then he got up and walked over and held out his hand and said, "Jennifer, it's time to go home." She thought he was a wonderful man and was sad that he and Frank never took to each other the way she would have liked.

Callum Macpherson, a recent widower, was a fond grandfather and a rigorous Presbyterian. He made the rearing of his son's daughter his new life's work. He drove her to school every day, to church every Sunday. Not sociable himself, he escorted her to church gatherings and, on the advice of Mrs. McKinnon, encouraged her to volunteer at Sunday school.

Jenny always loved children and wanted to protect them from all the bad things that can happen. She was everyone's pet. Poor little orphan girl, granddaughter of an upstanding church elder, polite, something of an heiress in a modest Cranbrook way. Some people considered her nigh on perfect, herself included. Certainly good enough for the town's most eligible bachelor, Mr. Mike Wilson. So as far as Frank was concerned, it turned out fortunate he hadn't notice she was already spoken for.

The church ladies had little faith in Mr. Mac's ability to guide Jenny towards womanhood, especially when it came to 'feminine matters'. Under their care she was spared the worst traumas of puberty and taught the mysteries of undergarments. At the age of fifteen, she was given a little talk by Mrs. Mac, as Jenny teasingly called her, and at its conclusion was presented with a book. "It's a bit old fashioned nowadays," she'd said, "but I found it helpful. Just ignore the snootiness and remember that the choices you make in the next few years will be with you for the rest of your life."

An Introduction To Married Life by Mrs. Sherwood Brandel: the wife of a clergyman, was packed full of sound advice on domestic arrangements, everything from how to manage a household budget to getting along with servants, as well as tackling the deeper questions of how to get, and keep, a husband.

Later, Jenny would laugh at most of it and blush to remember the nonsense she had taken for gospel but even the poorest nut has some meat in it as they say. There was one passage she learned by heart and it might have been true, way back when marriage could open a door for a woman or else put her in shackles for the rest of her life - like Frank's elephants.

"Courtship can be the most momentous period in a woman's life and is often the only one in which she has control over her own destiny. If she is to stay true to her vows to love, honour and obey, as well as to secure her own and her children's happiness, she must be certain that the man she accepts is himself loving, honourable, and trustworthy."

It was a different world. Even as young and sheltered as she was, she had seen enough to know how precarious life could be. Not only her own experience but others' too. Poor Mrs. Smith, her husband drank up the housekeeping money again or Mrs. Jones won't be in church until her black eye heals up. And if a husband decides to walk away or, heaven forbid, take up with another woman, what is a wife to do? Such high hopes they all had and many of them just put up with it and were miserable for the rest of their lives.

The hot August sun blazed down as Jenny hurried up Edward St., through Chinatown to the CPR station. She passed by the house where Mavis was drinking a last cup of tea with Mrs. Chou, having sworn her to secrecy and promising to write. She glanced down the alley towards The Green Door, where Lennie Chung was sitting on the stoop, still in his Sunday clothes, smoking a cigarette.

It was Francis Guimont's turn for Sunday duty at the telegraph office. "Mr. Ironsides' not here," he said. "He sometimes drops by in the afternoon after church. He'll be here to meet the night train to Vancouver for sure. The Coldstream Guards Band is on it - for the concert tomorrow. He's the welcoming committee. That would be about seven thirty. Anything I can do?"

Jenny hesitated. "No, I'll wait."

She sat in the waiting room for an hour. Francis came out to pass the time but she was fidgety and answered his questions distractedly. She seemed upset about something but he didn't like to pry. Then she got up, thanked him and said she might see him later. "If Mr. Ironsides does come," she said, "Tell him to.... Oh, I don't know, tell him to set fire to a train and I'll come running." She laughed and left.

She walked along Baker, dead quiet on a Sunday afternoon, then to the CPR manager's residence on Garden Ave. A neighbour told her the Ironsides had gone picnicking at Jimsmith Lake. Which left Bob and Jimmy at Gyro Park.

The usual Sunday pick-up game was just getting started. Everything was pretty informal and girls were allowed to join their boyfriends in the outfield although they weren't allowed to play the infield.

Mike Wilson had just struck out and was walking out towards left field. Jimmy was pitching and Bob was in centre standing alongside Eileen. Jenny went out to join them. She had decided to tell them the whole story, including what her grampa was up to, and then ask Bob to drive her out to Jimsmith.

Luckily, no balls were hit their way and nobody got out. When she had finished, Bob said, "Why don't you ask your boyfriend," pointing towards Mike. "His car's right here."

"He's not my boyfriend. Frank said you'd help."

"Look Jenny," Bob said, "I work Monday to Friday and half of Saturday. This is the most fun I get all week. When the game's over I'll go get my uncle's car if he's not using it. Or you can ask Mike not-my-boyfriend Wilson over there."

Miffed that baseball was Bob's most fun all week, Eileen took Jenny's arm and stalked off. "We could walk. It's only a few miles."

Mike and Bob were standing together looking in their direction. Bob was doing the talking, clearly telling Mike all about it. If Jenny didn't swear, she came close. "Never mind. I'll wait for Mr. Ironsides at his house. Tell Bob to keep quiet about it."

"Fat chance," Eileen said and went back to the game.

Jenny spent the rest of the afternoon sitting on the residence porch. Just before seven, she gave up and hurried back to the station. Mavis was sitting in the waiting room. They looked at each other, Mavis with suspicion, Jenny anxiously. If she finds out about grampa, Jenny thought, it will be all over town by tomorrow. If Bob doesn't blab first.

Francis came out of his office. "He hasn't shown up yet," he told Jenny.

She's come to stop him, Mavis thought. Why else would she be here? "Frank?" she asked.

Jenny looked at her. "No, I'm..."

"Have you seen him?"

Jenny blushed and looked away. "No," she said again.

"The train should be here soon," Francis said. "I'll take care of your bag."

"Thank you," Mavis said, "I'll wait out on the platform."

She can come out there if she has anything to say to me, she thought. She found out somehow and is trying to stop him.

Jenny watched her leaving. "Are you going to Vancouver?" she asked.

"Yes," Mavis said without looking back. "Either way."

What does that mean? Jenny thought. She decided to wait for Mr. Ironsides out front, away from prying ears.

Mavis watched Jenny go out through the front doors and pace anxiously up and down, stopping occasionally to look out across Van Horne St. She was obviously waiting for someone. Frank.

About ten minutes later, Ironsides came out onto the platform. He seemed agitated and kept looking down at his watch and then east along the train track. A far-off whistle sounded and he put his watch away.

Mavis looked in through the glass doors, across the waiting room and out towards Jenny. She was gone. No Frank either.

The train pulled up against the platform and the conductors stepped out, setting their step stools down at the car doors. "Hello Mavis," said Mrs. Morrissey, "Visiting Vancouver?"

"No," Mavis said. "I'm running away." Mrs. Morrissey laughed.

A crowd of soldiers in bright red uniforms, carrying instrument cases came out of a car further down. They lined up and at a word from their sergeant, marched towards the baggage car. Still no sign of Frank. And he'd sent no word.

He's not coming, Mavis thought, Jenny made sure of that. She walked back into the waiting room and across to the telegraph office. On the counter was a pile of blank forms and some pencils. She sat down at a desk in the corner and began to write. She meant to tell him how much his betrayal had hurt her, how sad she felt but the anger came pouring out.

Frank.

I guess you taught me a lesson I won't forget. I never should have told you I was leaving with or without you so then you saw your chance. What a skunk. I feel sorry for Jenny and I'm glad I escaped with only one night to regret. She'll end up with a skunk in her bed for the rest of her life unless she wises up.

I am planning on changing my name so you'll never know what you are missing until one day you'll see my picture on a movie poster. You can stick it up in the lunchroom at the lumber yard.

Sincerely and for the last time,

Mavis Weeks

She walked behind the counter and took an envelope from Francis' desk and put in the note, gummed it and wrote Frank Burton on the front. She took it out to Francis and asked him to give it to Frank the next time she saw him. He put it in his jacket pocket and handed her a baggage ticket. She took the conductor's hand and stepped up into the car. As the train pulled out, Francis looked across the platform to the window where she was sitting. He could see that she was crying and then a white cloud of steam drifted up from the engine and she disappeared into it.

Ironsides walked over and stood beside Francis. "Jenny Macpherson just told me she got it from Frank Burton that an elephant was seen over at Mayook. Are she and Frank......? Never mind. Do me a favour. I'm supposed to escort these fellows to the Mount Baker. Can you do it for me? If I grab the circus crew and take the Wardner road I can get there before dark."

Francis said he would. He helped his boss load some extra rope and chains into his truck. Then he turned back to attend to the waiting soldiers who had come out of the station and were forming up in front. They began to chatter and point. A Ktunaxa on horseback had just ridden up and dismounted a few yards away. He motioned to Francis to come over.

"I'm looking for the circus man. We got an elephant over

at Mayook."

"He knows already. Mr. Ironsides' heading out there as soon as he rounds up a crew."

The man swore. "My horse is worn out. I need a ride in his truck."

"I can't help you there," Francis said. "You could try waiting up on the Wardner road and catch him there."

The man swore again and rode off.

Francis spent the next hour getting the soldiers settled and working out the details of the little drama that he had just seen. What puzzled him was why Jenny was so fired up about the elephant that she would spend the entire day trying to get hold of his boss. Maybe that was only part of it. And what had upset Mavis? She'd been happy enough before Jenny showed up. He was itching to look inside her letter to Frank but didn't. When he got home he told his wife all about it.

Oh, that poor girl," she said.

"Which one?" he asked. "Jenny?"

"No, silly, she'll be all right" she said. "It's the one leaving town I feel sorry for."

The next afternoon Francis took his wife to the concert. They joined the crowd in the public school playground to watch the soldiers march by on their way to the arena. She nudged him and pointed across the street. Jenny was standing there holding her grandfather's arm. Mr. Mac was leaning heavily on a cane. Jenny seemed to be looking just about everywhere except at the band.

"Hello Francis, Mrs. Guimont." Mike Wilson raised his hat. "Have you seen Miss Macpherson?" She pointed. He thanked her and sprinted across just ahead of the band. Francis watched Jenny and it seemed to him that when she saw Mike, she looked distressed and shrank closer to Mr. Mac.

A minute later someone else came up behind them. "Hello, Francis," Frank said. There was a large red bruise on his forehead just over the eye. "Did Mavis... did Miss Weeks take the train yesterday?"

161

Francis nodded, reached into his pocket and handed him the envelope. Frank tore it open and stood reading without turning away. Francis could have shifted slightly to read it over his shoulder if he had cared to. As he read, Frank's shoulders drooped and when he had finished he slowly folded it up and put it back into the envelope. He quietly thanked Francis and walked away.

Francis and his wife enjoyed the concert very much. They enjoyed each other's company that day even more than usual. Francis found himself grateful that his life had settled into its comfortable groove and all the bother of youth was behind him. Not that he felt particularly old and when they got home, he dismissed the maid and took his wife straight to bed and they made love in the late afternoon which they had not done for a long time.

The Wrangler

On the Sunday afternoon the day before, Frank stood in the cherry tree, scanning the horizon like a shipwrecked sailor. Below him, Mr. Mac dozed quietly. "She'll wander off eventually," he'd said, without conviction.

Tilly remained close and vigilant. After about half an hour Hector returned and settled nearby on a large moss-covered boulder. Every so often he would sidle warily toward the tree and bark impatiently up at the two men, then retreat as Tilly began to stir.

Frank looked up at the sun and tried to guess the time. He figured he was quickly running out of it. He'd taken almost an hour to get to the head of the trail then one and a half more until he'd spotted Tilly. Almost another gone by since. That made it four thirty. If he started right away he might get back just in time to catch the train. A big if.

He figured he could wait until Tilly was turned away or distracted by Hector, jump down from the tree and hightail it back to town. Leaving Mr. Mac behind. With his bum knee there was no way he'd make it. Of course, if Tilly was diverted by chasing him, Mr. Mac might be able to make his getaway. But then what? It was his fault the old man was treed in the first place. He'd be a rat to run out on him now.

"Shit!" Frank said.

Tilly looked up at him. She's definitely not the one that knocked me out, he thought, forgetting that he's done that himself. This one has no tusks and mean eyes. Or maybe that's just the way she's feeling after ten days in the wilderness. She looks at home though. Smug.

"Shit!" Frank said again.

"Stop your cursing," Mr. Mac said, "It's a sign of weak character and a feeble mind."

That's where she gets it, Frank thought. Serve him right if I jump ship. Jump tree.

163

"You really went to all that trouble just to pretend?" Frank asked. "What were you going to do, say bang like a kid?"

Mr. Mac gave a snorting laugh. "Hadn't thought that far. Probably just pulled the trigger. Click." He thought a minute. "You're not very ambitious are you son?"

Frank looked at him.

"Dreams?" Mr. Mac prompted. "Mountains to climb?"

"I dreamt I played for the Cubs once. I was in my pajamas," He left out the missing bottoms. "I dropped the ball."

"Sounds about right. Isn't that blasted elephant ever going to leave?"

Why should she, Frank thought. She's having the time of her life, the first and likely last time she'll ever get to be what she is. "Maybe it would have been better if you had shot her," he said. "Can't be much of a life in the circus."

"Hard to know what goes on in the mind of an elephant. Got all those other elephants to keep her company."

Or share her misery. A while later, as the sun slipped behind the shoulder of Mt. Baker, "Listen! Horses."

Two riders appeared at the top of the road, turned and started down towards them. As they got closer Frank recognized the Ktunaxa man and his wife from Chinatown. They stopped and took in the scene, the two men in the cherry tree, Tilly standing guard and the dog perched on a boulder. The man said something to his wife and laughed. She laughed too. Then she said something and pointed back along the road.

They began to argue. Not violently but in the comfortable way married people are accustomed to. The woman said something that took a while to get through, slapping her hand several times on her saddle horn for emphasis. When she'd finished, the man sat thinking it over. Then he grunted assent, tipped his hat towards the two men, wheeled his horse around and trotted back along the road.

"Hey!" Mr. Mac shouted. "Where are you going? Get this elephant out of here!"

The man called back, "Be patient, old man. My wife knows

what she's doing."

The woman dismounted and led her horse to an apple tree at the far end of the orchard, keeping well away from Tilly who was watching intently. She tethered her horse, climbed up and began tossing down apples. When there were a couple dozen scattered on the ground, she climbed down, took a bag from behind her saddle and gathered them into it. Then she carefully walked halfway towards Tilly and sat down cross-legged on the grass.

She sat motionless for a long time while the prisoners, the dog, and the elephant watched. She had a pleasant round face with large dark eyes, a broad, stern mouth and black hair in a single thick braid down her back. She wore a green and white checkered dress that might have been made from a kitchen tablecloth, leggings and soft beaded leather boots. When she saw Tilly begin to graze again she took a pouch out of her dress pocket, rolled herself a cigarette and carefully lit it, tilting her head upwards to expel the smoke. Frank watched, fascinated, while Mr. Mac groaned in frustration. She looked over at them and carefully picked a piece of tobacco off her tongue.

Sometime later she began to sing. Frank had long given up hope of catching his train. He remembered what Mavis had said yesterday about taking it no matter what. But that had been before they'd become lovers and he hoped that would change things.

The song was incomprehensible to the two men. It was soft, like a lullaby, the same few words over and over, hypnotically. Mr. Mac had closed his eyes, an expression of grim endurance on his face. Frank found himself nodding off. He looked over at Tilly. She was swaying in time, shifting her weight from foot to foot, her trunk swishing through the grass. Like brush work on cymbals in a slow jazz piece, he thought.

He could understand why she was being so cautious. The circus men had made it clear that a rogue elephant was a dangerous animal and remembered the one at Jap Lake. He wondered if this was the same one. He couldn't remember seeing tusks. Still, he wished she'd get on with it. His rear end was getting sore and he was very thirsty.

On cue, the woman stood up, still singing. She reached into the bag beside her and retrieved three apples, holding one out towards Tilly. Stepping and swaying in time to the elephant, she edged sideways toward her, never facing head on. Frank read in the Herald that the circus trainers had taught them to dance and wondered if she knew that. Probably not, he decided. Like her husband said, she just knew what she was doing.

Gradually their dance brought them closer and closer together until she held the apple, flat on her hand, under Tilly's trunk. The elephant gently reached out with her lips and took it into her mouth. The other two went the same way as she danced Tilly towards her bag and extracted several more, leading her farther and farther away. "That's it," Mr. Mac said, easing his way down the tree. "Let's go." He stopped at the lowest branch and looked up at Frank. "Come on. Help me down!"

"Wait a second," Frank said. The song had changed, the words in English now. "Stop, stop, stop," she was chanting. "Stay still, old man. Stay still."

"She thinks the elephant's not ready."

"Nonsense," Mr. Mac scoffed. "Just be ready to help me run." He stretched out along the branch, dangling by his arms. "Come on!" he shouted.

Suddenly Tilly lurched around, squealing with anger, and charged. With the strength of desperation, Mr. Mac threw his legs back up into the tree just as Tilly passed under. But the maneuver had loosened his grip on the branch. He swung head down. "Jesus Christ! Help!," he yelled in pain and terror, holding on with both legs.

While the elephant regrouped for a second charge, Frank bolted down the trunk, hoisted Mr. Mac upright onto his branch and clambered back. Tilly circled the tree several times before stationing herself within striking distance once more. The woman yelled something, the contempt in her voice making it easy enough to understand. But when Tilly looked back at her she subsided and squatted down again in the grass. She reached into her pocket and began to roll a cigarette.

"I was calling on the Lord," Mr. Mac said. Sure you were, Frank thought, but it was me who answered.

Time dragged on, woman and elephant content to stay put. The two men had no choice but to do the same. The song began again, Tilly swaying gracefully in time. Another hour passed. And half another. The light had steadily faded, crickets were chirping in the grass. A flight of swallows and a pair of bats darted back and forth through the chilling air. Every once in a while Mr. Mac would glare up at Frank and mutter, "Pinhead!"

Tilly grew restless and began to wander around them in ever widening circles. The woman stood up and motioned to them to come down slowly. Then they heard the sound of a truck....

Jenny wasn't very good at lying so it hadn't taken Ironside long to get the whole story out of her. She started out with the bald statement that an elephant had been spotted at an abandoned farm somewhere along the Mayook trail.

"Who told you that?"

"An Indian."

"An Indian told you?"

"Well, he told grampa."

"When was this? This morning?

"No, yesterday."

"And your grampa only sent you to tell me today? At six thirty in the evening?

"I'm sorry, Mr. Ironsides, I've been looking for you all day. Frank said...."

"Frank? Frank Burton? What's he got to do with this?"

"Frank told me where grampa... I mean, Frank must have spoken to the same Indian and found out...."

"Found out? Found out what?"

"Where he went," Jenny said lamely.

"Where who....your grampa? You mean he went after the elephant? When was this? After church?"

That was too much for Jenny. "No. He didn't go to church. He took his gun and when Frank found out…."

"His gun! That big elephant gun?" Everyone knew the story.

"Oh, Mr. Ironsides, please don't tell anyone. Please just go and find him and stop him from doing something foolish."

"Goddamn it, Jenny, I can't… oh, excuse me…I can't… I have to meet the train. All right, don't cry. I'll see what I can do. I'll have to get a crew together and get out there. I'm sorry but I don't see how I can keep this quiet if he….. Well, I promised your young man he could come along next time we went after an elephant. Maybe he can help keep a lid on it."

"My young man?"

"Mike Wilson. My wife and I were playing bridge last night with Mr. and Mrs….. He is your young man, isn't he? I thought…"

"It doesn't matter. Please just get out there!"

As Jenny walked disconsolately home and the train was carrying Mavis away from Cranbrook forever, Ironsides drove around town rounding up his crew. That was easy enough because he knew a couple of them were playing ball at Gyro Park. Mike Wilson would be there too and that should be enough. As it turned out that damned reporter from the Courier was there too and insisted on coming along. He'd have to have a word with him. Fortunately, Betts the editor was a bridge player too.

Jimmy and Bob ran home and borrowed Uncle Henry's car and raced to catch up to the circus truck and Mike's Studebaker. By the time they turned off the highway there was quite a convoy. The boys were surprised to see a man holding a horse in the back of the truck which they were pretty sure hadn't been there before.

Mayook itself was just a flag station on the rail line and a cluster of farms connected to a water line running down from Mount Baker. They pulled up outside a house about half a mile in. A boy who might have been twelve told them there was a burned-out homestead with an old orchard another mile up. When he found out they were hunting an elephant he begged to come along. Ironsides said no but the kid hopped onto the back when they started off and grinned back at Mike as they bumped along.

The plan was to drive the last quarter mile as quietly as possible, stop short and reconnoitre. They hoped the elephant, if it was there at all, would be hungry and glad to see them after two weeks in the bush. Opinion was divided on that.

Frank and Mr. Mac, being higher up, heard the truck first, then the woman and finally Tilly. Hector was asleep. It was a sound Tilly was used to and associated with the company of other elephants and a regular supply of food and she moved slowly toward it. But it also came with circus men who shackled her inside stalls and sometimes whacked her with sticks. As their smell reached her she slowly backed away and stood hesitating at the edge of the orchard. The woman walked along with her, keeping her distance, chanting softly and eying her carefully.

The two circus men, Ironsides, Mike, Jimmy, Bob, and the boy came in a bunch to the top of the road. There was enough light to see the fruit trees and the dim outline of the stone chimney. They halted at the gate and peered down the tunnel of grass. The Ktunaxa followed, leading his horse. One of the circus men, tall and skinny, wearing overalls and a cloth cap, pushed forward and led the way. Suddenly he stopped and pointed. "What the hell's that squaw think she's doing? Hey," he yelled, waving his arm, "Get the hell away from that elephant. You're gonna get yourself killed."

Her husband came up behind. "That's my wife you're yelling at," he said. "And you don't call her that."

The circus man turned to face him. "Says who?"

Ironsides pushed between them. "Calm down, Bill."

"No Indian's telling me what…"

"Listen," Ironsides said. "If you start something don't count on back up from me."

Bill looked at the other circus man who shrugged and examined his boots.

"It's just a word," Bill said, looking away.

"So's arsehole," the Ktunaxa said. Everybody laughed, except Bill.

"Okay, smart guys. How do we catch that elephant without his... Mrs. getting killed."

They looked back towards the orchard.

"Hey," Bob said. "Where'd they go?

Tilly and the woman had disappeared. The men ran to the orchard, reaching the cherry tree just as Frank and Mr. Mac were climbing stiffly down. Frank limped back and forth rubbing his rear end while Mr. Mac collapsed on the ground with a groan.

"Over there," Frank said, cocking his thumb towards the remains of the farmhouse.

"Well, well...Frank Burton, The Great White Tree Climber!" Mike laughed. "Something to tell the grandkids about. Or maybe Jenny can. Did I ever tell you about the time one of my old beaus, can't remember his name, got treed by an elephant...."

"Knock it off, Mike," Bob said, unable to suppress a smile.

A path led from the orchard, behind the house and continued through a field surrounded by a broken-down fence. It was full of thistles and tansy and must have once been a garden. They could see where the fugitives had trampled through the weeds onto a logged slope that dropped down towards the road and the parked truck.

The woman and the elephant were walking side by side, winding their way between stumps and piles of slash. Hector trailed a few yards behind. The circus men ran ahead, Bill across to the truck, the other after Tilly. As he got closer, he circled around them and blocked their path, waving his arms nervously. Tilly stopped and began to back away.

Bill started up the truck and drove slowly up the slope. The woman began to walk quickly towards him, yelling something and waving at him to stop. He ignored her, turned away and bumped over the rough ground in a long curve that took him between Tilly and the lower edge of the clearing. Hector raced along beside, barking furiously. The truck stopped at the bottom of the field. Bill jumped out and began to pull ropes and netting from the back. Tilly swerved and lumbered away toward the trees higher up. Hector followed.

By this time, Ironsides, Mike, Bob and the boy had come through the garden and stood watching. Frank limped up behind. The other circus man waved them closer. They obeyed, reluctantly inching down the hill. Tilly saw them coming and made a dash to her left but her path was blocked by a tangle of slash and junk logs. She made a noise between a trumpeting and a squeal that Frank thought sounded like despair. She turned again and dashed across the hillside towards the road.

She might have escaped that way except the Ktunaxa rider came galloping down onto her and she veered away. Hector raced past and took up station beside the horse, barking constantly.

Tilly tried to get by again, but the man, the horse and the dog, working together, forced her back. After two more tries, she turned away into the field where the circus men were waiting. They had pegged a net to the ground and as she rushed past a slash pile, they threw it over her. A moment later, as she struggled to free herself, Bill came up from behind and wrapped a rope around her hind leg and pulled it back so that she had to lift it in the air to keep her balance. She knew from long experience that she was caught and so gave up the struggle.

After they had loaded Tilly into the truck, the horseman rode up. It was almost dark. He pointed up the slope to where his wife had gone to retrieve her horse. "My wife says you didn't have to do that. They were going to the truck. They had decided it was for the best. The elephant knew cold nights will come soon and she had to go back." He looked down at the circus men. "She said the elephant doesn't deserve men like you. If you don't change, the spirit of the elephant will haunt you when you die."

He leaned down closer to them. "I'm not sure I believe her but she might be right too." Then he turned to Ironsides. "I'll come tomorrow for the reward."

"The hell you will," Bill said.

"Last I heard, that's my decision," Ironsides said. "See you tomorrow, Mr....."

The Ktunaxa turned his horse and rode off without answering.

The Interlude

They watched the circus truck drive away with Tilly in the back, the grinning farm boy hanging on behind. Back at the orchard Mr. Mac was waiting, leaning on his gun.

"That's a hell of a weapon, Mac," Ironsides said. The old man grunted sourly, hobbled towards Mike's convertible and got in. "So long, Pinhead!" he said as they drove off. Jenny's going to hear all about it, Frank thought. I'll be the town joke.

To his relief, Ironsides said, "I'm going to have to ask you to be discreet here, Jimmy. There's no point in holding up a prominent citizen to ridicule. I mean Mr. Macpherson," he added with a smile toward Frank.

You could tell Jimmy wanted to say, "And I'm going to have to ask you to stick it" but of course it came out, "Yes, sir. I can appreciate that for sure."

"We don't want every Tom, Dick and Harry thinking they can tame an elephant like that woman just did. Somebody could get killed. You wouldn't want that on your conscience."

"No, sir."

"The gun wasn't loaded," Frank said to no one in particular.

They crammed into Bob's car for the long trip home. It was not a comfortable ride for Frank and Jimmy in the back seat with the dog. At some point, Hector had found something he like the smell of and rolled in it. After dropping Ironsides off at the arena the three boys drove over to Bob's and sat on the porch drinking his uncle's home-made beer.

Swearing them to secrecy, Frank told them all about it. When he'd finished and the laughter had died down – Frank always enjoyed telling a story against himself –Jimmy said, "To hell with it. It's too good a story to sit on. The Edmonton Journal's been running my stuff the last couple of weeks and they offered me a job. I'll take it with me."

After his third beer, Frank said he had to take a walk

to clear his head. He took Hector home and headed up Edward St. The Green Door was still closed, not surprising on a Sunday night, but the key was in its hiding place. He let himself in, listened and called out. No answer. As he passed the kitchen he realized how hungry he was. He hadn't eaten since the bread and cheese the day before. There was a paper bag full of apples near the stove. He took two and ate them both, including the cores.

Up in the loft the bed was as he'd left it. He realized there was no point looking for her anywhere else. If she was still in town, this was where she'd be, waiting for him. With open arms. The faint hope he'd been nursing drained away and he lay down on the bed, sore and tired, still hungry. He thought he could smell her on the pillow.

Sometime in the night a dog started barking in the alley and he woke up. It was another Monday and dawn was lighting up the tops of the Steeples to the north. He let himself out, grabbing another apple on the way, leaving a dime beside the bag. He walked through the empty streets to Hanson's garage, got the key and continued to the constituency office. His letter was gone. "Well, shit," he said, out loud, then thought about Mr. Mac's weak characters and feeble minds. He laughed. "Well, shit", he said again, defiantly.

He went home, slept for a couple of hours, had a bath and breakfast, confessed to Mrs. McKinnon about the stolen bread and cheese, and went out again for one last, hopeless search for Mavis. He got down to Baker and Fenwick just as the Coldstream Guards were forming up in front of the hotel. He followed along behind until he saw Mike Wilson sprinting across the street and stop beside Jenny and Mr. Mac. Not wanting to be seen, he ducked into the crowd lining the edge of the school yard. But Jenny had been on the lookout and spotted him as he worked his way through the crowd.

She watched him talking to Francis and could tell by the nervous way he walked that he was anxious about something. She saw Francis hand Frank a letter and knew it must be something personal because Francis made a point of turning away when he opened it. She was just a small-town girl but she wasn't stupid. Two and two added up to four as clear as day and she knew it came from Mavis. Mavis at the station talking to Francis, asking her if she'd seen Frank. Then she wondered why she'd lied about it.

By the way he read it through, looked away and read it through again, Jenny could see there must have been something between them and she was telling him goodbye. He seemed pretty upset about it, but she couldn't say she was.

As she watched, she was hanging onto her grampa's arm. All morning he'd been bothered about something. He wouldn't tell her what but then Mike did. It was funny because Mike started talking about it like she already knew the whole story. Mr. Mac tried to shut him up but Mike went on and on about what an idiot Frank was landing the pair of them up in a tree. Little did he know but the old man never liked him nearly so much after that.

Jenny never blamed Frank for two-timing her with Mavis although she wouldn't have used such an expression which she considered vulgar and American. How could she object to Frank doing what she had been doing all along herself. She supposed she could have objected to his keeping quiet about it but things were different for a man. A woman was expected to have suitors but a man's motives might easily be misconstrued. He is supposed to have already made his choice and stick to it. Not fair really but when she considered how many advantages men had in these matters, she didn't lose any sleep over it.

The violence of Mavis' letter hit Frank hard and he walked away head down, hunched over like a whipped dog. She had called him a skunk and believed he had seduced her knowing she was leaving town the next day. He could see how she would think so. Why hadn't he told her he was going to try to stop Mr. Mac from shooting that elephant? Because somewhere in the back of his mind he hoped doing it would set him right again with Jenny? Seeing her yesterday at the farm he knew she was the one he loved. Maybe Mavis was right. He was a skunk. A coward and a skunk.

"Hello, Frank," Doc King said, taking him by the arm. He steered him away from the crowd towards the centre of the yard. "Not left yet? Since you didn't have time to tell me in person, I assumed you were in a hurry." He reached into his jacket pocket and pulled out Frank's note. "I picked this up yesterday after church so you've had at least a day to find me."

Frank stared at the ground where some schoolgirls had scratched a hopscotch game in the dirt. He couldn't think what to say. He remembered watching girls play, years ago when he was a kid, thinking what alien creatures they were. His eyes followed the pattern of the squares, up and back. He saw them jump from one to another, their bodies spinning, then landing on one foot, waver and balance as they reached down for a pebble, the flutter of their dresses, the glimpse of their legs above laced up boots.

"Got an elephant story for me, Frank?" Doc King prompted. "I hear you had quite an adventure yesterday."

Already? Frank thought. Still his tongue wouldn't work and his eyes moved up and down the boxes. His face was hot. He felt humiliated.

"Okay," Doc King said. "Just tell me one thing. Do I need to look for a new driver?" Frank managed to shake his head. Doc King patted him on the shoulder. "Eight-thirty sharp," he said and walked away. Frank, afraid he'd be blubbering any minute, ran for home.

When he got there Mrs. McKinnon was in the garden picking tomatoes for canning. Rev. Mackay had dropped by for fruitcake the day before so she had a pretty good idea how things stood with Frank and Jenny. And Jimmy had told her all about his run-in with Tilly and Mr. Mac. She was, she liked to say, "all gossiped up." She could see he wanted to get past her but knew a sad face when she saw one. "Give me a hand with these, will you, Frank," she said pointing to a basket of tomatoes. She chattered away until she'd steered him into the kitchen and set him to work washing jars.

The table, covered in a bright yellow oil cloth, was piled with more tomatoes, another bushel basket half full of string beans and a bouquet of dill weed. The Kerr mason jars were arranged in rows beside the sink. A pot full of screw tops and lids was simmering on the stove beside the big blue canning kettle. It was the same job his mother used to give him. "This'll save us a ton of work," she'd said when they first came out during the war, although Frank couldn't see the difference at his end.

They worked away for a couple of hours, blanching beans, skinning tomatoes, mixing vinegar, mustard seed and dill, stuffing the beans into jars headfirst and the tomatoes up to a half inch from the rim. While they worked, they talked, mostly Mrs. McKinnon, keeping her head bent over her hands, working expertly, her voice soft and musical, a mother's voice.

She talked about what a difficult summer it had been for tomatoes, too many cool nights, but planted up against the house they had done well enough. She told him what a good gardener Mr. McKinnon had been. "We had the finest garden on Garden Avenue," she said.

"This would have been our twentieth anniversary. Arthur was hired to teach in the high school here. We were very young. I was nineteen and Arthur was twenty. It was a struggle at first. The things we didn't know!

"We bought this house with a bit of money he inherited, part of a dairy farm divided into lots when the son died and the family moved away. The yard was a mess. Imagine, they kept their cows penned up right outside the back door. I was horrified when I first saw it and didn't want to have anything to do with the place. But Arthur said it was a blessing in disguise.

"The mess and the smell kept the price down so we could afford to fix up the house a bit. Plank floors and the ugliest wallpaper you ever saw. But with all those years of manure in the yard, once Arthur had dug it in, sewn grass on the lawn and alfalfa where the garden was going to be, you never saw such abundance. I still think he's out there sometimes, just out of sight by the lilac bush."

She stopped, laid down her knife and looked out the window. "I couldn't bring myself to go to the concert today. It would have brought back the day they all marched away.

"You're a sweet boy. Jenny will be lucky to get you even if you don't amount to much in the world's eyes. Give her children and pray they'll live to see a better world. Now off you go and please don't be late for supper."

Frank started driving again next morning. It was a busy week. They went back to Kimberly one evening, to talk to the managers and shop keepers this time, over to Yahk next day to shake hands in the lumber yards. They drove to Fernie the day before Arthur Meighan came to speak and spent the night in Wardner a few days later.

Frank figured the old man was still feeling cautiously optimistic. If nothing else, he kept saying, they would go down fighting, which sounded like touching wood. He had fun with his elephant stories too. People came to expect them and gave him a cheer as soon as he said, "Now about those elephants...." Sometimes it was Meighan up in the tree and sometimes it was himself. And as for going out hunting with a big gun and no ammunition, "Well, wasn't that just like the Tories all over!"

Frank kept thinking about what his landlady had said about giving Jenny kids and praying for a better world. He was all for giving her kids, at least the first part, now that he knew he could manage it without embarrassing himself. But he didn't see the point of praying for a better world since he didn't believe in God. He was willing to keep his fingers crossed though and hope that socialist principals would catch on before it was too late.

He sometimes thought about taking a train to Vancouver to look for Mavis. It didn't seem all that difficult. She was bound to show up at a jazz club. It was something he kept in the back of his mind for after the election - once Jenny had made her choice - and chosen Mike.

His day started at six and went late so he didn't see Bob until the next Sunday afternoon at the ball game. Jimmy had left town by then. He endured the expected razzing from the boys about his tree climbing exploits but it was friendly enough and a sure sign that life had returned to normal. Another week passed. They made another trip up the Columbia Valley to Golden. He drove Mrs. King to teas and strawberry socials when Doc had committee work. Otherwise he was kept busy running errands, putting up posters and handing out flyers.

Labour Day came and suddenly the election was only a week away. All three campaigns had heated up. Dr. Rutledge had brought in the former B.C. premier, Bill Bowser, and Sims had been holding rallies night and day since late August. Frank turned twenty-one towards the end of August and was on the voters list. He didn't have any proof of his age but Harry vouched for him. He tried his best to keep his mind on the task at hand and if thoughts of Mavis or Jenny did pop up, they quickly turned into imaginary conversations that drifted along without much being said.

Myrtle and Charlie Ed had disappeared without a trace. Zack Terrell had returned and taken over the search from Ironsides but he was not hopeful and gave himself a week before giving up. "Most likely hunger and these cold nights have finished them off," he told the Courier. "One of these days somebody's going to stumble across a heap of elephant bones in a ravine somewhere and then you can write the end of this story."

The Prison

All the lights were out at the Macpherson house except the one in Jenny's room three stories up under the peak of the roof. She had pointed it out to Frank once, telling him it ran the whole length of the house and she could look down onto the garden in front and across to the mountains behind. She told him it was awfully hot up there in the summer. He immediately turned red as he pictured her lying naked on her bed, glistening with sweat.

Now the house was a dark silhouette against the night sky with the one bright eye. As he opened the gate, he saw that a board had been nailed below the 'No Salesmen Allowed' sign on which her grampa had written in red paint 'And Pinheads!'

He tiptoed up the path through the garden towards the porch. There were rows of cabbages, carrots, and potatoes at right angles one side, parallel beds of irises and day lilies on the other. Just before he reached the porch he saw a shadow move across the lighted window. He stepped back and called up to her in a loud whisper.

The shadow stopped and then she was there, the dark shape of her naked body against the light, leaning out to him. "Oh Frank!" she said, exactly the way she had the day he'd gone looking for her grandfather.

The screen door flew open with a bang and Mr. Mac stood looking down at him, a huge gun in his hands. He raised it to his shoulder, pointed it straight at Frank and fired. Frank yelled and woke up.

He lay there recovering for about five minutes which was all the time he had if he was to get any breakfast before heading off to work. His job for the day was to drive the Kings up to Kimberley for the Labour Day celebrations. Harry had called in some personal debts and got them invited to hand out prizes. It was a long day but worth it for all that good will just before the election.

They got off to an early start, giving them time to make

a detour to the St. Eugene Residential School which was just a couple of miles out of their way. If the Tory Prime Minister had been French-Canadian they wouldn't have bothered. But with Meighan blaming the customs scandal on corrupt Quebec politicians, Doc King thought it was worth reminding the priests that their mother province had voted Liberal ever since Laurier. He had no idea if the nuns would be voting at all but figured if he could get them on the voters list, Harry could arrange to ferry them a few at a time up to the polling station at Wycliffe.

As they turned off the main road towards the reserve, Nellie said, "I feel sorry for those poor children. Taken away from their families."

"I was," Doc King said. "Can't see it did me any harm. I was homesick for a few days, then I got over it."

"Going to boarding school with a lot of over-privileged boys is hardly the same thing Horace. They can't even speak English."

"Exactly. And they're not likely to learn at home either or become civilized and earn a living. The days of the noble savage are over, Nellie."

As she sometimes did when she thought her husband in the wrong, she asked Frank what he thought.

"Well, Ma'am," he said, "the last time I saw one, I was up in an apple tree feeling kind of foolish and he looked pretty noble to me."

Doc King laughed. "That's because he was in his element out there in the wilderness. But the modern world has closed in on him. He can't hunt and fish the way he used to. He can't follow the game up and down the countryside. The countryside's not his anymore."

"Because we took it away from him," Nellie said.

"Yes we did and don't tell me you're sorry. Fifty years ago most of this province was empty except for a few thousand Indians. All this country, timber, minerals, pastureland going to waste. Fifty years from now there'll be a million or more coming from all over Europe, starting a new life, towns, cities, roads, farms, mills, prosperity. Only a fool would be sorry about that."

"Or an Indian," Frank said.

"Then he'd better get over it and join the parade. This is the way it's always been. One day it will be our turn too if we don't keep the Chinese out."

The road took them down into a broad valley, the steeple of a church in the distance. Grain fields and grazing land stretched away toward a low ridge to the north. "Reserve land," Doc King said, mustering up some tour guide enthusiasm. "We'll make farmers out of them yet."

Further along they came to a cluster of small log houses arranged every which way on a couple of acres of dry, pounded earth. There was no sign of electricity or running water except what might come from a small creek to the left of the road. No sign of human life either except a boy of about ten, a brown, short-haired dog at his heels. There's always a boy and a dog, Frank thought, remembering the one in Mayook and wondering how Hector was doing. Just past the village, they came to St. Eugene church. "Pull over," Doc King said, "I don't believe you've been here before, Nellie. It's worth a look and we're in plenty of time."

The church stood behind a picket fence at the north end of the village. They stood looking up at a square, elegantly proportioned tower below an eight-sided steeple flanked by two smaller ones, all topped by crosses. The central spire was maybe a hundred feet high. The front doors had a pitched roof supporting a life-sized statue of the virgin. Above her was a smaller statue.

"Who's that guy?" Frank asked, pointing up. "St. Eugene, I suppose, whoever he was."

"Correct," Doc King said. "He was a seventh century pope. Poor old fellow got caught up in Byzantine politics I understand. Didn't last long and God only knows why they made him a saint. Pun intended. Politics again, I guess. I believe it was politics that got his moniker on this church in the first place."

They tried the door, found it open and went inside. It was

dim and cool after the glare of the day. The only light came from four narrow stain glass windows along each wall. Painted statues were suspended near the ceiling. The nave held a statue of Jesus, arms spread wide, a large heart with shafts of light radiating from his chest. A Ktunaxa woman was scrubbing the floor on her hands and knees in front of the altar, a bucket of water beside her. She was singing to herself and didn't seem to notice them. Once again, Frank was taken back to the day they captured Tilly, the woman singing under the apple tree.

They sat together in the rearmost pew. "Politics" Doc King repeated. "The first priest, Father Coccola, was a member of the Order of Missionary Oblates of Mary Immaculate, founded by a Frenchman, Eugene de Mazenod a little over a hundred years ago. For the last thirty or so they've been trying to get him made a saint." He chuckled. "Like being appointed to the Senate.

"When I was first elected back in '03 Father Coccola invited me to tea. He provided something stronger, bless him, but the invitation said tea. The purpose of his hospitality was to ask me to drop a word about the wonderful work his mission was doing whenever I came across an influential catholic in Victoria. Leaving no stone unturned on the road to sainthood. He confided to me that naming this church after that obscure seventh century pontiff was part of this same campaign, on the principle that one saint deserves another."

"And did you?" his wife asked.

"Of course I did. Every chance I got. It was the truth after all, more or less."

"More or less?"

"Look at this fine church.. Brand new at the time, shipped over in pieces from Italy."

"And look at that squalid village," his wife said.

"Exactly. And the fellow who paid for it, the church I mean, died last May. Old Indian Pete. We'd have gone to the funeral, Nellie, if we'd been here instead of Ottawa."

They left the church and walked to the car, Nellie dropping a dollar into the poor box on the way out.

"Indian Pete," Doc King continued as they settled into their seats, "was one of old Chief Isadore's fiercest warriors, one of the braves who busted those fellows out of jail way back when. He hated white men like the devil. At the time Father Coccola took over the mission, the miners and the Indians were at each other's throats. They called in the Mounties, but it was Coccola who kept the peace until they showed up. He had spent the previous five years ministering to the miners and railroaders in Golden and was as tough as old shoe leather. When Pete tried to scare him off he didn't back down. They ended up the best of friends. Turn here, Frank.

"Indian Pete found the ore that started the mines at Moyie. He took it to the priest and they staked claims together. When they sold them, Coccola got Pete to hand over his share and he used the money to build the church. Maybe it's my Baptist prejudice but I can think of more useful ways to spend it."

They drove through a wrought iron gate between concrete pillars with crosses carved into them and up an avenue lined with railings. At the end was a broad, three storied building made of concrete blocks moulded to look like stone. It was massive, maybe two hundred and fifty feet wide, Frank guessed, gray and silent with rows of narrow windows running from side to side like bars. It might have been a prison except there was another cross perched on a small tower at the centre of the roof. The avenue led to a circular turn-around with a stone statue of Jesus at its hub, the heart on his chest emitting more rays of light. Behind him were broad stone steps.

A young nun came out and stood waiting for them. She wore a heavy black dress with wide sleeves, her hands reaching out and clasping each other over her belly like a pair of hooks. Her shoulders and chest were covered by a second heavy cloth, a wimple, also black. A silver cross was suspended from a chain around her neck. Her face was narrow and pale, pretty, Frank thought, framed by an oval of white linen wrapped tightly around the sides and across her forehead, held in place by a close-fitting hood.

She tilted her gaze down towards Frank as he walked around to open the door for Mrs. King. He looked up at her, cocked his head to one side and offered his best smile but she shifted her eyes quickly away to the back of Jesus' head. The hot August sun blazed down on them and he wondered what it felt like under all those clothes.

"She's used to it, I suppose," Nellie said, reading his mind and smiling when he blushed.

"Go stretch your legs, Frank," Doc King said. "Be back in an hour."

He watched them climb the steps and follow the nun into the school, Nellie's hand resting lightly on her husband's arm. The door clanged behind them, adding to the impression of a prison. He parked the car and strolled around towards the rear.

There was a large barn, some cattle pens and a vegetable garden where a couple of nuns were hoeing and chattering in French. They stopped when they saw Frank. Beyond them was a fenced pasture containing some black and white cows. The grass looked greener here and he could see some irrigation ditches and the St. Mary River. Its bank was marked by a line of trees and off to the north he saw a cluster of tipis. He figured he had enough time to walk across to take a closer look. He'd never seen a tipi or an Indian camp before.

He had worked up a thirst by the time he reached the river. He pushed through a line of alders to some rocks above the water, knelt down and leaned out to take a drink, just saving himself from tumbling in. He walked along a path at its edge towards the camp, suddenly feeling awkward like he'd just stepped into someone's house uninvited. A man came out of the nearest tipi, giving Frank a look that said that was exactly what he'd done. And then he realized he'd seen him before, at the abandoned farm above Mayook.

"Hello, Pinhead."

Frank stopped short and stared at him. Where had he heard that?

"My real name's Frank," he said, "Frank Burton." And stuck out his hand.

The man was too quick for him and had already turned away, giving him the chance to take it back. Frank kept it out. "I didn't get a chance to thank your wife for what she did. She's a brave woman."

"I guess." He looked down at Frank's hand then leaned forward and shook it. "Ned Harris. The wife's Eva. We never could figure out how you two got stuck up there."

Frank told him the story. As he talked he looked toward the camp. There were four tipis, three grouped together farther away among a grove of big cottonwoods where a small creek ran into the river. They were made of brown canvas, about twelve feet across at the base. The doorways were open and they had flaps at the top like sails, covering the smoke hole when it rained. In the space between them was a frame of poles for drying, either clothes or meat. There was a fireplace and some logs for sitting and some sort of woven matting on the ground. He couldn't see into the tipis.

"You believe him?" Ned asked. "About the gun not being loaded?"

"I guess so," Frank said. Then he remembered the cartridges on the kitchen counter. "Maybe."

"Calling you a pinhead was a good way to get you to think so," Ned said.

"Thanks," Frank said. "I feel better already. Maybe I saved that elephant's life after all."

"There's another big one dying out in the bush the end of Gold Creek Road. I told the old man about it too but he wasn't interested. Tell it to Pinhead, he said. They've been cutting a track into where he's holed up. Should be getting him out in a couple of days."

"Her. If it's big it's female. Her name's Myrtle."

"Yeah," Ned said, "like mine's Ned Harris." It took Frank a while to figure out what he meant. "You want some water?"

Frank told him he'd drunk from the river.

"Bad idea. You got a mine upstream. Water's no damned good except for washing. We get ours out of that creek. Tailing pond's been leaking into the river for the past year. You keep saying you'll fix it."

"Not mine," Frank said and just stopped himself from saying, "I wish it was."

Ned looked at him.

"I work for Dr. King. I could talk to him about it."

"Yeah, you could."

Frank got back to the school just as the Kings were coming out, accompanied by an older woman, probably the top nun. Doc looked pleased so he'd probably picked up a few votes. Nellie didn't look so happy but managed a polite smile as they said goodbye. When they pulled out onto the highway she looked back across the fields towards the long grey building flickering between the trees.

"I wouldn't want to send any child of mine to that place," she said.

"Well, since we don't have any children...."

"You know what I mean, Horace. They talked about those children as if they were," she searched for the words, "as if they were determined to be wicked. Where was the kindness?"

"Oh, they'll be all right," Doc King said. "Those good ladies are Christians after all."

The Charge

"Hello Jenny," Frank said.

He'd recognized her as soon as he stepped inside the bank even though her back was turned. She was wearing a shapeless black dress a size too big, topped by an ungainly black cap. It reminded him of yesterday's nun. She was standing at the customer desk writing something on a slip of paper. As he came up behind her, she dropped her pencil and snatched it up. He could see a torn envelope lying in front of her with 'Fink's Mercantile' stamped on it. That explained the dress. It was the uniform worn by the girls working their lunch counter.

"You got a job!"

She turned to face him. "Don't sound so surprised. I'm eighteen."

"Don't remind me."

"What's that supposed to mean?" she said, her chin going up. Already the conversation was getting heated.

"Nothing. I guess I'm surprised, that's all. I mean that your grampa would let you."

"Like I said, I'm eighteen. This isn't the Middle Ages."

He looked down at his shoes. "Three more years."

"Two and a half," she said quickly, then turned away and picked up her pay packet and stood twisting it in her fingers, thinking she shouldn't have understood what he'd meant quite so fast.

He reached over and spun the pencil and leaned back so he could see her face. "Only two and a half. Well a fellow can wait two and a half, easy."

"Some fellows wouldn't have to wait at all if they…."

"Some fellows!" he exclaimed, loud enough to turn heads including Bob's who looked up from his desk with a smile and a wave. Seeing Bob made it worse, sitting there in his new office with Mr. Robert Lewis, Loans Manager, stencilled on the glass.

"You're making a scene!" She stepped back intending to

leave but he snatched the pay packet out of her hand, squeezed it open and peered in.

"How much are they paying you? Not half what you're worth, I'll bet. All those *fellows* coming in to buy sodas and grilled cheese sandwiches and ogle you in that swell dress."

"Give that back, Frank Burton," she whispered angrily, "or I swear I'll slap your face, bank or not!"

"Wouldn't be the first time," he said handing it over and shifting gears. "Aw Jen, let's not fight. I'm going elephant hunting today and they're dangerous beasts. This may be the last time you see me alive. Myrtle...."

"It'll serve you right if she stomps you to death!" Jenny hissed and stomped out herself.

After a long Labour Day in Kimberley, Doc King had given him the Tuesday off and he decided to join the gang of young townies recruited by Ironsides to help with Myrtle's capture. Maybe his boss had let him go because he hoped for another story, or maybe he was feeling guilty for not doing anything about that mine waste spilling into the St. Mary River. Frank had brought the subject up on their way back, thinking he'd be in a good mood after the prize-giving and hoping Mrs. King would back him up. She did too.

"Why that's awful! Horace, you must speak to Geoffrey about this. His manager is cutting corners." Frank noticed they were on a first name basis with the owner.

"I doubt it. Ed wouldn't sneeze without permission. Look you two, between a soft-hearted wife and a socialist chauffeur I could lose this election. I just spent last Friday night at the Board of Trade eating rubber chicken and listening to bad jokes while trying to convince them a Liberal government is not entirely disastrous for the country. But if Geoff starts telling them I want to shut down his mine...."

"He wouldn't!"

"Oh yes he would! After the election, *if* I win, I'll have a talk with him. If I lose, you two can form a committee and talk to him yourselves. Now shut up the both of you and let me doze."

After depositing a portion of his own pay, Frank strolled out of the bank to the CPR station where the elephant posse was gathering. There were five other townies, three circus men, Ironsides and Terrell. He had hoped work would prevent Mike from joining them but there he was with the same old taunt. Frank didn't know the other men particularly well but he could tell by their smiles they knew the story.

Before they set off, Terrell made a speech from the truck bed. "I want to thank you men for volunteering to help us out," he declared, with a slight emphasis on 'volunteering', to make it clear no one was getting paid. "A couple of Indians tracked Myrtle to a timber landing above Gold Creek. She's in rough shape. Some damn fools took a shot at her a while back and hit her in the leg. She won't let anyone near enough to see how bad it is but it looks infected. Left to herself she'd stay there until she dies. We've cut a trail in and the plan is to coax her out into the open where we can get some nets and ropes on her. Once we've got her under control we should be able to walk her out.

"You may think she's too weak to cause trouble but don't be fooled. I seen one once in Chicago was on his last legs. As quick as lightning he charged a man and killed him. Next minute he dropped dead himself. So you never know. Okay? Let's go."

With most of them in the back of the circus truck and Mike and two friends in his Studebaker, they drove through town and along Gold Creek Rd. Mr. Mac was out hoeing in his garden. Mike, who had been leading the way, honked and waved. The old man straightened up and waved back but when Frank waved too, he quickly dropped his hand, snatched out his hankie and blew.

The road ended at an old mill site full of fire weed and thimble berries. Ropes, nets and leg irons were handed out, mostly to the townies, Frank noticed, and they set out in single file, the circus men leading the way. It reminded him of a jungle movie, the hunters up front, the native bearers strung out behind.

A rough track took them around mounds of sawdust and

rotting slash then through a grove of cedars at the edge of a creek. The ground had been recently leveled, holes filled in. Through the trees they could see large moss-covered fir stumps from the old logging operations thirty or more years before, like tombstones in an abandoned cemetery.

Soon the path began to rise as they skirted a narrow gully lined with pines where the creek fell away into a series of waterfalls. A flock of crows flew on ahead, announcing their presence with raucous caws.

Frank was carrying a thick coil of rope slung diagonally across his chest and a heavy sledgehammer. Every few yards he shifted it to his other arm until both were aching badly. Mike Wilson and his friend George were just ahead wrestling with a large piece of netting that sagged and swayed between them. It smelled of tar in the heat. The sun beat down on them from straight overhead and flies flew up from the bear grass, attracted by the salt of their sweat. He began to regret coming. Some people collect stamps, he told himself. I collect elephants. Heck of a hobby.

To keep his mind off his aches, not to mention the itching from those damn flies, he began to wonder why. It was that look from Myrtle right at the get-go that started it, he guessed, some kind of bond between them. So now here he was helping them catch her, as if that made any sense. He told himself she'd die out there on her own. But being dragged back to the circus in chains? Was that any better?

They came to a log bridge over another creek. Beyond was a landing where felled timber had been collected and skidded down over the snow by horse teams. You could still see the track but in summer it was too steep and rocky for an injured elephant. Where it disappeared into the trees, two young Ktunaxa men wearing identical red plaid shirts and stained grey overalls sat with their backs against the stump of a giant fir, smoking pipes. In front of them were the remains of a cooking fire and a pile of cedar boughs and ferns covered with blankets. They must have been keeping watch, Frank thought.

He recognized one of them from the bunch he'd seen at the station.

At the far edge of the landing there was a dense stand of young hemlock. The flat feathery branches fanning out from their trunks reminded him of the fringes on Mavis' dress, the thought immediately swept away by the sight of a large elephant watching them from deep in the shadows. Yep, that was Myrtle all right, thinner, the cloth with her name on it torn away except for a tattered red strip circling her neck.

"Right where we want her," Zack Terrell said, pointing to a low rock bluff behind her. Bright green moss covered it, streaked with dark lines where water seeped through cracks near the top, the reason she had taken shelter there.

"She's hemmed in," Terrell continued. "You boys go get yourselves some lengths of tree branch and station yourselves either side so her only way out is straight ahead. We'll set up here while Bill climbs those rocks and gets in behind. When I give him the signal he'll start climbing down and you start tapping with your sticks. That should bring her out. Chances are she'll come slow but if she charges, we'll have these nets pegged down and ready. You fellows just stay the hell out of the way."

While Terrell was explaining his plan, Frank had thrown down the sledgehammer, unloaded the rope from his shoulder and collapsed exhausted onto a boulder. Several weeks of mostly sitting behind the wheel of a car had taken its toll. The other townies seemed to be feeling the same way. Mike and George had dropped the netting and were sitting on the ground a few feet in front of Terrell, their heads drooping.

Terrell and Ironsides exchanged looks "Come on now, boys," Ironsides said. "Let's get a move on. She won't stay in there forever." The men began to rouse themselves but not fast enough to suit the circus boss. "Rise and shine," he yelled. "Chop chop!" And for emphasis he clapped his hands together twice and hard. Which was a mistake.

Frank had kept his eyes on Myrtle and could see she didn't much like the sound of Terrell's voice, flipping up her trunk when he started talking and moving restlessly from side to side. When he yelled and clapped his hands, she gave a squeal of anger and despite what must have been stabbing pain in her legs, she charged.

The two Indians sitting on the other side of the clearing opposite Frank were the first to react. They jumped to their feet and yelled. Everyone turned to look, first at them, then to where they were pointing. Myrtle was coming out from the hemlocks, head down, trunk swinging, quick and determined. Everybody froze.

Terrell stood facing her, his hands still raised, seeing her come out of the trees straight at him. He looked around at the scattered, useless piles of nets and chains and ran for it. Ironsides and the other circus men dropped their tools and followed on his heels. They scrambled up a large mound of slash, cursing the thistles that grew out between the jumble of logs.

It took the townies another few seconds to realize what was happening, then they too scattered. By this time Myrtle was well clear of the trees and coming as fast as her injured leg and weakened condition allowed. It was fast enough. She had already covered half the distance between her shelter and Mike who was still sitting on the ground right in front of her. Frank was well off to the side. He took a step forward and watched her come, awed by her size and power, pitying her as she squealed and grunted each time her injured leg slammed down.

Frank saw George jump up and run after the others. Mike twisted around to watch him go then took a quick look back at Myrtle. When he saw how close she was he pulled himself up and scrambled frantically over the bundle of ropes at his feet. Halfway across, it slid sideways and he crashed down onto it with a yell. He struggled back up and cried out again. The tendons of his right ankle, caught in the netting and bent under the weight of his body, had torn away. He jerked upright, grabbed his knee and tugged at the ropes entangling his foot. He looked up. Myrtle was barrelling down on him less than a hundred feet away. His cry of pain turned to a scream of terror as he threw up his hands to ward her off.

When Frank saw Mike go down, he stopped thinking straight. He wasn't concerned about Mike at all. He was worried about Myrtle, afraid if she trampled Mike and killed him, or even if she didn't kill him but just broke a few bones, they would shoot her for sure. And then, somehow, he convinced himself she would stop if he told her to. If he went out there and told her to stop, she would.

When he came to tell about it later this is when he would pause, lean forward with a little twinkle in his eye and say, "Well, as a matter of fact, she did."

A charging elephant doesn't gallop like a horse. It moves in the same way it walks, only quicker. A healthy one can get up to fifteen miles an hour which is the same as a four-minute mile. Given her condition, Myrtle must have been going less than that when Frank stepped out in front of her. Which only gave him more time to consider his position.

A healthy female Asian elephant can weigh up to three tons. Myrtle was big, but not healthy and so probably only weighed around two and a half tons although weight and speed were not the calculations uppermost in Frank's mind. In the last few seconds left to him, ninety percent of his brain was running through the possible ways to make her stop. The remaining ten percent was trying not to think about what would happen if she didn't.

In the end the best he could come up with was to wave his arms and shout, "Stop!" When she was just a few yards off, he couldn't watch anymore and shut his eyes.

The Hero

In the darkness behind his eyelids, Frank could hear Myrtle's squeals and grunts coming steadily closer, the pounding of her feet keeping time with his heart. He could feel the sweat on his forehead turning cold and, behind him, he heard Mike's despairing cry of "Oh God!" He waited, his mind telling him she would stop, his body tensed for the impact. Then silence. Then Mike again, "Jesus...." and a moment later a warm stream of sweet moist breath on his face, a snuffling sound followed by soft touches on his neck and cheek.

He opened his eyes. Myrtle's trunk, stretched out towards him, circled around his face, breathing him in and coming to rest on his left shoulder. They looked at each other, both smiling – at least Frank did, and he thought maybe she did too.

The silence continued while everybody watched, taking in what had happened, slowly accepting the evidence of their eyes. Frank Burton had stepped in front of a charging elephant, had stopped her with a single word of command, had saved Mike Wilson's life. For Frank it was blissful. He and Myrtle continued their quiet communion, her trunk still resting on his shoulder, his hand rubbing up and down her forehead.

It ended with a commotion behind him as the spectators recovered. He could hear Terrell giving orders. At the sound of his voice Myrtle withdrew her trunk and jerked her head up. Frank raised his arms but kept his eyes fixed on the elephant's. "Shut up, Terrell," he said as loudly as he dared. He stepped close to Myrtle and pushed her head gently to the right. His hand pressed into the hollow behind her ear he led her away towards the two Ktunaxa men.

Behind him he heard George hurrying over to his friend. "Mike! What happened? You could have been killed." And Mike saying, "For Christ's sake, George, control yourself!"

Frank and Myrtle walked around the edge of the landing back towards the bridge, the two young trackers falling in behind. Myrtle's breath came in short bursts, her chest hardly moving, the muscles of her belly heaving up convulsively. She gave the occasional harsh liquid cough and there was a bubbling in her throat. Every few steps she stopped. "You can make it, girl," he said. "It's okay, sugar." remembering his mother's endearment when he was very young. He was close to tears and tried to catch Myrtle's eye but she was staring dully at the ground, gingerly picking out painful steps between rocks and exposed tree roots. He felt his own heart bursting.

When they came to the bridge, Myrtle stopped and reached with her trunk toward the water. Frank could see she was too weak to climb down. He remembered seeing someone carrying a bucket and looked around but one of the young men was already heading down the bank. A minute later he was back. They exchanged a smile of satisfaction as she eagerly sucked the water into her trunk and brought it up to her mouth.

Terrell pushed his way through the group behind, but Frank intercepted him. "She's doing fine. We don't want to get her upset. She trusts me."

Ironsides took the circus boss by the arm. "He's right…," he began but Terrell cut him short, already convinced by the look on Frank's face. "All right, just be careful," he said, keeping his voice low, "don't move her too fast. She's at death's door."

It took an hour to lead her down to the mill site. A couple of times it seemed like they wouldn't get her even that far. Her pace became slower and slower, the rest stops longer. Once she sat down on her haunches with a grunt of pain. A mix of blood and pus oozed from the abscess on her hind leg. She would have toppled over right then but Frank and his two companions leaned into her shoulder and somehow kept her upright.

It might have been a coincidence, Frank thought later, but when they got into the open and could see the circus truck up ahead, Myrtle let out a rasping sigh and went down for the last time. He knelt beside her head, putting his hand at the top of her trunk and she looked up at him with one steady, amber eye. Terrell came up from the other side and bent over her, laying his ear against her chest. "Yeah," he said, "Pneumonia. We'll never get her into the truck." He stood up. "Time to put her out of her misery." He turned to walked toward the truck.

Frank jumped up and grabbed his shoulder, spinning him around. "What the hell, Terrell."

Later, Ironsides would say, "I always thought Frank was a nice enough boy but a bit of a Milquetoast. Shows how wrong you can be. When he stopped that elephant in her tracks, he sure got everyone's attention. And when he stood up to Terrell... Well Terrell's a bit of a roughneck, and the way Frank grabbed hold of him, I thought he was going to bust him one. So did Terrell and I could tell he didn't much like the idea. I mean Frank was a substantial fellow too. It was just that we hadn't noticed it before with him being so generally mild mannered but, I tell you, his eyes were blazing."

Terrell stepped back and held up his hands. "Woah," he said. "Calm down. I'm no happier about this than you are. I appreciate what you did up there son, but," he pointed down at Myrtle, "look at her. She's done."

"He's right you know, Frank," Ironsides said. They looked down at Myrtle. Flies had settled on the goop around her eyes and the sores on her body. There was a second bullet hole, swollen and scabbed-over, on her hip above the abscess. "My telegraph dispatcher, Francis Guimont, has a gun that should do the job, a Westley Richards Express. Bought it a couple of years ago from a British army officer. Wants to bag a grizzly with it but I don't think he has yet." He laughed grimly. "His wife won't let it in the house."

"Couldn't we get Doc Rutledge to take a look at her? I bet he'd be glad to." Frank said. "You could send a man for him at the same time." He didn't mention another elephant gun a lot closer than the CPR station.

"Can't hurt, I suppose, if we can find him quick," Terrell said. "But don't get your hopes up."

They sent a couple of townies off in Mike's car and settled down to wait. Frank crouched beside Myrtle. He brushed the flies away from her exposed eye and she blinked up at him. He felt the tears coming back and he looked away. The other men had gathered around them in a circle. "That was a hell of a thing you done up there," one of the circus men said. "You saved that fellow's life." There was a murmur of agreement.

Frank wanted to tell them that they'd got it wrong, that he'd known all along that Myrtle would stop when he told her to, but they wouldn't have believed him anyway. Besides, the more he thought about it the less he believed it himself. Maybe it was just another dumb thing he's done like waltzing the mayor's wife out from the Victoria Café. Maybe a lot of the things people thought of as brave were just spur of the moment foolishness that give you the shivers when you think back on them. Remembering the eyes-closed wait for Myrtle to stop, or not, sure gave him the shivers now.

He looked down at her again. Her gaze hadn't shifted but seemed more distant, less focused. She was not so much looking at him as using him to hang on. There was a powerful stillness about her despite the wheezing of her lungs and the occasional cough and grunt of pain. He could see she was going to die. Her ribs showed like curved sabre blades beneath the tight grey shroud of her skin. Doc Rutledge wasn't going to do a damn thing for her. He felt trapped. He couldn't leave her, but he dreaded the thought of being there when the gun came. He closed his eyes and listened to her breathing and felt the weak tremors running through her body beneath his hand. He began to pray she'd die soon.

After a while the men wandered off and sat smoking on the back of the truck. He lost track of time and he might have dozed off. He was aware of some cheers and laughter when George and Mike came limping in. After a while he became aware of someone close beside him, the familiar scent of lilac soap and a soft hand pressed down on his. "Hello Jenny," he said sleepily. He could have been dreaming.

Jenny looked at him anxiously. She thought he must have taken a blow to the head when the elephant hit him. "Are you alright?" She looked around. The circus men were standing by the truck, talking and laughing. Mike and George were sitting at the back, feet dangling. "They said you were hurt."

"Not a scratch," Frank said. "Mike's the one got hurt when he tried to get out of her way." He took his hand out from under hers and ran it down the elephant's trunk. "Myrtle's dying," he said but she didn't hear him.

"*Mike's* hurt?" Jenny said. "Oh!" Then again, "Oh!"

When the townies who had been sent for the gun drove by Mr. Mac's place he was still out in the garden, weeding. They slowed down and stopped. The one in the passenger seat called out, "We caught the elephant. She's in real bad shape though. We're going to get the vet and a gun. Tell Jenny her boyfriend got hurt."

"What do you say?" Mr. Mac said. "Who? What are you doing in Mike Wilson's car?"

While they were repeating their news, Jenny, who had been washing carrots at the kitchen sink, came out onto the porch and heard "in bad shape." Then, "Hey, Jenny, your boyfriend got hurt. He's up at the old mill site." He pointed back down the road. "Gotta go fetch the doc." Then they were gone.

"Frank!" Jenny cried. "Grampa, get the truck. Frank's hurt." She ran out onto the road.

"Now Jennifer, calm down…. Jennifer, come back here!"

"I'll walk if I have to," she called back and kept going. She'd gone about half a mile before Mr. Mac caught up and took her the rest of the way. As he slowed down to make the turn into the mill site, she saw Frank sitting slumped beside the prostrate elephant and opened the cab door. When her grampa hit the brakes, she jumped out.

"I thought…," she now exclaimed. "They said….," She stopped as she realized she was the one who had put Frank's name together with 'boyfriend'.

As usual, Frank misunderstood her and concluded, with some bitterness, that Jenny was more concerned about Mike's sprained ankle than the dying elephant. "Oh, Mike's all right.

He's over there somewhere if you want to go nurse him."

Mr. Mac walked over. "Looks like Mike will survive, Jennifer. Hello….," he hesitated. "Hello Frank. I hear you had another run-in with an elephant. Looks like this one got the worst of it."

Frank looked up at the old man smirking down at him. What the hell, he thought. "You plan on shooting this one too?"

"Frank!" Jenny said.

"Listen here, young man. I told you that gun…."

"I don't believe you. Francis Guimont has the same calibre. I bet you got shells from him."

Whatever Mr. Mac was about to say next was interrupted by the arrival of Ironsides. "Mac, Jenny," he said. "I guess you heard Frank here is quite the hero."

As neither had, both looked at the train master in surprise and, in the old man's case, disbelief. "Come to think of it, there's no reason why you should. Frank's not the sort of fellow to blow his own horn." He smiled down at him. "Stepped into the path of a charging elephant. Stopped her in her tracks. She would have trampled young Wilson to death if he hadn't. The rest of us were just standing there with our thumbs up our…. well, our mouths open."

He collected himself and tried again. "Wilson was down on the ground, you see, tangled up in some netting and Myrtle here was charging down on him full bore." They all looked at the dying elephant. "She couldn't hurt a fly now, I know, but let me tell you, she shot out of those trees like an express train. Her last gasp, I guess. Frank led her all the way down, tame as a kitten."

As she digested this news, Jenny remembered the expression 'reckless courage' applied to soldiers during the war, often posthumously. She wasn't sure she liked the idea of Frank being the sort of man who died bravely and would have preferred that virtue in a more modest form. Still, she couldn't help a swelling of the heart when she looked at him now and pictured him standing undaunted between Mike and certain death. That he did it to save his rival she considered so much icing on the cake.

Under the guise of caressing Myrtle, she reached out and bushed her hand against his. Frank had been concentrating on tracing the furrows circling the elephant's trunk and on its next pass slid his hand up over Jenny's. Their eyes met and despite certain formalities which had yet to occur, both would later consider that moment the true beginning of their marriage.

Mr. Mac, meanwhile, had been observing and thinking. His observations told him that Jenny had made up her mind once and for all and his thinking told him that the combined determination of his granddaughter and a young man capable of standing up to a charging elephant would be almost impossible to overcome. He would resist for the next two and a half years, of course, since he had the law on his side. Besides, she was far too young. Whatever Frank's true colours, he told himself, there was time enough for them to be revealed.

Continuing to think over his personal history with Frank and elephants, he surprised them, especially Frank, by saying, "Now that's exactly the darn fool thing you would do. I don't believe for a second you were trying to save Mike Wilson's life. If I was a betting man, which I'm not," he went on, glancing towards Jenny, "I'd wager it was the elephant you were trying to save just like the last time we met."

In the last few minutes, Frank had gone up considerably in Mr. Mac's estimation and now it was his turn. "That's just what I've been trying to tell everybody. Not that Mike isn't worth saving but I guess I didn't have time to think of that. I didn't have time to think of anything."

"It can be our secret," Mr. Mac replied dryly. "Saving a man's life, that's heroic. Risking your own trying to save an elephant, especially a dying one, well, I'd say the general verdict would be just plain foolish." They all looked back at Myrtle. Her breathing had fallen away to practically nothing, her one visible eye almost vacant. She seemed to be sinking slowly into the earth. Mr. Mac took Ironsides by the arm and led him away. "I doubt we'll be needing that gun, or Doc Rutledge."

Alone together for the first time in weeks and suddenly finding themselves in the relationship they had been fumbling towards for the past eight months, Frank and Jenny grew shy. Their hands strayed apart, keeping contact only through the medium of Myrtle's trunk. Frank wanted to tell her that he was sorry he had made fun of her outfit the day of the stampede but luckily he couldn't find the right words and it was a subject that never did come up.

After a while Jenny said, "Poor thing," and quietly began to sing. She sang Loch Loman; the song her grandfather had sung on the day he came to take her home to Gold Creek Road.

Ye'll take the high road, and I'll take the low road
And I'll be in Scotland afore ye
For me and my true love will never meet again
On the bonny, bonny banks of Loch Loman

Although she had loved them at the time, Jenny had since thought the words not particularly appropriate for that occasion but now they struck her as sadly perfect. Her sweet, clear and gentle voice was the last sound Myrtle heard.

The Speech

"I see you have recovered from your ordeal, Frank," Nellie King observed.

They were sitting at her dining room table two days later. Doc King was in his office putting the finishing touches on a speech he planned to deliver that afternoon to the Fort Steele Board of Trade. Frank was devouring a plate of ham sandwiches washed down with lemonade.

"Ordeal?"

"Mrs. Weeks was telling the church ladies all about it this morning . You were almost trampled to death by a charging elephant and providentially escaped with nothing more than a broken leg.

"Oh, I know," laughing at Frank's expression, "that's not quite how it happened. I had already heard three other versions but I like Mrs. Weeks' the best. She capped it off by observing that the Devil looks after his own. Well, I couldn't let that pass without asking just what she meant." She paused. "Can you guess?"

Frank could but preferred not to and said, "No." with a guilty examination of his sandwich.

"Now, since there is very little truth to her first story, I shouldn't give much credence to this one either, I suppose, but she claims to have documentary proof. You know Mavis, her daughter, of course – the one who ran away to Vancouver a few weeks ago? Well, that's how she put it although I believe Mavis is over twenty-one. Apparently she left her mother a note saying she was 'running off' with... you!"

Frank carefully pushed a slice of pickle around the perimeter of his plate.

"Obviously not true.," Nellie pursued, smiling. "Still, there's one thing that puzzles me. I asked Mrs. W. exactly when her daughter left town and it turns out to have been the very same evening you spent up that apple tree with Mr. Macpherson.

You weren't planning to leave Horace in the lurch, were you Frank?"

He was spared having to answer by the return of her husband. But later, as they motored along Baker St., Doc King brought it up again. "Nellie been grilling you, Frank?"

"Yes, sir," Frank said, keeping his eyes on the road. "It was a mistake all round."

"I'll agree with you there. Miss Weeks would be an attractive proposition in some respects, I imagine, a very talented young lady. Ambitious, I'd think. But hanging around backstage is not for you. She'll break a few hearts before she's through."

"I thought I'd broken hers."

"For a week or two maybe." As they slowed down at the corner of Fenwick Ave., Doc King pointed across the intersection. "There's Rutledge and his daughter. I delivered her, as a matter of fact." He chuckled. "There's gratitude for you.

"A bit late in the game to be handing out leaflets, I should think. Nobody reads them anyway. Still, we all do it. It's like fishing. You reach into your tackle box, pull out a lure and if it catches something, you're a genius. Only the fish knows what he's going to bite on. We only find out after he's hooked."

"You still think you're going to lose?" Frank asked. It was no longer an idle question now that Jenny was back in the picture.

"I've stopped thinking. Hurts the brain. This is a queer district and a queer election. The country's trying to figure itself out and most people are tired of being told what to think. Back east in New Brunswick, ridings stayed the same for decades. My father was the MP for Queens for nearly twenty years and then he stepped straight into the Senate…."

But Frank wasn't listening. He was thinking about where he would be next week. Out of a job for one thing because Doc King would be heading back to Ottawa or back to doctoring and either way wouldn't be needing a chauffeur. And he would be right back to square one.

"Then in '16," Doc King prattled on, "Harlan Brewster asked me to run again. Harlan was a dyed in the wool Reformer. With a capital R. Votes for women, workmen's compensation, employment standards, you name it. He was going to put an end to patronage in the civil service for heaven's sake. The glue that holds this country together, some wiseacre said. He did manage to bring in women's suffrage. Then he had a heart attack and died, poor fellow.

"Which reminds me. We'll be parting company next week, rain or shine. Did you finish high school?"

The question took Frank by surprise but he could guess what it meant. "No sir."

"Well, you may have to take some night classes. If I'm elected I can guarantee you something. Maybe not in Cranbrook right away but I imagine we can get you installed back here in time for the wedding."

Frank looked blank.

"To Miss Macpherson. She's eighteen, I believe. That's less than three years to wait even if the old man won't consent. If I lose, of course, the prospects might not be so rosy."

Frank knew from discussions with Bob that something like this was to be expected once Doc King was re-elected. The trouble was, the more he thought about it, the more he didn't want to vote Liberal. Despite Mr. Sims mockery at the Fernie meeting, he agreed with most of what he'd said. So how was he supposed to look himself in the mirror having taken the job without giving his vote in return? It was easy to say the two shouldn't be connected but they were.

His boss interpreted his silence correctly. "This isn't a bribe, Frank," he said. "You can vote however you want." Another couple of miles down the road, he exclaimed, "Damn it, Frank! Why won't you vote for me?"

"It's not you! I'd be glad to vote for you but that's not the way it works, is it? I mean it's not personal and I guess I think that's the way it should be."

They returned to uncomfortable silence the rest of the

way past Wardner then over the Kootenay bridge and onto the road through Bull River. It was pretty much a ghost town by then except for a couple of lumber operations, having had its heyday about sixty years before.

"About this charging elephant you stood up to, Frank. I need something to warm up the crowd...."

Frank tried to talk him out of it, first by asking him to drop the idea entirely, then at least leaving his name out of it. But Doc King wouldn't budge. "I've stood by you, Frank," he said. "The elephant bulletin was a great idea and you got a hefty raise out of it. But on the other side of the ledger, you've screwed up more than once and I've still kept you on. You owe me."

Reluctantly, Frank told him what had happened, with emphasis on his concern for Myrtle and conviction that she would stop. "We already knew each other," he explained, "so getting her to stop was no big deal. I'm no hero."

"Hooey," Doc King said. "My story needs a hero and you're it. Tell you what. I'll leave your name out of it if you promise to vote for me." He laughed. "Never, mind. I wouldn't trust you anyway."

A couple of miles shy of Fort Steele they dipped down onto a long plank bridge spanning the banks of Wild Horse Creek. In the space of two years, thousands of miners, mostly American, had panned, dug, and scoured every inch of it for several miles up. They took out over seven million dollars' worth of gold and left it looking like an abandoned gravel pit. Then the Chinese moved in and worked it all over again. Nobody knows how much they took out but it was enough to bring them back year after year. From the middle of the bridge they could see a fountain of spray from a hydraulic operation upstream. "They're a hardworking people," Doc King observed, "I'll give them that."

As the town's water tower came into view, he sighed and wiped his brow. "Well Frank, I think I've got it worked out. I'll keep it folksy and if there are no ladies present, I hope to do it in my shirt sleeves.

"You may have noticed," he continued, "I've been steering

clear of Mackenzie's quarrel with Governor General Bing. As far as I can see, he had every right to ask Meighan to form a government and the fact he's an Englishman doesn't matter a damn. Most people around here would agree, too. But I've been told there's a sizable number up this way, mostly with American antecedents, who think it's time we poked a stick in Britannia's eye and they want me to do the poking. And that, my friend, is why I need a good story, so the ones who don't think that way won't lynch me!"

In its heyday, The Odd Fellows Hall had been a handsome building, wood panelling on the walls and a high ornate ceiling. The furnishings, a carved oak table at the far end with one leg that didn't quite match and several rows of chairs with well-worn leather seats, gave it an air of faded grandeur. Like the town itself. The windows had been thrown open in a futile attempt to reduce the afternoon heat. As he entered, Doc King took Frank's arm and said, "Stick around. That's an order." Then someone shouted, "Hello Doc!" which got a laugh, some cheers and a round of applause.

Whether they were going to vote for him or not, his years of medical practice had made Doc King a popular and well-respected man. It took several minutes of back slapping and hand shaking before he was seated at the head table and the meeting was called to order. After a half hour of routine business he rose to speak, the applause, much thinner this time around, affirming the audience's partisan divide. It was one thing to welcome a neighbour and quite another to listen to him tell them how to vote. Unfazed, Doc King swept the room with his warmest smile. "My fellow Canadians," he began, "I thank you for your kind invitation to speak here today."

Frank usually let his mind wander during the litany of Liberal virtues and Tory vices, tariffs and freight rates, old age pensions and Senate reform. Better yet, he might have sneaked a sandwich off the buffet table and slipped out. But today he had strict orders to remain and a sinking feeling that soon all eyes would be turned on him. He knew the speech by heart and could see it coming, the moment Doc King would pause, examine the ceiling for a moment, chuckle quietly to himself and launch into an elephant story which inevitably led to a clever and amusing illustration of the afore-mentioned virtues and vices. Well, he only had himself to blame.

"Some of you may have heard of the recent capture of the elephant, Myrtle, who fled the Sells Floto Circus over a month ago. Myrtle, you understand, was advertised to be a most accomplished pachyderm who could dance the Charleston. A month on the run in the wild, however, harried by trackers, wounded by youths armed with pop guns, plagued by insects during the day, cold and hunger by night, had turned her into a much different beast. By the time a pair of Ktunaxa scouts had cornered her two days ago at the base of Moyie Mountain, she was pertinacious, downright ornery and ready to sell her freedom dearly.

"A crew of wranglers and local volunteers marched off to retrieve her. Among them was that young man there." He flung out his arm towards Frank who almost ducked as everyone turned to examine him, his face red with embarrassment. "His name is Frank. He's my driver. I gave him the day off for this express purpose because I had a feeling they would need him. And I was right."

By this time sweat was pouring down Doc King's face and he began to remove his jacket, exposing a pair of bright red braces whose colour exactly matched the ensign behind him. As he wiped his brow and neck then slowly rolled up his sleeves, he said, "As a medical man, I strongly advise you all to follow my example. Ladies, my apologies. I suggest you also take whatever measures modesty permits.

"As I was saying," he continued, raising his voice above the clatter as they all, the ladies included, followed suit, "the circus crew had cornered Myrtle and was preparing to lasso her into submission when….." he stopped mid-sentence and waited for the noise to subside…, "when she beat them to the punch and charged!

"Imagine! Three tons of angry elephant bearing down – oh yes, ladies and gentlemen, for bearing down she was, straight at a young man directly in her path not fifty yards away, down on the ground tangled up in a pile of ropes and netting from which he was desperately attempting to escape. Now I don't know what you would have done in such a situation but I would have yelled blue murder and I believe the young man did in fact do just that. Everyone watched in horror. Everyone, that is, except that man there." He flung out his arm towards Frank and, as anticipated, everyone turned to examine him again.

"What Frank did, my friends," he resumed in a quiet voice quivering with emotion, "what he did next, he has begged me not to reveal. His modestly forbids me from uttering a word. Perhaps I shouldn't." Smiling faces turned towards him. "We know you better than that, Doc!" someone said to universal laughter.

"Do you, sir? Very well, since you've found me out, I shall. I'm an old politician who can't resist the temptation to associate myself with a bit of glory. Sorry Frank.

"Now imagine," he continued, pointing to a large man standing at the rear of the hall, that that gentleman is our elephant." He's always voted Tory, Doc King later explained, so no harm done. "And this young lady over here to my right," indicating a middle-aged woman in the front row, "is about to be trampled to death by that gentleman, excuse me, I mean by that elephant....

"They haven't even been introduced!" someone interjected to roars of laughter.

"When suddenly, out of the blue, Frank calmly stepped into the path of that onrushing beast. With a noble and commanding gesture and the single word, "Stop!" he brought her to a standstill so close that she could reach out and caress him with her trunk. Which she proceeded to do!"

The laughter and general hubbub which accompanied this last speech erupted into cheers and applause as everyone again turned towards Frank with grinning faces. He turned and fled.

As he pushed through the door and into the open air, he could hear someone strike up For He's a Jolly Good Fellow. A hearty chorus joined in, gradually fading away as he clambered down the bank towards the Kootenay River.

The Baby

"Are you sulking, Frank?"

"No. sir,"

"Glad to hear it. When my chauffeur refuses to acknowledge the best wishes of his admirers, stares grimly ahead and drives five miles in silence, I may be forgiven for supposing he is sulking. But no doubt you know best."

"Yes, sir."

"Don't you want to hear how I did it?"

"I could see where you were going. Some.... thing," (he wanted to say nonsense), "about Mackenzie King standing up to Governor General Bing like I stood up to the elephant. Saving the country like I saved Mike."

"Exactly! And you can sneer all you like but it worked. It always does. They saw right through it of course, which is part of the charm. Makes them feel smart. Half of them probably think I made the whole thing up. You running out at the end was perfect."

When they stopped by the office, Harry handed Frank a note from Mr. Mac. "We need to talk," it read.

"Maybe the old boy's coming around," Doc King offered. "I can spare you tomorrow morning. That is if you want to accept his invitation. Up to you."

That night he fell asleep thinking about the look Jenny had given him the last time they were together. They were still holding hands, hers on his and his resting on the dead elephant's trunk. There were tears in her eyes, which was to be expected, but also love for him and the promise of more to come. A couple of hours later he woke up in a sweat, tangled in his bedsheet, having run up and down a long dark hallway lined with closed doors. He was convinced Mavis was lurking behind every one of them.

Next morning he drove out to the farm. He couldn't get back to sleep after his dream so he was feeling a bit rough. He told Mrs. McKinnon where he was going and she did her best to fortify him with an extra strip of bacon and a heavy dollop of cherry jam on his biscuit. "What's the worst that can happen?" she asked. "His bite is much worse than his bark." She laughed. "I mean the other way around." But Frank wasn't so sure.

On the way over he went past the Whitmore house. The fence had been repaired and there was a long black car parked outside. Hector was sitting on the sidewalk beside it. Frank stopped to say hello and give him a pat for luck. Just then the front door opened and two men came out, carrying a coffin. Mrs. Whitmore followed them onto the veranda and stood with folded arms, watching. Frank realized the car was a hearse. As the men slid the coffin into the back, Hector began to howl.

"Oh for God's sake, Hector!" Mrs. Whitmore cried. She turned to Frank. "He's been howling all night."

"Is that Mr. Whitmore?" Frank asked. "I'm sorry for...."

"Yes, that's him. Hector, shut up, you're driving me crazy!"

"I could take him with me," Frank said. "We're friends."

"You can keep him for all I care. He's Al's dog."

"I'll take him for the day, anyway," Frank said.

Hector wouldn't move until the hearse drove away. He was thinking about following until Frank grabbed his collar and steered him into the McLaughlin-Buick where he settled onto the front passenger seat. Frank was glad of the company.

Mr. Mac was sitting on his front steps. As soon as Frank pulled up Hector ran over and sat in front of him wagging his tail. Hector never jumped up on anybody, Frank noticed, which was just about the best thing you could say about a dog.

They went into the kitchen, Hector going straight through to the back porch. Frank sat nervously at the table fiddling with his hat while Mr. Mac poured some coffee. "I suppose you take milk and sugar."

"Cream and brown sugar if you got it."

Mr. Mac snorted, filled the order and handed Frank his cup. He sat opposite, stirring his own meditatively for a long minute although it was black. Frank sipped his. It was very hot and a long way the strongest he'd ever tasted.

"Jennifer's at work, if you're wondering," Mr.Mac said at last, placing his spoon deliberately on the table and pressing his forefinger onto it as if to keep it from running away. A couple of more minutes went by, taking their time doing it. Frank wondered if he was supposed to say something but couldn't think what.

"Good," he muttered.

"What? Oh, the coffee.... railroad style. Grounds in the pot, stir it up with a few eggshells and simmer until they settle. Keeps you awake on a long haul. You get used to it."

Frank doubted that.

"All right.... Look here," Mr. Mac said and cleared his throat. He was struggling. "Before I came here to look after Jennifer I was an engineer with the CPR. Before that I was a fireman, a stoker. Mostly it was shovelling coal into the furnace. Sometimes if we got held up and were running late we had to build up a big head of steam to catch up. It was back breaking work. Finding a man who could handle it wasn't easy. Sometimes we'd take on a new man, big strapping fellow, didn't last a week. Couldn't take it. I figured you were like that. I told Jennifer, he looks good but he won't last." His eyes flicked up to Frank and then down again to the spoon. Another minute trudged by.

"The last couple of years there've been a few youngsters come round. Not just you and Mike though you two were the only ones she took to. They'd show up at church on Sundays and I'd give them the John Knox treatment. That got rid of most of them. You and Mike stuck to it, though you were the only one joined the social club. I don't suppose his old man would have let him anyway, being a staunch Anglican... if there is such a thing. We saw through you right away, of course."

The old man pushed back his chair and stood up. "So that's the way things stand." he said and reached out his hand. "Are you going to finish that?" Frank gulped the coffee down, burning his throat and handed the cup over. He stood up too but Mr. Mac waved him back down. Frank tried to figure out what had just been said and what he was supposed to say in return. He thought maybe he could ask Jenny and stood up again.

"Well, thanks for the coffee," he ventured and picked up his hat.

Mr. Mac pointed at the chair. "Sit down, sit down," he said testily. "That Indian came by yesterday. He's tracked down the last elephant, the little one, Charlie Ed. He wants you to help bring him in."

"Indian?" Frank said. "You mean the one whose wife…."

Mr. Mac scowled. "Yeah, that one. He seems to think you have a way with elephants. And from what he said about the circus boss short-changing their rewards, he figures it would help if you came along. Makes sense."

"I'd have to ask Dr. King. The election's on Tuesday and he may need me every day. Where is he anyway? The elephant, I mean."

"He said somewhere over by Jimsmith Lake. Anyway, don't worry about your boss. He's making a speech at the Legion."

That was all Frank could get out of him besides, "Just be ready to go tomorrow afternoon. And keep quiet about it. It's a surprise."

Tomorrow was Saturday and as predicted, after a morning trip out to Lumberton, Doc King gave him the rest of the day off. He hadn't asked what Mr. Mac wanted to talk to him about and Frank didn't mention Charlie Ed. He wasn't sure if telling his boss about it mattered but since Mr. Mac asked him to keep quiet he might as well.

The old man picked him up just before noon in the truck he used to take cattle to the slaughterhouse. Jenny was in the cab wearing her uniform. Frank noticed she'd managed to find one that fit.

"Get in and keep your hands where I can see them," Mr. Mac said.

"Grampa!"

"I mean it," he said, then added, "By the way, you forgot your dog yesterday. Al's dog, I should say. I dropped him off on the way over. Mrs. Whitmore says you can have him if you want. Too bad about Al."

They drove downtown, Frank keeping his hands well in view. As they came to a stop, he felt a sharp pinch on his thigh. He got out and held the door open as Jenny climbed down, stumbling into his arms. "Good luck, Grampa," she called and skipped away. She smelled of wild roses this time.

At the CPR station, a wiry, dark-skinned man in coveralls and a cloth cap was standing near the entrance. He tossed a coil of rope into the back and opened the cab door, squeezing in beside Frank. The smell of whiskey and tobacco came with him, a large wad of the latter wedged in his cheek. His few teeth, which he displayed in a wide grin, were stained a brownish yellow.

"This is Mr. Griffin," Mr. Mac said. "He's with the circus. That's Frank."

They shook hands. "Spot Griffin," the circus man said. "Care for a chaw?" Frank declined with thanks.

The road to Jimsmith Lake wound steadily upwards along the track of an old logging railway. Near the top they caught up with Ned Harris riding a big tan horse. At the top a clearing looked down through a screen of lodgepole pines to the lake and picnic grounds. Waiting there were the two young Ktunaxa men who had helped Frank lead Myrtle down to Gold Creek Road.

Jimsmith Lake is about half a mile long and deep at the Cranbrook end where it curls around out of sight into a broad marsh full of water lilies, painted turtles and ducks. Ned dismounted and walked over. "We'll have to leave our horses and the truck here," he said. "There's a track takes us where the elephant comes down to drink. Any time now." He pointed at Spot. "What the hell?"

"It's all right," Mr. Mac said. "He's working for me. He knows elephants and I want him along to make sure this one won't die on us. I'll keep it in my barn 'til Monday when we take him into town and turn him over. Don't worry, Frank will make sure you get your money."

"Why wait?" Ned said. "I don't get it."

It dawned on Frank. "The election parade!" he said. "But I thought…"

"Never mind," Mr. Mac snapped. "Come on, stop wasting time jawing."

They set off single file down the track. One of the young men was carrying a burlap bag. He reached in and extracted a couple of apples and tossed one to Frank. Ned was carrying a rifle, he noticed, but none of them had brought any nets and Spot had the only piece of rope.

Black clouds were building up in the west. Frank wondered how the elephant would react to thunder and lightning. He also wondered what Mr. Mac was up to. His first thought was that it was to help Doc King who was planning on having a parade on Baker St. Monday afternoon. But suddenly he wasn't so sure. Doc Rutledge was a vet after all and it would be a good laugh at Doc King's expense if, after making such a fuss about elephants, it was Rutledge who finally brought home the last of them. Either way, there wasn't much he could do about it right then.

It was easy-going along a ridge trail to the far end of the lake. A short drop took them down to the marsh. Ned crept quietly ahead then motioned them to follow. A few dozen mallards and buffleheads flew up with a noisy rush and several turtles plopped down off a log sticking out from the shore. "He comes from over there." Ned pointed towards a clump of birches. "Cools himself off right here. It's a sight."

As far as Frank could tell, the plan was for him to work his magic on Charlie Ed and charm him into walking back to the truck. Maybe, since Charlie was only a baby, they thought he wouldn't give much trouble. He couldn't remember seeing him at the stampede and began to wonder just how little a little elephant could be.

The posse settled down to wait behind a patch of

thimbleberry, Mr. Mac peering out from time to time through the leaves. After about twenty minutes he began to wave his hand behind his back. Like a pack of gophers popping out of their holes, everybody stretched up behind him. They watched Charlie Ed slip out from the alders and step delicately into the water. Swirls of mud rose to the surface and washed against his body as he sank slowly into it. He reached out with his trunk towards some lily pads where the water was clear, sucked it in and squirted it, first into his mouth and then back over his head and down the length of his body. He floated further out, giving squeals of delight.

Charlie Ed was small, but not that small, standing maybe six feet high at the ridge of his back. He was round like a beach ball, the upward curl of his mouth giving him an expression of permanent good humour. He looked like he wouldn't hurt a fly although he must have weighed close to a ton. Unaware of his stalkers, he was well out into the marsh and wallowing contentedly, water flying in all directions. When the men were directly behind him, Spot, who had brought up the rear and was farthest up the slope, gently called out, "Charlie.... Chaaarlie.... Come to daddy."

Lost in his aquatic revery, Charlie didn't hear him, but Mr. Mac wasn't taking any chances. He waved at Spot to be quiet. "Damn it, man, you'll startle him!" Unfortunately, as an unfamiliar and urgent voice, this one got through to Charlie. He jerked up his head and twisted around as his old keeper spread his arms and called out again, "Chaaarlie, it's Spot!" With an excited squeal, the baby elephant plunged through the lily pads towards the shore.

Mr. Mac turned to Frank and yelled, "Stop him!" Without thinking, Frank obeyed, once again stepping in front of a charging elephant. This time common sense prevailed. At the last second he jumped out of the way, knocked sideways as Charlie brushed past.

There was a log sticking out into the water to his left and he tried to reach it with his leap. He would have too if Mr. Mac hadn't jumped onto it an instant before. First Mr. Mac and then, as Frank threw his arms around him for balance, Frank himself, sprawled headfirst into the swamp.

It took them a good deal of thrashing and spluttering to regain their feet. They wiped away the mud and water lily stalks and looked about them. Charlie Ed was standing quietly in front of Spot who was slipping a loop of rope loosely about his neck. Frank began to laugh, joined by the others. All except Mr. Mac.

The Parade

Frank woke up Sunday morning from a dreamless sleep and got quickly out of bed. He hadn't been to church since Jenny had banished him and he didn't want to miss seeing her. He'd put his alarm clock on the windowsill at the far end of the room just to make sure. There was too much at stake.

Jenny had still been at work when they returned to the farm with Charlie Ed the day before, everybody cold and soaking wet because of the downpour that started almost immediately after they set off back to the truck. The elephant was the happiest of the bunch, Spot a close second. "We always got along," he told them. "I'm the one who taught him the Charleston."

The rain and a tarpaulin over his back made sure nobody saw Charlie between Jimsmith Lake and Mr. Mac's barn. He was a little nervous of the cows at first but soon settled in. It was part of the deal that Spot would spend the night and all Sunday keeping Charlie company. Frank headed home to do some heavy thinking. For his part, Mr. Mac hadn't said a friendly word to him since they'd both gone into the marsh.

There was nothing special about the church service that day, but Frank always remembered it with fondness. Mr. Mac was in his usual pew, still not speaking to him, which suited him fine. When it was over, the old man stalked down the aisle without a sideways glance and Frank headed into the garden. He sat down on the arbour bench and waited, figuring if Jenny wanted to talk, she'd look for him there. He wondered whose side she would be on if her grampa turned out to be a secret Tory after all?

When she arrived, he jumped up and kissed her. She let him, just once, and said, "Stop it now and listen. Grampa's up to something. He told me to walk home or catch a ride with Mr. and Mrs. Chesley. He wouldn't tell me where he was going but I have a pretty good idea. He was on the phone last night talking very quiet, not like him at all. Then when I asked him who it was, he told me to mind my own business. After he went out to the barn to check on Charlie, I called Letty at the exchange. She told me it was Doc Rutledge and she heard them talking about Charlie until Grampa told her to get off the line."

"That old... so-and-so," Frank said, remembering who he was talking to. "Doc King's planning a parade up Baker tomorrow afternoon to cap off his campaign. Doc Rutledge is too. They always do that. I thought your grampa wanted Charlie for Doc King's, but it looks like he's gone over to the Tories. Come on, I'll walk you home.

"I guess you're wondering why I care who gets Charlie," Frank said, "after saying I'm not voting for either of them."

"Not to mention staying in Grampa's good books," Jenny said with a smile.

"I wouldn't know about that. Never been in them as far as I can tell. It's just that Doc King's my boss and it wouldn't be honest to let it slide. But darned if I know what to do about it. I guess I could bribe the circus fellow to help me steal him."

Jenny stopped and looked at him. "All right," Frank laughed, "just a thought. Although it wouldn't really be stealing... All right, all right."

They walked on. After a while Jenny said, "I have an idea. It's a bit complicated so you're going to have to get Doc King in on it too."

As she explained her plan, Frank marvelled. He had his doubts about it working but since he couldn't think of anything better, he agreed to give it a shot. Besides, she's smarter than me, he told himself as he kissed her at the garden gate, one eye out for Mr. Mac.

"I'll come along for the ride with Grampa and Charlie tomorrow," Jenny said. "I want to see the fireworks." Then she pushed him away. "Now go."

His boss wasn't at home but Nellie directed him to the office where Frank found him shuffling papers in the back room, Harry Bennett leaning over his shoulder. He told them his story. Their reaction was the same as Frank's although the adjective

Harry used was stronger than so-and-so. "And here I thought he was coming round," Doc King said. "What's the plan?"

"It's Jenny's idea," Frank said, as the two men raised their eyebrows. "We're engaged... I think," he explained. "Anyway, she's on our side. She says I need to go see Mr. Terrell tomorrow morning and tell him we've caught Charlie and where to pick him up. We've also got to find out where and when the Tories are starting their parade. There'll be phone calls about it tonight, Jenny says and Letty at the exchange will pass it on to you once she finds out. Someone can call Mr. Mac Monday morning pretending to be from the Tories and tell him there's been a change of plans and he's to bring Charlie to...."

"The CPR station, Harry cut in. "We can hide in the garden. He won't see us until it's too late. We can start the parade down Baker."

"As long as the Tories aren't meeting anywhere nearby," Frank said.

"Born conspirators!" Doc King laughed. "I'll make the phone call. You're sure MacPherson has switched sides?"

"Looks like it," Frank said. "He's had a bee in his bonnet about the customs scandal from the get go. Jenny says it's because he claims to be a teetotaller and tipples on the side. Says he's got a guilty conscience."

Next morning, after an anxious night, Frank was up early and went straight to the office, missing breakfast. Doc King was already there, looking pleased with himself, feet propped on his desk. "They're meeting in front of the Court House at ten o'clock which couldn't be better. You were right about Mac. I pretended to be Sam Hershmer and told him to meet us at the CPR station. The quickest way is up Lumsden and Edwards, away from downtown."

"She's a smart girl, Frank. You're a lucky fellow. Now go tell Terrell we want to borrow his elephant."

Frank found the circus boss at his hotel having breakfast. He sat down opposite and signalled the waiter. "Morning, Bill. Ham and eggs with a side of baked beans, toast and coffee," he said, "and put it on Mr. Terrell's bill."

He grinned at the circus boss' look. "We found Charlie. He's in good shape. Dr. King wants to borrow him for his parade. It'll just be a couple of hours, up and down Baker."

"Sure, sure," Terrell said. "Thank Christ you found him. I'll be glad to get out of this burg – no offense. So where is he?"

"I'll get to that once we settle about the reward. It's for Ned Harris. He tracked him down and helped with the capture. Two hundred dollars. Canadian."

Terrell looked like he was ready to argue. "American," he said. "And I don't have that much cash on hand."

"You can write a promissory note to Mr. Ironsides," Frank replied, "and I'm not bargaining. Two hundred Canadian or I make a phone call and Charlie's back in the woods." He motioned to the waiter. "Bill can witness it."

It was a little after nine by the time everything was settled. Frank was feeling pleased with himself as he strolled along Baker, Terrell's note in his pocket. Harry and Doc King were to drive up and meet him around ten, enough time to let his supporters in on the joke and tuck them away in the station garden. It was like arranging a surprise party and he was looking forward to seeing Jenny again, not to mention the look on Mr. Mac's face. But you know what they say about the best laid plans of mice and men.

Jenny and her Grampa were just finishing breakfast and he was heading out the back door to supervise the loading of Charlie onto his truck when the telephone rang. She went to get it but he beat her to it and started in on a conversation which she heard with mounting distress.

"That's right…. Yes, she's here…. Too bad, nothing serious, I hope…. Just like that? Not very considerate…. The lunch shift? Sure, no problem. I'll tell her. I'm heading out in a few minutes anyway and I'll drop her off…. Not at all. She'll be glad to help…. You too, Goodbye." Then he turned to Jenny and said, "They want you to cover the lunch shift today. Mary somebody is sick and somebody else who's name I didn't catch, up and quit. Seems she just got engaged and her young man doesn't want her to work. Quit without notice. Not very considerate. I'll drive you in. Better hurry and get changed."

She knew there was no point in arguing and any attempt to get out of it would only rouse his suspicions once her plot came to fruition. And that was the last thing she wanted. Well, the second last. The last was that in driving her into Fink's, he'd take the route he always took, across Garden Ave. to the corner of Baker, a short block from the Court House where the Tory meeting really was.

She watched her grandfather cross the yard towards the barn and picked up the phone. Letty would be off this morning so she'd have to let somebody else in on it. At this rate half the town would find out. The operator was Judy which couldn't be worse.

"Hi Judy, I'm…. Fine thanks. I'm in a…. Yes, so I heard. Listen Judy…. Judy, this is an emergency. I can't talk. You need to get a message to Frank…. I can't, I told you. I can't talk…. Try him at Doc King's office. Then try him at the train station. Ask Frances……Judy, there's no time to lose. Whoever you get make sure they know where Frank is and get them to pass on this message….Yes only Frank, or maybe Doc King or Harry Bennett if you can't get Frank. Tell him I got called in to work and my grampa is driving me…. Yes that's the message…. I can't tell you…. That's right, it's code. You're so smart…. Keep trying until you get him. And hurry…. yes, you can borrow it anytime you want. Thanks, Judy, you're a champ." She hung up and ran upstairs to her room.

Half an hour later, Mr. Mac was fuming at the foot of the stairs. "Can't you wear something else or borrow another one when you get there? We're going to be late. We are late!"

"Sorry Grampa." She picked up the apron that had lain on the bed in front of her for the past ten minutes. "Oh, here it is. Sorry, I'm so flustered, this morning. Be right down." Five minutes later she got into the cab while Spot Griffin hopped in the back with Charlie. "Take it slow," he said, for which Jenny blessed him.

Another ten minutes passed before they got to Garden and Baker. Jenny wondered if there was anything she could say or do to prevent her grampa looking to his right towards the Court House. But then she saw Frank standing beside the McLaughlin-Buick right there on the corner. And he waved to them!

Beyond him Jenny could see a crowd of people carrying placards although it was too far away to read them clearly. "Over here!" Frank yelled. "You can unload him over here!"

Mr. Mac laughed. "I don't think so, Pinhead," he muttered and laughed again. Then he turned a sharp left and tore up Baker St. towards Fink's Mercantile. Oh, Frank, Jenny thought, You're a genius. "Grampa, that was Frank," she said. "You can drop me off here, I'll walk the rest of the way. Go unload Charlie."

"That's all right, Jennifer," Mr. Mac said, and laughed again. "Plenty of time."

Frank watched Mr. Mac's truck drive up the street, stop briefly in front of Fink's and then continue on to the CPR station. He walked over to the crowd of Tories gathered around Dr. Rutledge. "I'm sorry, sir, but it looks like Mr. McPherson has switched sides again."

By the time Frank reached the station, the cattle truck was backed up against the loading dock at the side of the platform and Spot was leading Charlie out towards Zack Terrell and a bunch of other circus men. Ironsides was talking to Mr. Mac. As Frank pulled into the parking lot, Doc King walked out of the garden followed by a crowd of men and women who began to cheer as Charlie came into view. Foremost among them were two men carrying poles supporting a banner with CHARLIE VOTES FOR KING! painted across it in red letters.

Frank decided he might as well keep his distance and pulled in behind a row of cars. He got out and stood on the far side, watching. Mr. Mac was towering over Doc King, waving his arms and yelling. Doc King pointed up towards Terrell who came down to join them. Mr. Mac yelled at him too then turned on his heels, got into his truck and tore out of the parking lot, spitting

224

gravel. When he passed Frank he braked, thought better of it and tore off again.

"I take it your plan worked," Doc King said when Frank joined him. "I can't for the life of me think what objection he can possibly have to you as a son-in-law."

"Neither can I," Frank grinned.

The parade was a great success. Charlie was in his element and feeling frisky after a couple of days in a warm barn with good food and the company of his keeper. Tied across his back were a pair of rough placards reading KING OF THE ELEPHANTS! on both sides. A man in a clown costume followed behind with a garbage cart and shovel. By the time they reached Norbury the crowd had more than doubled and every store window and doorway was bulging with onlookers.

A block further on, at Fenwick, they met the Tory parade coming in the opposite direction. Doc Rutledge and his daughter were in the lead with about thirty dejected followers. As they passed grimly by, they were greeted with taunting cheers from the Liberals.

The Winner

"It's all up to your friend Sims," Doc King said. "If he takes enough votes away from me, Rutledge wins. About fifteen hundred should do it." He looked at Frank meaningfully.

Frank pretended not to notice. "Do you want me to drive you down to the Court House?" Then we could vote together and I'll cancel yours out, he almost added, but didn't think his boss would appreciate the humour.

"I'll walk," Doc King said. "And I know what you're thinking. Go vote on your own time." He took an envelope from his desk and tossed it towards Frank. On the outside was written, In appreciation for services rendered, your friend, Horace King. Inside was a cheque for five hundred dollars. "If I do win, I'll have you to thank. At least that's what I told the committee last night." He stood up and held out his hand. "It's always a nuisance to know what to do with the surplus. Harry will have your regular pay. Come and see me Thursday once the dust has settled. Nellie will want to see you too."

Frank left the office and drove the car over to Hansen's Garage. It wasn't looking as splendid as it had seven weeks before and he winced to see the dent in the front fender. He spent the next hour washing and polishing, then went inside and handed over the keys. Sean wanted to speculate about the election but the topic made Frank nervous and he escaped after a few polite words.

When it came to dealing with her grampa, Frank had decided that Jenny was the boss and didn't argue when she told him to lie low for a few days. "He'll be as mad as a rooster but it serves him right. After he calms down we'll get together and have a talk about the future. You finding another job would help."

At least now he had five hundred dollars in the bank although it had taken a bit of doing to get it in. The teller had looked him over and asked him to wait while he walked over to the manager's office. Pinky came out, scanned the cheque, then Frank. He took it across to Bob's office and called him out. Bob looked at it and whistled, then composed himself, said something to his manager and walked over to Frank, grinning. "Mr. Rockefeller, I presume?"

Walking down Baker to the Court House, he felt more like Charlie Chaplin than John D. Finding another job was easier said than done, at least to support a family. Holy cow, he thought, scarcely believing that supporting a family wasn't miles down the road but already breathing down his neck.

Frank joined the line crawling up the Court House steps. He reached into his pocket and brought out the card Harry had given him when he registered to vote. Now that it came to it he started having doubts. He knew Doc King was right that voting for Sims was only going to help Rutledge. On the other hand, why shouldn't Rutledge and his cute daughter get a trip to Ottawa. Doc King MD would probably do more good for the citizens of Cranbrook than Doc King MP, especially if, as seemed likely, Meighan won the election. Besides, he, Frank Burton, was a socialist, wasn't he?

The most important thing in his life was to get a job and Doc King had promised to find him one, making it clear that winning Kootenay East was a big part of the equation. And what kind of a bum takes a job from a man he won't even vote for?

Frank's card was in bad shape by the time he handed it to the clerk at the desk. "Sign here," he said with a paternal smile. "First time? Nothing to be nervous about. Just mark it with an X," which annoyed Frank, although he did just that a minute later beside the name Sims, James. Relieved, he jogged back down the Court House steps, passing his boss and Harry Bennett deep in conversation. They didn't notice him

Next stop was the Victoria Café where he'd promised to meet Bob for lunch. His favourite table by the window was occupied by a trio of ladies drinking tea so he took a stool at the counter to get a closer look at the girl behind it and ordered coffee. Then, remembering he was practically a married man, he checked an impulse to flirt and kept his eyes on his cup, freeing up his ears for the conversation behind.

The lady with her back to him was doing most of the talking. Naturally, it was about the election. "Tom," she said, "is convinced Rutledge is going to win but I told him not to count Dr. King out just yet. The parade yesterday with that funny little elephant made quite a stir. People like that sort of thing and they like whoever's behind it. I'm told he sent his chauffeur out to find the poor thing. That's the young man who stopped the wild elephant, the one that died."

"Wasn't he the one who knocked you down, Louise?" another lady asked.

"The elephant? Oh, the young man. No, no. He didn't knock me down. It was the funniest thing. Right here at the door. I was just coming in for some tea and he was going out when he tripped. But he didn't knock me down. He took me by the waist, to steady himself, you know. There was no impropriety. Well, I'd thrown up my arms to protect myself and he took my right hand in his left and my left reached up to his shoulder, to steady myself you know, and we went backwards, well I did at any rate, and it was just like we were dancing. It was most gracefully done and he was very apologetic. An extremely attractive young man. I wouldn't mind dancing with him in earnest sometime."

A few minutes later, as the ladies were gathering up their gloves and handbags, Bob came in and swung onto the stool beside him, slapping down a hefty manila envelope. "Two hundred smackers in tens," he said, explaining that Ironsides had come in after he'd left and asked Bob to pass it on.

Frank told him who it was for. "I'll need a ride out to the Mission."

"Hell, you can afford to buy your own car."

"Afraid not. Jenny and I are getting hitched."

"No kidding! Me too. Say, maybe we should shoot for a double wedding. Save a bundle."

"Sure, if you want to wait a couple of years," Frank said

bitterly. "No job, her grampa hates me, she's only eighteen, well nineteen in three months, so no licence without his permission. We could elope, I guess. Save a real bundle."

"No go there," Bob sighed. "Eileen's set on the works. And it's got to be quick the way things have been going."

"Eileen's....?"

"Not yet but you know how it is. Only a matter of time before we slip up."

Frank, of course, didn't know how it was – another reason to envy his friend.

"Cheer up," Bob said. "I'll buy you lunch. Doc King find you a job yet?"

Frank explained his qualms. Bob laughed. "You voted for Sims? Geez, if Old Pinky found out my best friend is a socialist.... Hey, Miss, a couple of Swiss steaks for me and my pal. And make his red."

There was a dance that night at the auditorium with election results to be announced as they came in. As part of their plan to lie low, Jenny decided to skip it. She said her grampa wouldn't go anyway, especially after his recent humiliation. Even so, when he arrived just after nine o'clock and paid his dollar, Frank kept an eye out. The last thing he wanted was a dust up with his future grandfather-in-law.

It was mostly the younger crowd out on the dance floor and the music was upbeat. The dance was supposed to start at ten but they always got going early. The Bluebirds, a five-piece orchestra, was playing watered down jazz, more Paul Whiteman than King Oliver. Later on it would be foxtrots, waltzes, and polkas for the old folks.

Off to the side was a roll of newsprint that ran about fifteen feet across the wall. The names of the three candidates were written at the left-hand side, one above the other. Francis Guimont sat at a table beneath, holding a glass jar full of black ink with a small paintbrush sticking out.

Frank stood near the door watching the couples and thinking about Mavis. Some time that night she would walk up to him, hold up a couple of train tickets and say "Hello, Valentino, I'm just passing through on my way to New York. Coming?" He knew if he turned around she'd be there, so he didn't.

Later, making his way between the rows of tables in search of a dark corner, he almost tripped over the outstretched leg and crutches of Mike Wilson. He was pouring the contents of a leather-bound flask, disguised as a notebook, into a glass of soda water. After showing him the spine, down which was printed Rum Tales in gold letters, he tucked it inside his jacket, "Old family heirloom," he said.

Frank tried to step around him but Mike reached out and caught his sleeve. "Sit down and have a drink. You can't save a fellow's life and not have a drink with him. Make room, George. You know George, Frank? Old pal from St. Andrews." George nodded without smiling and looked away. Frank sat uncomfortably between them and went back to watching the dancers, the men's feet in particular. He had a feeling it was one of those things that was harder than it looked.

"I never thanked you," Mike said. "Thanks. Get Frank a glass, will you George?" George got up and walked away. "Old pal from St. Andrews," Mike said again. "What the hell made you get in front of that elephant? The only thing I can think of is you wanted to impress Jenny. Is that it? You wanted to impress Jenny?"

"I wasn't thinking. I just did it. Kind of stupid, I guess."

"You mean stupid not to let me get trampled to death? I wouldn't worry about that. I'm out of the picture anyway. But I suppose you're already aware of that. Was she in on the Charlie caper by the way?"

George rapped a glass down on the table. "I'm going to dance," he said and walked away again.

"Caper?"

"I'm on Rutledge's committee. I know Gramps was supposed to deliver Charlie for the parade. I saw you wave him over. Smart move. Stupid old bugger. I saw Jenny with him in the truck. Was she in on it or not?"

Frank didn't answer and Mike let it go. Some older citizens began arriving. The music became more sedate and the younger couples drifted out into the night. It got noisier with shouted greetings and speculations about the election. Cheers and applause met Dr. Rutledge, his wife and daughter, as they took a table near the orchestra. Smiling jauntily, he waved and led his wife out onto the dance floor.

When the music stopped, Ironsides stepped up to the microphone. "Ladies and gentlemen," he announced, "first results from some smaller polling stations have come in over the wire. Leancoil: Sims one, King two, Rutledge 3." Cheers and laughter erupted. Someone yelled, "A landslide!"

Francis stood up and wrote the numbers beside the candidates' names. Mike had extracted a real notebook from his pocket. "Last time King won Leancoil eight to four," he said, squinting at a column of numbers.

Ironsides continued to read out totals, all from small towns like Beavermouth, Wasa, and Flagstone, eight in all. Francis copied the numbers in three rows across the newsprint. Then he slowly added them up, wrote down the totals and circled them. They read Rutledge; 108, King; 59, Sims: 26. Mike beamed across at Frank and consulted his notebook again. "You can expect Rutledge to be ahead in most of these places, but last year it was closer." He added up a second column, "It was ninety-three to eighty-six. Sims is the difference. Not looking good for your boy."

The music started up again. "Seems like you've got two choices," Mike said, pulling out his flask again and waving it in Frank's face, "Either you try and catch up with me or you go find a sympathetic bosom to rest your weary head on."

"I can't dance and I doubt if there's much left in that thing."

Mike smiled mournfully. "Too true. I'm sorry we came to blows, Frank. A shame to lose a friendship over a woman. Such a cliché."

"There's no reason we can't…"

"Afraid there is. I'm leaving town as soon as this thing works." He held up his leg. "I'm fed up with the lumber business, the old man breathing down my neck. So, for the son of a gentleman, that leaves the church or the army. I picked the army. He can't cut me off for that and a fellow can drink more."

"You're enlisting?" Frank thought about his brother, then about Mike's panicked scramble over the nets to get out of Myrtle's way. Maybe Mike did too because he added, "Not planning to enter the hero sweepstakes. I'm going to military college. Be an officer as well as a gentleman. Anyway, that last one was supposed to end them all, wasn't it?"

They returned to watching the dancers. George was partnered with Alice from Hanson's and they seemed to be enjoying each other's company. "Don't get your hopes up, girlie," Mike muttered.

Two dances later Ironsides was back at the microphone. Rutledge had taken Meadow Lake sixty-three to five and Harmer's Lumber Camp thirty-five to fourteen with Sims a total of ten for both. Francis wrote the numbers, added them up and circled the new totals. It was beginning to look like a rout. The Bluebirds moved on to polkas and the Tories rejoiced. So much for elephant stories, Frank thought, and began to wonder what he would say to his boss.

Right on cue, just before eleven, Doc King entered the hall trailed by a knot of supporters, smiling bravely. Spotting Frank, he gave him a thumbs up. Beside him, Nellie waved to friend and foe alike. As they approached Rutledge's table all eyes followed. Would he shake hands and concede then and there? Poor Nellie, Frank thought, there goes the dining room furniture. He almost regretted voting for Sims.

But as it turned out, that was the high-water mark for the Blues. As if he knew it, Doc King strolled past his rival and took a seat beside him. Crossing his legs, he tilted back in his chair and said something to Rutledge. They both laughed. Then they sat companionably together, quietly conversing like two elderly spectators at a lawn bowling tournament. Forty-five minutes later, several more announcements produced a string of circled numbers, the last three reading: King 2678; Rutledge 2487; Sims 1097.

With seven polling stations scattered around the city, plus the advance poll, Cranbrook had the most votes and by tradition reported last. As everyone knew, the Tories always won Cranbrook. The year before, when it was just the two of them, Rutledge had won the city by fifty votes. Now, with Sims in the mix and probably getting most of his votes from King, they were virtually neck and neck.

Ironsides looked down at the slip of paper in his hand. "Ladies and gentlemen, the results from Cranbrook and the advance poll are as follows. Sims; 253, Rutledge; 618," He paused. "King; 674."

Some people began to cheer but it wasn't clear who they were cheering for. The slower witted crowded around Francis as he wrote down the new numbers, adding them to the previous counts. He circled the result and stepped away. Sims 1340; Rutledge 3105; King 3352.

Mike swore. Just about everyone else began to cheer because, of course, everyone likes a winner and wants everyone else to think they backed him. The band struck up For He's a Jolly Good Fellow as Doc Rutledge stood up and offered his hand to Doc King. His daughter stood beside him, crying. Nellie and Mrs. Rutledge, standing on either side, patted her shoulders. Frank could see Mrs. Roberts beside her husband looking bored. He wondered if he should ask her to dance but thought better of it. Then he and Mike shook hands too and that was the last they ever saw of each other.

The High-Striker

Frank woke up with a hangover. Down in the kitchen, Mrs. McKinnon said, "I heard you stumble in at some ungodly hour so I kept the coffee hot. And would you look at that." There were a couple of inches of snow on the lawn. "Earliest I've seen in years. That little elephant gave himself up just in time."

Frank told her Charlie was going to be the star attraction at the Fall Fair. Doc King had announced it from the balcony of the Canadian Hotel at the end of his victory speech. "I'm grateful to all six of those escaped elephants for giving me something to talk about during my campaign besides tariffs and senate reform," he declared. "I'm particularly grateful to Charlie Ed for his support here in Cranbrook. I've spoken to Mayor Roberts and Mr. Terrell of the Sells-Floto Circus and they have agreed to change his name to Cranbrook Ed in honour of this fine city. Unfortunately, Nelly and I will not be here for the ceremony as we are needed in Ottawa. However, we look forward to seeing you all again at Christmas."

Frank could see that the hot coffee was bait. She wanted to quiz him about his future now that he was out of a job and engaged to be married. He pleaded urgent business and made his escape. That business was taking the two hundred dollars out to Ned Harris. But since he needed Bob to drive him to the mission and Bob didn't get off work until four, it was hardly urgent. That gave him most of the day to kill. He decided to see what his other best friend was up to.

Hector was tied to a tree in his back yard looking glum, until he caught sight of Frank peering over the fence. His joyous barks brought Mrs. Whitmore to the kitchen stoop. "He's been miserable since Al died," she said. "I thought I'd seen the last of him a week ago when you took him away. Then he showed up again the very next day. I've been asking around and nobody wants him. I was thinking I might have to…." She looked away.

Frank explained that he was boarding and couldn't keep a

dog. "But I'll come and take him for walks when I can. And I'm getting married soon," he added, "so I could take him then."

"All right. He's your dog. I'll hang on to him for a month and then you'll have to come and get him no matter what. You can pay me something for his food until then." Frank gave her two dollars and promised two more every week. Mrs. Whitmore untied Hector and held out the rope. It was the first time he had seen her smile. She didn't ask him who he was marrying.

Heading back to town, he was passed by a line of trucks with Conklin and Garret All-Canadian Shows painted on their sides. That would be the Fall Fair midway being set up beside the arena. He followed and caught up to them parked in a line out front. A dozen hefty men were rolling carts loaded with steel pipes out of the trucks and pushing them towards the centre of the park where another gang was busy putting up amusement booths. Beyond them a Ferris wheel was beginning to take shape.

As Frank watched, one of the workers turned towards the booths and hollered, "Hey Haaarr-iet!"

A woman came out of a caravan. "Whadayah want?"

"Bring us some water would ya." The man's voice was familiar, also the name, and when she dipped a pail into a barrel and started towards him, Frank realized who it was. He quickly ducked behind a truck, pulled his collar up, his hat down and sneaked away. Just what he needed.

When Bob came out after work they dropped Hector off home and drove out to the reserve. But the only thing they found at Ned Harris's camp was open ground and a bare tipi frame. They drove back to the village and asked around but no one would talk to them. All they got was don't knows and shrugs. "A couple of white men in a car asking after an Indian aren't going to get much," Bob said. "Besides, they'll all be out deer hunting this time of year. He probably thinks you're going to keep the reward anyway."

"No he won't," Frank said.

The next day was a Thursday when the Herald came out.

The paper boy whizzed by on his bike at about seven and for once Frank was up and waiting for him. He wanted to see the election results from across the country which hadn't been clear on election night.

The headline read "May Not Get Clear Majority" but a closer examination showed that the Herald, being a Tory paper, was trying to make the best of a bad hand. The truth was the Liberals had won 116 seats to the Tory's 91. That was out of a total of 245. After you threw in the 11 Progressives, 8 Liberal-Progressives 2 Independents and the lone Independent Liberal, all bound to vote with the government, they had more than enough. Frank's political education had progressed far enough to tell him Doc King, as the only Liberal elected in BC, was sure to get into the cabinet. And if he kept his promise, Frank was guaranteed a place on the government payroll too. But did he want it?

Nellie always kept a good table so Frank waited until noon to pay his call. "You owe me a dollar," she said to her husband. "Horace thought you'd come this morning but I said you had patience enough to wait for lunch."

After they had started in on the shepherd's pie, Doc King asked, "Did you pay off that fellow?"

Frank told them about his attempt to find Ned. "I guess it'll have to wait."

"No it won't," Nellie said, retrieving the Courier from the sideboard and reading aloud from the back page. "The last of the lost elephants caught today...."

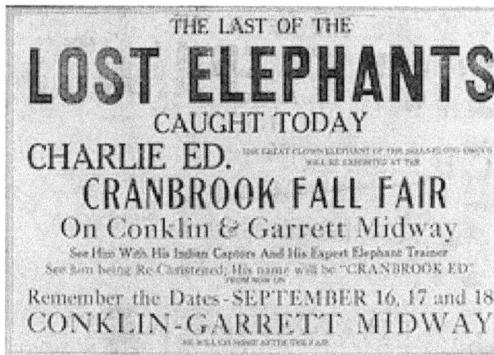

THE LAST OF THE
LOST ELEPHANTS
CAUGHT TODAY
CHARLIE ED. THE GREAT CLOWN ELEPHANT OF THE BIG SHOW CIRCUS WILL BE EXHIBITED AT THE
CRANBROOK FALL FAIR
On Conklin & Garrett Midway
See Him With His Indian Captors And His Expert Elephant Trainer
See him being Re-Christened; His name will be "CRANBROOK ED" FROM NOW ON
Remember the Dates - SEPTEMBER 16, 17 and 18
CONKLIN-GARRETT MIDWAY
HE WILL GO HOME AFTER THE FAIR

"See him with his Indian captors... You should be able to find him at the fair."

"I hope our little escapade didn't get you into too much trouble with the old man," Doc King said.

"I've been lying low," Frank said, "but we're going to tell him about our marriage plans as soon as he simmers down." At the same time, he was wondering how he could find Ned at the midway without bumping into Harriet and her big husband.

Doc King smiled. "You realize you're going to need his permission."

"Jenny says he'll come round once he knows we're serious."

"And how will she convince him of that?" Nellie asked.

"I don't know and she won't tell me. But she did say me having a job...."

"Ah, yes," Doc King interjected, "You remember Harding, the Regional Postmaster up in Golden? I put a call through to him yesterday. He's set to retire in three years and agreed to take you on as his assistant. Teach you the ropes. After a couple of years on your own, you'll be in line for a place back here."

So that was it, five years in Golden. His heart sank, which made him realize his qualms about taking the job were so much hot air. He'd been hoping all along there'd be something too good to turn down. Then, like it or not, he'd have to take it. And by most standards it was a good offer, except he knew Jenny wouldn't go for it. She's stand up to her grampa by marrying him, but she wouldn't turn around and move to Golden. That was too much. She'd ask him to wait before she'd do that.

Seeing Frank's expression, Doc King said, "Well that went over like a lead balloon."

"No. I'm grateful. It's more than I deserve."

"People rarely mean it when they say that. So…?"

In that moment Frank realized something else. He couldn't please himself anymore. He was a man with responsibilities. "I'll have to talk it over with Jenny."

The rest of lunch was uncomfortable - Doc King miffed that his offer hadn't been embraced with open arms and Nellie excessively cheerful trying to smooth things over. But they got through it, mostly talking about their return to Ottawa.

"I received a telegram from Mackenzie last night, offering me the Ministry of Soldiers' Civil Reestablishment. Bit of a mouthful. Paquet lost his seat, poor fellow. I'll be responsible for the Department of Health too. I imagine we'll be making it a full ministry this term. A lot of work for yours truly."

The Kings were due to leave next morning and Frank volunteered to help with the luggage. He could hardly do less. Then he went home and lay down to think. Still tired from tramping several miles with Hector the day before, he did most of it while asleep. He dreamed he was with the Yankees. He's been traded for Babe Ruth and the atmosphere in the dugout was hostile. To make matters worse he struck out his first time at bat. On one pitch, which was very humiliating. Instead of returning to the dugout, he took the train to Vancouver with Mike Wilson. As they passed through Nelson, Jenny and Mavis were standing on the platform, but the train didn't stop. "Looks like it's just you and me, kiddo," Mike said. Then he woke up. After pondering it for a while he thought that just about summed it up.

By the time he'd washed, shaved and suited up, it was almost five o'clock and he realized he hadn't told Mrs. McKinnon he wouldn't be eating supper at home. To make up for it, he peeled the potatoes and set the table. Then he set off to find Ned.

The fair was at the north end of the midway near where he had spotted Harriet and her large husband. Once inside he was funnelled past booths selling rolls of tickets for a nickel each. Different rides or games cost between one and three tickets. To get to the exhibits you had to run the gauntlet of midway attractions set up much like they had been in Invermere, a corridor of booths with strings of electric lights criss-crossing overhead. But instead of band music playing in the distance there was a pneumatic calliope blasting circus music from a stage beside the Ferris Wheel. The nightly dance was held at the auditorium several blocks away, featuring the Sid Syncopators which the Herald promised would "furnish a class of music that will please the fastidious."

A passage between carts selling cotton candy, hot dogs and ice cream led the way to the arena housing the exhibits, including Charlie Ed. Frank bought a couple of dollars' worth of tickets. He'd made a date with Jenny for Saturday night and thought he might as well get in some practice.

There was a chill in the air and the breeze made it feel even colder. He was grateful for it because he could wrap a scarf around his neck and cover the lower half of his face without looking out of place. Thus disguised, he worked his way past a shooting gallery, a ring toss and a carousel, stopping every now and then to reconnoitre. There was no sign of Harriet or her husband. He tried his luck pitching baseballs at a pyramid of milk cans but mostly missed. He wished he knew which booth was theirs. He'd gotten it into his head that it would be a High-Striker where you tried to ring a bell with a mallet. The big man would be good at that.

Oddly enough he was right. As he approached the far end of the arcade, he heard a loud clang and some ragged cheers. Off to one side he saw a small crowd gathered around a low platform with a wooden tower on it, maybe twelve feet high, painted yellow with red stripes, like a tape measure. There was a firehall bell on top. Peering through the circle of spectators he saw Harriet, her husband beside her, a hefty, long-handled mallet slung over his shoulder. "Who's next?" he bawled. "Who's next to show what a real man can do. Step up to win a prize for your best girl. Only one ticket a try. Come on, don't be shy. You sir…"

He was holding out his hammer towards a youth who had been pushed forward by a gang of laughing friends when Harriet caught sight of Frank. The scarf hadn't fooled her. "Fred!" she said, pointing and laughing. She leaned closer and said something else that made him scowl, first at her, then at Frank who pulled his scarf away and scowled back. But there was no telling what a jealous husband might say from the safety of a crowd. Or Harriet for that matter. Nothing spread quicker than small town gossip. He knew Mrs. Weeks was already saying Mavis had left town because he'd jilted her. Tangled up with a married carny girl would be icing on the cake. He turned to walk away.

"Frank"! It was Jenny. And as if that wasn't bad enough, Mr. Mac was standing beside her. Caught between a rock and a hard place. He could see Jenny was wondering what he was doing there without her but with Mr. Mac listening he didn't feel like explaining he was on his way to give Ned Harris his reward.

"Grampa's going to try the High Flyer," Jenny said, getting the name wrong. "And his cabbages came in second!"

"I said I'd think about it. Waste of money if you ask me." Mr. Mac looked at the shelf of prizes, gnome-like wax figurines, paper cut-outs, lollipops piled haphazardly around a small collection of more attractive dolls and stuffed animals. You could see he was trying to figure out how they made any money off it, maybe thinking hitting the bell was harder than it looked. With Frank watching, the stakes had gotten higher.

"Well, nice seeing you," Frank said, suddenly terrified that Harriet would realize Jenny was his girlfriend and say something.

"Aren't you going to watch?" Jenny asked. Then she added, mischievously, "I wonder which one of you two strong men can make it ring louder?"

The two strong men eyed each other. For a second it

looked like Mr. Mac was going to say something unpleasant but after a brief glance at Jenny, he thought better of it. His expression softened and he almost smiled as he looked back at Frank. "All right. You have a few years on me but on the other hand I've put in a lifetime of hard work. But let's wager something on it and Jennifer can be the judge. I win, you muck out my barn. You?"

Frank was tempted to say, "You let me marry Jenny," but knew that wouldn't fly. Instead, he said, "You stop holding Charlie Ed against me."

Mr. Mac looked surprised, and annoyed at the reminder. Then he laughed and stuck out his hand. "You're on."

By this time the young man ahead of them had been persuaded to take a swing. Making a show of it he spat on his hands, rubbed them together and lifted the mallet high over his head before bringing it down hard onto the pad. His friends cheered as a small metal ball flew up towards the bell, then groaned as it slowed to a stop beside a red stripe marked Nice Try!, and slid back down again.

"Good for a warmup," Fred said. "Now put your back into it. That'll be another ticket."

This time the mallet arced up with a mighty swing and crashed down. Cheers turned to groans and jeers as the ball barely reached Almost But Not Quite!. The kid dropped the mallet in disgust and started to walk away.

"You're not a quitter are you," Fred called after him. "You almost made it. Why even my wife can do it."

The young man turned and looked at her. "Yeah sure, " he said. "In a pig's eye."

"If she can, you can," Fred said, handing the mallet to Harriet and stepping back. With a graceful and powerful swing, she sent the ball soaring to the top of the tower where it gently struck the bell. More cheers, and laughter at the young man's expense. Red faced, he slapped another ticket onto Fred's outstretched palm. This time there was no mistake. The ball flew up, hitting the bell with a resounding clang. Disdaining the proffered doll, he strutted away.

At first Frank had scarcely been watching the little drama, consumed with anxiety and unable to escape. Harriet was bound to guess who Jenny was and find some way of making trouble. He needed to convince her that Jenny was his sister.

Taking the bull by the horns he pushed forward and thrust himself in front of Fred, leaving Jenny and Mr. Mac a few paces behind. The trick, he realized, was not to say it outright– they probably wouldn't believe him - but to make them come to that conclusion on their own. He handed over two tickets and took the mallet. "I'm going to have a contest with my grandfather," he said. "This is for both of us."

Then, as Jenny and Mr. Mac came up behind, he snatched up the mallet and said, "I'll go first," which he knew Jenny wouldn't like. Right on cue she frowned at his bad manners and said, "Is that all right with you, Grampa?"

"Sure. Why not."

Frank saw Harriet put two and two together, come up with brother and sister and frown in disappointment. He swaggered over to the High-Striker knowing exactly what would happen. With a swing worthy of John Henry, he slammed the mallet down. Sure enough it scarcely made it past Nice Try!. Looking sheepish and avoiding Jenny's eyes, he handed the mallet to Mr. Mac.

The old man frowned. having rightly judged that Frank's swing was as good as anything he was likely to produce. "Good luck," Frank said, stepping a couple of paces behind him and directly in front of Fred. Catching the big man's eye, he pointed at his foot and gestured for him to move it away. At first Fred pretended not to understand but when Frank shrugged and turned as if to address the crowd, he quickly stepped back just as Mr. Mac brought the mallet down. Clang!
He gave Frank a puzzled look. "Am I missing something?"

"My hand must have slipped," Frank said. "It doesn't matter, you win. I'll be over bright and early. And I'm counting on lunch." Then, with a jaunty wave at Jenny, who had already figured out he was up to something, he made his escape.

In the summer before leaving home, Frank had worked the midway at the C.N.E. in Toronto where he learned a few tricks of the trade. All the arcade games were rigged, including the High-Striker. The striker is a metal ball with a hole drilled through it that slides up to the bell on a wire. The wire should be tight and straight. If it's loose and wobbly, it's almost impossible to get it to the top. The operator stands beside the tower with his foot on a loose floorboard hiding a lever. When he presses down, it raises the base a few inches and loosens the wire. Fred had played that game with the kid who ended up needing three tickets to hit it. Then he was so relieved at finally succeeding he didn't even bother to collect his prize. Frank had caught on as soon as Fred stepped back to let Harriet take her swing.

He was feeling pleased with himself as he headed towards the arena. He'd fooled Harriet, put one over on Fred, and worked his way a bit further into Mr. Mac's good books, even if the price was mucking out his barn

The Ultimation

Clustered around the entrance to the arena were the four Popular Girl contestants selling raffle tickets for a new Chevy sedan. He bought one from each, another dollar gone, then went inside. It smelled the same as the last time he'd been there, hay and fresh dung. But now the hypnotic stillness had given way to the murmur of voices, the occasional laugh, and the lowing of cattle. Rows of trestle tables displayed vegetables, fruit, jars of preserves and pickles, needlework, quilts, and pottery. A couple of hundred people wandered up and down the aisles, pointing and exclaiming as they recognised a friend's contribution, some sporting ribbons of blue, red, or gold. Among the cabbages was a red ribbon pinned to a card reading MacPherson Farms. Further along, he found a blue one tied to a large jar of pickles labelled Mary McKinnon and wondered if that was the batch he'd worked on.

Pens containing cows, horses, sheep and goats had been constructed across the back wall with stacks of smaller cages filled with chickens, turkeys, ducks, and rabbits. Charlie's pen was in the centre, by far the largest, and overhung with a banner printed in bold circus script, CHARLIE ED and HIS INDIAN CAPTORS.

Charlie looked in good shape and happy, or at least contented, working his way through a pile of fresh alfalfa. One of the young men who had watched over Myrtle was asleep on a blanket over a heap of straw. Ned Harris sat cross-legged on the ground close beside Charlie, staring at the far wall, his face as expressionless as a face could be.

A boy of about twelve had climbed onto the railing and was leaning in. "Hey, mister Indian," he said, "did you catch him?" and when Ned didn't answer, turned back to his father laughing. "Does he speak English? Speakum English, mister Indian?"

"Come on," his father said, "Let's go look at Uncle Dave's

bull."

While this was going on Frank stepped away to the side, not wanting Ned to know he'd been watching. He felt ashamed to hand Ned his reward as though it made him a participant in his humiliation. "Not said a word since we got here," said a man sitting on a bale of hay in the shadows. It was Spot Griffin. "Paying him twenty-five bucks for the three days. You'd think he'd want to earn it. Just sits there and stares at the damn wall."

Frank thought about the two hundred dollars in his pocket. Maybe Ned would tell them to go to hell if he had it. A young couple came up, the man holding a toddler. Charlie swung a wisp of straw above his head and stuffed it into his mouth with a flourish, much to their delight.

Frank extended the envelope towards Ned who ignored him. He was chanting softly to himself. "Ned," Frank whispered, "Hey, Ned, I got your money."

For a second, Ned's eyes flickered towards him, his head nodding to the blanket beside his leg. Frank tossed down the envelope. "Nice knowing you, Ned. See you around," he said.

As he walked away, he remembered what Doc King had said about the Ktunaxa letting the land go to waste. He remembered reading about Lord Argyll over in Scotland who owned thousands of acres that he hunted on for a few weeks a year. Different worlds he guessed. Then he thought, "No, it's the same world, more's the pity."

The next day he went to pay his debt to Mr Mac. It turned out that his hired hand had left Cranbrook a week after Frank had put him on the voter's list. He and his boss had gotten into an argument about politics and Mr. Mac had fired him – not because of his politics, which he was willing to tolerate, but because he had sworn at him and refused to take it back. The upshot was that when Frank pushed his wheelbarrow into the barn Friday morning, it had not been properly mucked out in six weeks.

"You're late," Mr. Mac greeted him.

"I was helping the King's with their luggage," Frank

explained. "They took the train to Ottawa this morning."

The old man grunted. "You better get cracking. Honest work for a change."

Backbreaking and odorous, more like it but Frank was determined to do the best job he could. Three hours later there was a large and steaming pile of cow manure behind the barn, clean, straw-covered stalls inside.

When he presented himself at the kitchen door, Jenny said, "Just in time for...oh Frank, you stink!" She handed him a block of soap and a towel. "There's a water tank out back. I'll bring you some of Grampa's clothes. Scrub good. Remember this is our chance to talk to him."

Frank stripped and stepped into the water. Summer had long gone and it was freezing. He was scrubbing away, still trying to think of a plan when Jenny came up behind. He snatched up his shirt to cover himself. "That's better," she said, giving him the once over while handing him a neatly folded pile of clothes. "Let me do the talking!" she called out, giggling as she ran away.

When Frank entered the kitchen dressed in Mr. Mac's shirt, socks and overalls, Jenny was just serving up lunch. Their eyes met, a twinkle in hers. He could feel his face getting red and wondered how long she'd been watching him and what exactly she'd been looking at.

Lunch was Mr. Mac's favorite, bacon and tomatoes on fresh bread with real homemade mayonnaise made from a recipe Jenny got out of The Canadian Home Journal, dill pickles on the side and a glass of lemonade. Her grandfather looked down at his plate. "I can see what you two are up to." The fact that he made them a couple seemed like a good start.

They ate in silence, through seconds. A couple of times Frank was about to say something but was deflected by Jenny's toe against his ankle and turned it into a cough. She didn't say anything either. As she explained later, "I figured, let him get full of his favorite lunch first. And let him do the talking."

When he did, it was, "How old are you, Frank?"

"Twenty-one."

"Barely, I'm guessing. Anyway, old enough to know your own mind and make it up for yourself." When Frank opened his mouth, he cut in, "Jennifer, of course, can make up her own mind too. Always has, quick as lightning. It's less certain she's old enough to know it. Three years is a long time."

"Which is why we want to..." Frank began, cut off by another ankle kick.

"Want to what, Frank?"

Frank glanced sideways at Jenny who looked daggers back. "Get on with it," he mumbled lamely, to the tablecloth.

Mr. Mac smiled benevolently. "I completely agree, depending on what 'getting on with it' means. Now to my mind, Frank, it means settling down to a steady job, putting aside some money, going to church on a regular basis. And for you, Jennifer, it means learning how to be a good wife. Mrs. McKinnon can teach you that. There's lots of things you don't know about married life. At least I hope there is."

Mr. Mac stood up and looked down at them. "I'm sure you've got your reasons for getting married right away – or Jenny has anyway – but fortunately I'm the one with the say until she's twenty-one. If you've done all I'm asking by then, Frank, you have my blessing. If you haven't, I'm pretty sure Jennifer wouldn't want you anyway. That's my last word. And now I'm going out to the barn to see what kind of a job you've made of it."

After he'd gone they sat staring at the door for a couple of minutes. Then Frank said, "I suppose we could always elope."

"Frank!"

"I'm serious. Doc King says there's a job waiting for me at the post office in Golden and I've got a little over six hundred dollars in the bank. What do we care what that old goat says."

"Grampa is not an old goat! He's looking out for me. He doesn't trust you, that's all."

"You're going along with him? You want us to wait? That's your plan?"

"Well, would you?"

"Wait? Of course I would," Frank said, not altogether sure he was telling the truth. "I thought...."

"Do you love me, Frank?" she broke in, reaching across the table and taking his hand. "Would you work your fingers to the bone to keep food on the table? Are we going to have lots of children? Will you promise to stand by me?"

"Sure," Frank said. "All of it. Except I've just about run through every decent job I'm likely to get around here. I guess you wouldn't want to move to Golden and leave your grampa behind."

"Of course not. Now promise me. Properly."

Frank tried to look solemn and almost succeeded. He extricated his hand from hers and stood up. "I promise. Cross my heart and hope to die."

"Good. Then as far as I'm concerned, we're as good as married. Now listen. When Grampa comes back, you let me do the talking and sidle over to the hall door. When I give the word, run for it."

"What?"

"Do as you're told. Quick, here he comes."

Mr. Mac was smiling as he stepped back into the kitchen. "You have a bright future as a hired hand, son," then laughed at Frank's expression. "Well, maybe not. This place doesn't pay anyway. More of a hobby."

He sat down and leaned back expansively. "But I tell you what. When Angus and Bertha died, they left Jennifer their hardware store. Maybe she told you that. She'll own the building as well as the business when she comes of age. I was ready to retire at the time anyway, had my savings and pension from the CPR so I kept Carl Wiggins on to run it. I told him he could have it for ten more years. He pays me a share, of course, and we agreed that when Jennifer turns twenty-one, we'll see where we stand."

He turned to Jenny. "I thought maybe you would keep him on if he wanted to stay or hire someone else if he didn't. Or most likely you'd get married, and your husband could run it."

"What about me?" Jenny said.

Mr. Mac laughed. "I never met a woman yet who knew anything about hardware, let alone business. Besides..."

"I could learn just as well as any husband," she said indignantly.

"All right, calm down. The point I'm trying to make here is if Frank wants to learn the hardware business, he's got three years to do it in, with Carl teaching him, and if he makes a go of it...."

As Mr. Mac was talking, Jenny kicked Frank one last time and nodded towards the door.

"Where are you going?" Mr. Mac asked.

"I'm not sure," Frank said, looking confused, "Stretching my legs, I guess."

"Well, if Frank is going to learn the hardware business," Jenny said, standing up and leaning in towards her grandfather, her voice getting louder with every word" I don't see why we can't be married at the same time. I don't want to wait three years and neither does Frank. We're ready now!"

"I'll tell you when you're ready, young lady," Mr. Mac said, letting his temper go. "You'll be ready when I say you are and that goes for him too!"

Jenny looked meaningfully at Frank then back at her grandfather. "I love you, grampa," she said, "and I'm grateful to you. But life is too uncertain. I learned that when Momma and Poppa died. Frank and I are getting married. You can't stop us."

"Of course I can," Mr. Mac said.

"I read in the Herald..." Jenny began.

"The Herald! What's The Herald got to do..."

"If you'll let me finish, Grampa. I read in The Herald that a young couple in Ontario, just like Frank and me, even younger than me, seventeen, I think. They wanted to get married, but their parents wouldn't let them. They applied to a judge and because she was in the family way..."

"The what!!"

Jenny blushed and looked at Frank. He thought she looked very beautiful at that moment. "The family way," she repeated softly.

Then she yelled, "Run, Frank!" because Mr. Mac had picked up the lemonade pitcher and was yelling too.

"You bastard! You put her up to this. I'll see you in hell…." And he threw the pitcher but missed Frank who was already halfway down the hall and hit the framed lithograph of Daniel in the Lion's Den that had been hanging there since the house was first built.

When Frank got out onto the road he stopped and looked back. He felt like a fool and a coward and thought about going back if only to make sure Jenny was all right. But then Mr. Mac came out onto the porch and stood looking at him. They stared at each other, but Frank couldn't think of anything to say except "It wasn't me," but didn't.

"Mr. Mac ran back into the house. It occurred to Frank that maybe he'd gone to get his gun, just like in his dream, and remembered that adage about discretion and valor. He looked around and decided to hide in a clump of lilacs a few yards up the road but before he could move he saw Jenny up at her bedroom window. She waved and threw something towards him. It smashed on the path just in front of the garden gate. He ran over and picked up one of the pieces, pink porcelain. There were some coins scattered on the ground too and he realized it must be her piggy bank. Then he saw the note and grabbed it. He didn't stop to read it though because by then he could hear Mr. Mac clumping back down the hall. He ran for it.

He ran until his legs started to give out and then he trotted along for about a mile, looking over his shoulder every now and then and wondering what he would do if Mr. Mac came after him in his truck. He was also wondering what Jenny meant by being in the family way. At first, he thought she must have been confused about what it meant. Next, he had a bad moment thinking Mike Wilson might have had something to do with it but decided that couldn't be true, almost for certain. Almost. At last, he decided she must have just made it up and he was filled with admiration. Although how she was going to get a doctor to say she was knocked up when she wasn't was beyond him.

When Frank got to town, he sat on the government building steps and read Jenny's short, hastily scrawled note.

I am determined. Love Jenny

She hadn't had much time to think what to say, write it, stuff it into her piggy bank and throw it out her window but he couldn't help wishing she'd been a little clearer. Determined to do what? Marry him? He knew that already. It couldn't be elope because she had already told him she wouldn't. Making Mr. Mac believe she was... the thought made him tremble... pregnant? But that wouldn't work either because he'd make her prove it. Unless...

Frank jumped to his feet and began to walk quickly up Baker St. His mind was a jumble and he couldn't think straight. He found himself filling up the blank space in his head by counting footsteps and measuring off each block to see if they were the same length.

When he got all the way to the bank, his brain suddenly cleared. He went inside and took out two hundred and fifty dollars. Hanson's had some used cars for sale and it occurred to him that if he was going to get married and have a baby, he should have a car too.

Hanson's was still open and Alice told him Sean was out back. "Speak of the devil," he said as Frank came through the gate. "I just sold your old chariot to Doc Rutledge." He pointed to the McLaughlin-Buick Frank had been driving for the past six weeks.

"Did you show him the dent in the fender?"

"I said she's as you see her, not going into details. I doubt he noticed. You buying or just looking?"

When Frank said, "Buying," Sean suggested Mike Wilson's Studebaker. He was tempted, for lots of reasons, but had sense enough to decline. An hour later and a hundred and eighty dollars lighter, he came away in a shiny black three-year-old Chevy roadster with a retractable canvas top, no dents that he could see.

He took a couple of turns up and down Baker, honked in

vain at Bob's office window, drove over to Mrs. Whitmore's and picked up Hector. He thought about taking a run up Gold Creek Rd. but lacked the nerve. Finally, not knowing what else to do, he drove around town, then dropped Hector off and went home, just in time for supper.

After they had eaten, Frank followed Mrs. McKinnon into the kitchen, picked up a washcloth and told her what had happened. "Good gracious, Jennifer said that?" she exclaimed. Then she gave him a searching look.

Frank waved his cloth like a white flag. "I had nothing to do with it," he said. "Honest."

"Are you sure? Sometimes...." Mrs. McKinnon set a plate carefully into the rack and picked up another and began scrubbing it slowly. "Sometimes...."

"No," Frank said. "I could count the number of times I've even kissed her on the fingers of, well maybe both hands, but that's it. I mean," he continued, feeling pretty sophisticated to be having a conversation like this with an older woman, "not that I didn't give it a try a couple of times but Jenny wouldn't let me so much as...."

"All right," Mrs. McKinnon said, thrusting a dripping plate towards him, "I get the picture."

"I mean, we've only been engaged, well, had an understanding, I guess you'd call it, for a week and she's been clear all along that she wanted her wedding night...."

"But she said as far as she was concerned you are already married. Is that right?"

"Yes, but..."

"And you think she would go through with it if that's what it takes?"

Frank reached into his pocket and handed her Jenny's note. "Good gracious," she said again. "What's got into her."

"Nobody.... yet," Frank said to himself with an inward smirk, then, out loud, "Her grampa might listen to you."

"I'm not so sure I don't agree with him. I know it feels hard, but you're both so young."

"But would you want anyone to take three years away from the time you had with Mr. McKinnon?"

She smiled wistfully. "Oh Frank," she said, "That's clever. A little cruel to remind me of it.... All right, I'll talk to him. Perhaps we can work something out. But you must promise...."

There was a knock at the door and Mrs. Mac asked Frank to send away whoever it was. Except that it was Jenny. She pushed past him and rushed into the kitchen throwing herself, crying, into Mrs. McKinnon's arms.

"It's so unfair," she sobbed. "Why is he treating me like this? Haven't I always been good?" She pulled herself free, went to the sink and picked up a plate which she brandished over her head. "I've always been good, damn it!" Then she quietly seated herself at the kitchen table and placed the unbroken plate carefully in front of her.

The Dog

"He said I was ungrateful," Jenny said. "He called me names and made me go to my room. I told him it wouldn't change anything, so he locked me in. Like an old witch in a fairy tale." She laughed. "Except it's never worked very well and took me no time to get it open with my nail file. I sneaked downstairs and I could hear him talking about me on the telephone to Reverend MacKay."

"Oh dear," Mrs. McKinnon said.

"So I came here."

"I'm glad you did, dear. We'll go and talk to him. Goodness knows who was listening in on that conversation. Frank, you stay here. I'll take Jenny home in your car."

"You can drive?" Frank exclaimed.

"You bought a car?" Jenny said.

"Of course I can drive! Come along."

"I'd rather stay here with Frank. Grampa will just call me names."

Mrs. McKinnon thought about that. "Perhaps it would be for the best. But...." She hesitated, looked sideways at Jenny, then meaningfully at Frank. "Remember, now," she admonished him.

As they watched Mrs. McKinnon and the Chevy weave unsteadily down the street, gears grinding, Jenny asked, "Remember what?"

Frank walked back into the house, Jenny following. "Remember what?" she repeated when they reached the kitchen.

"I guess she meant promise not to...." Frank realized he wasn't sure how you were supposed to talk about such things. In cold blood, anyway, to a girl. "You know, the family way stuff." Then he added, "I didn't promise though. You knocked on the door just as she was asking me. I guess she didn't want to talk about it in front of you. I never got around to promising."

"It's none of her business anyway," Jenny said angrily. She looked at Frank with an expression he had never seen before, looking straight into his eyes. Then it shifted and went right through him. He could see her hands curl into tight fists, relax, curl again. "Let's go up to your room," she said softly.

When they got there – Frank wasn't sure how, his feet clumsy on the worn carpet as they climbed, his mouth dry, watching her body brush against the inside of her dress, Jenny closed the door and turned the key. "Let's hope this one works better," she said and sat down on the edge of his bed.

Frank leaned against the door, wondering if he hadn't promised, really, because he had meant to. It felt kind of cheap to take advantage of Mrs. Mac's confusion when she was only trying to help. Jenny was looking down at the floor in front of her, at the small rag rug that he was always grateful for on a cold morning. He sat down beside her. They sat examining the rug together, counting the circles and not touching.

After a while, Frank put his arm around her. She tensed up for a second and then leaned her head against his shoulder, although her back was still stiff and upright. Her hair tickled his nose, but she smelled good. He twisted awkwardly around to kiss her. He wasn't sure what was supposed to happen next but he figured Jenny would put a stop to whatever she didn't want. He told himself that getting her in the family way would be like stepping onto a long, long road that would take them to the end of their lives.

Outside in the yard a dog started barking. Frank reached down and took Jenny's right hand and moved it towards him. Then he ran his own hand up her arm and brushed it across her small breast and up to her neck. She began to respond to his kiss. The dog continued to bark, getting louder and then it began to howl mournfully.

Frank pulled away and laughed. They looked at each other, smiling. "Who's dog is it?" Jenny asked. Frank got up and walked stiffly to the window keeping his back to her because of the way he was and pulled the curtain aside. "Oh for... goodness sake. It's Hector!"

The movement of the curtain caught the dog's eye and

he redoubled his barking, crouching down and springing up towards the window. Across the alley, a man yelled from his back porch, "Shut that dog up!" Frank slid up his window and called down, "Sorry. Hector, good boy, go home." That quieted him until Frank closed the window. Then he started up again.

They went back and forth with that a few times, the man across the alley joining in, until Frank said, "I'm going to have to take him home. It's only a few blocks."

"I'll come with you," Jenny said.

Hector happily led the way as they walked along Garden Avenue. The air was cold and Jenny had come away from home without her coat. Frank wrapped his jacket around her shoulders. It made him feel like she was really his. He was happy they had gotten out of his room and he felt grateful to Hector for making it happen. "Good boy," he said. Hector looked up from the base of the tree he was sniffing and wagged his tail.

They walked hand in hand, both trying to think of something to talk about besides what was on their minds. A fat half-moon hung low in the southern sky, the last of the light fading. Finally Jenny said, "You bought a car?"

"I thought it might come in handy, you know, if we had to..."

"We're not running away!" Jenny snapped, which brought them back to the subject they were avoiding. "Can we afford it?"

Frank loved the 'we'. He told her about the bonus and how he had been saving up his pay. They talked about the job in Golden and agreed that neither of them wanted him to take it. They liked the idea of taking over the hardware store. "I've been handling the money at Fink's," Jenny said. "I'm good with figures."

"Well you've got a good one, anyway," Frank said, slipping his arm around her waist. They tried walking like that for a while, bumping along, then going back to holding hands which took them to the corner of Fenwick.

"I was taking him out to the yard to do his business," Mrs. Whitmore told them after Hector's bark brought her to the door.

"He just took off. That's the last straw. You can take him now or not but my cousin over in Lumberton says he'll take him first thing tomorrow if you don't. If you want him, you gotta take him now. No ifs ands or buts. I've had enough. He was Al's dog anyway."

Frank looked at Jenny. "We'd better take him," she said decisively. On their way back, it occurred to Frank that adopting Hector was the first important decision they had made together. They were a family now.

Mrs. McKinnon had not returned so they sat on the porch waiting, but after half an hour it got too cold. Frank couldn't imagine what his landlady would say if she found Hector in her living room, or even her kitchen for that matter. They decided to take him up to his room. He was glad it was a Friday night and none of the other boarders, all young single men, were at home.

As soon as they opened the door, Hector jumped onto the bed and curled up. "What's that expression the French use?" Jenny said, "Menage a trois?"

"Manage a what?"

"Never mind. I guess we better wait and see what they worked out," she said and lay down beside Hector, wrapping herself in the bed cover and smiling up at Frank. "I hope he doesn't snore." She closed her eyes and Frank sat on the edge of the bed holding her hand until she fell asleep. He felt partly relieved. After a while he got his winter blanket out of the closet and shooed Hector off the bed. He lay down beside Jenny and fell asleep too.

When Mrs. McKinnon got home after midnight and found Frank's door locked, she suspected the worst and went to get her key. She listened for a minute and quietly opened the door. Seeing them sleeping chastely side by side was a relief. She locked the door again and tiptoed away.

Next morning she let them sleep in until her other boarders had all gone out. As she was climbing the stairs, Mr. Mac knocked on the front door and poked his head in. She ushered him into the kitchen and told him what she had seen the night before. "I think they are going to be sensible," she said. "I hope you are too" and went back up the stairs.

"There's breakfast, you two," she said, knocking on Frank's door. "Jenny, your grampa's here."

Frank and Jenny listened to Mrs. McKinnon's footsteps as she retreated downstairs. They were lying naked in each other's arms, Frank wondering what was going to happen next and Jenny remembering what had happened the night before.

When Mrs. McKinnon looked in on them, they had both been almost asleep but Frank was keeping an ear out and the click of the lock had awakened him. By this time the moon had gone down and the room was dark. He lay there listening to Jenny's breathing. His belt buckle had shifted around and was biting into his hip. He tried to twist it straight, then decided to take it off. As he was pulling it stealthily through his pant loops, Jenny shifted closer. "Frank," she whispered, "I think we should do it."

He nearly said, "Do what?" but went dumb instead. The silence stretched out until Frank realized that if he didn't say or do something it would be all over. It felt like the moment before he had stepped in front of Myrtle. He closed his eyes. In the darkness, he saw her face, reached out and felt her arms slide around his neck, her body pressing into him.

As they kissed, both became aware of a regular thumping within a few feet of the bed. They stopped to listen. The sound stopped with them and then started up again. It was Hector's tail hitting the floor. They pulled apart and began to laugh which, when they eventually subsided, made it easier to undress without awkwardness. "I wish I could see you better," Jenny said. Frank got up and took a candle out of his side table and lit it. She lay on his bed looking up at him, the sheet tucked under her chin, naked arms by her side. "I read about that," she said, pointing....

"Now what?" Frank said next morning as they listened to Mrs. McKinnon's tread fading away down the hall. "I guess we'll have to tell them." They thought about that, trying to think of the words.

"It's none of their business," Jenny said stubbornly.

"But wasn't that the point?"

She looked at him, the tears starting to come. "Is that what you think?"

"It was your idea!" Realizing how that sounded, he turned towards her, grabbed her by the shoulders and pulled her on top of him, wrapping the sheet around them. "Best idea you ever had." Then, out of nowhere, "I keep thinking about those circus elephants. Dragged from pillar to post all their lives, never getting a chance to be what God made them. Makes me sorry I ever had any part in catching them."

"They would have died out there if you hadn't."

"Sure, but only because they shouldn't have been here in the first place. Come on, let's get it over with."

They untangled themselves and got up on opposite sides of the bed, dressing with backs turned. Hector came out of the closet where he'd been curled up for the night, stretching and wagging his tail.

"He's part of the family now," Frank said and later, in the hall, "You go first. He won't throw anything at you."

"I'm not so sure," Jenny said.

Mr. Mac was sitting at the table, cradling a coffee mug. Frank eyed his fists nervously and stopped just inside the kitchen, leaning against the door jam. Jenny took a seat across from her grandfather, hands folded primly on her lap. "Good morning, Mrs. McKinnon," she said, just as primly. "Thank you for taking me in last night. Good morning, Grampa."

The old man grunted, his eyes fixed on Frank as if trying to read what he and his granddaughter had been up to. Frank tried to hold his stare but wavered.

"How did he get in here," Mrs. McKinnon burst out. "Did you...?"

"Hector's Frank's dog," Jenny said, as their best friend wagged greetings from the doorway. "Our dog," she corrected herself. "He's adopted us. Mrs. Whitmore was going to give him away after promising him to Frank. We had to take him. He was howling outside..." She stopped, blushing as she remembered the circumstances.

"Leave him be for now," Mrs. Mackinnon said. "Your grandfather and I have been talking and he's prepared to acknowledge that Frank...."

"Frank's got me over a barrel is the long and the short of it," Mr. Mac cut in. "Jennifer's made up her mind, for better or worse, and that's that. I know you think the world of him, most women do, it seems to me. And Ironsides likes him. Doc King too for what that's worth." He peered down into his mug, then up at Frank. "I'm told you behaved yourself last night. That's a mark in your favour so I'm willing to settle for next spring. If you can make a go of the hardware store...."

"I'm sorry," Jenny said, "but no."

"No?" Mr. Mac said, temper rising.

"You're right, Grampa, Frank did behave himself last night or he tried to. But I wouldn't let him."

"Jenny!" Mrs. McKinnon exclaimed.

"What do you mean?" Mr. Mac asked, slower on the uptake.

Frank decided he'd been on the sidelines long enough. He took a step into the room. "We'll get married properly some time or other," he said, "whenever you're ready to sign the papers. Or we'll wait until she's twenty-one. But that's all we're waiting for."

Mr. Mac stood up and pointed his finger at Frank. "I'll get a court order against you!"

"Callum, for heaven's sake be reasonable," Mrs. McKinnon cried.

Frank reached out and took Jenny's arm and steered her out into the hall, walking backward and keeping an eye on Mr. Mac. Hector got up and joined them as they walked out. Seeing his Chevy parked out front, Frank laughed as he realized Mrs. Mckinnon still had his keys. Greatly daring he ran back into the house and snatched them up from the hall table. He could hear angry voices coming from the kitchen.

"Come on," he said. "We can beat him out to your place and pack up a few of your things."

Jenny sat quietly beside him as he drove. When they arrived, she said, "I'm not running away. I'll stay and wait for him. You go. Seeing you will only make him mad."

They argued about that for a while but of course Jenny won. They agreed to meet the next day, Sunday, when she'd be singing in the choir.

"We'll go say goodbye to Charlie," Frank said. "They're shipping him back to the circus tomorrow afternoon."

The Christening

From time to time over the years Frank would talk about taking a trip to India to see an elephant in the wild but he never did. And whenever the circus came to town he always stayed away and even busied himself in the back of the store to avoid seeing the parade. That Sunday was the last time he ever saw one, except occasionally in his dreams.

It rained most of Saturday and Frank spent the rest of the morning walking around town with Hector. Bob and Eileen had taken the train to Nelson for a weekend getaway. Boredom finally took him to Doc King's constituency office. Harry was addressing a bunch of thank you notes that his boss had signed before leaving for Ottawa.

"You not left yet?" he asked. Frank had to bring him up to date on everything since the election. It seemed a long time ago and he had a hard time explaining why he was turning his back on what Harry clearly thought was the chance of a lifetime.

"You're trading a career in the Post Office, halfway up the ladder to being your own boss, for working in a hardware store with that old buzzard breathing down your neck. I hope she's worth it." Frank said she was and after an exchange of views on the weather, he left.

He truly did think she was worth it but wasn't nearly as sure that passing up Doc King's offer was a good idea. It gave him a restless night and was still on his mind next morning in Knox Church. He usually sat up front so he could swap glances with Jenny and signal he wasn't afraid of Mr. Mac across the aisle. There had, however, been occasions when he'd stayed further back. This time he arrived late and slid into the first pew he came to. He spotted the back of the old man's head and busied himself with a prayer book.

The choir was already well into the opening hymn. It took him a minute to find Jenny squeezed between two robust ladies in the back row. She looked so slender beside them that he found it hard to imagine her with a baby inside. He realized he was a bit unclear about how all that worked and wondered if it had already started. He'd asked her about it that night and been startled by her answer.

"I can't be sure, of course" she told him with a business-like air that got his attention. "But it's my time. I read about it in a book. The one that had the pictures. A bunch of us girls shared it around a couple of years ago. A real eye opener." She smiled and ran her hand over his ribs to show her recent experience had been another.

He asked her where she'd got it. "I'm not sure I should tell." Then, "Well I guess it doesn't matter since she's left town. Mavis Weeks."

When Frank didn't say anything, she added, "I know you liked her. I always thought you and she…" She hesitated.

"What?"

"I thought she might catch you before I did."

That had set off a round of denials and assurances that ended up in the usual place, remembering which took Frank most of the way through the service. When it was over, he ducked out quickly to avoid Mr. Mac and walked around to the garden. When she came out and sat down beside him, she looked haggard and her eyes were puffy. "I don't want to talk about it," she said. "It was awful. Let's go say good-bye to Charlie."

Frank thought the rechristening was a lot of tomfoolery. He'd just about gotten over the entire elephant business by now. There was no doubt the last few weeks had changed him, made him a better man, he guessed, but he didn't want to think about it – kind of like a snake who has no more use for his old skin once he's shucked it off.

In the beginning he'd been caught up in the excitement of the stampede and that first night of elephant hunting with Hector. Then he'd come up with the idea for Doc King's Elephant Bulletin. After that there'd been the roller coaster ride between Mavis and Tilly followed by Myrtle's death. It had been exhausting.

They walked over to the Royal Bank for the ceremony. Frank didn't want to talk about elephants which seemed to be the only thing Jenny did want to talk about. He wanted to know what had happened with Mr. Mac, which was the last thing she wanted to talk about. So they didn't talk about much of anything.

There were about a hundred people on hand including a reporter from each paper, photographers in tow, as well as Mayor Roberts, Ironsides, Zach Terrell and a couple of handlers. Mrs. Roberts was there too and they exchanged friendly waves that drew an enquiring look from Jenny. Most of the rest seemed to have at least one kid in hand. Frank looked at them with new interest and a prickle of trepidation.

As reported in the Herald the following Thursday, Charlie was led forward between two burley circus men and, with the granite pillars of the Royal Bank as a backdrop, presented to the crowd. As Charlie tossed his head and waved his trunk in acknowledgement of the cheers, Mr. Roberts produced a bottle of "real honest champagne." He poured it over the elephant's head and declared his name to be henceforth Cranbrook Ed.

'The christening over (as everyone thought), a presentation to the winning lady in the Cranbrook Gyro auto contest then took place," The Herald continued. "Mayor Roberts, having kindly consented to make the presentation, asked Miss Marie Patterson to come forward. Standing in front of Cranbrook Ed, His Worship complimented her on the excellent work she had done and asked her to accept with her $200 wardrobe, a bouquet of flowers. In his most gracious manner the mayor was handing the flowers to Miss Patterson when the newly christened, apparently thinking he could show His Worship how such presentations should be made, grabbed the flowers and making a pass with them to his mouth as if to eat them, then waved the bouquet on high, much to the surprise and delight of those present, then dropped them at the feet of the honoured young lady who, picking them up made suitable acknowledgement to both His Worship and Cranbrook Ed.

"The next stop was at the Victoria Café where he was the guest of the proprietor Mr. Geo Anton, for breakfast. Here, standing in front of the café, Miss Lopeter of the Victoria staff brought out a tray bearing some delicacies, which, judging by the manner in which he proceeded to relieve the tray of its burden, was much to his liking. This was Cranbrook Ed's last meal in the city of his adopted name.

"From the café the march continued to the CPR depot where Mr. Ironsides purchased a ticket for Cranbrook Ed, writing a cheque for $1200. For this Ed got a whole baggage car to himself in which to ride all the way to San Francisco where the Sells-Floto Circus is now showing. Here he will join Tillie, doubtless telling her about the sad fate of Myrtle and the wonderful sendoff from Cranbrook."

Frank and Jenny, in no hurry to get back to the complications of their lives, stayed to the end. As the train pulled out of the station, Frank said, "It's funny. All along I've been thinking what a shame those elephants never got to live their lives in the wild, out where they belong, but Charlie didn't seem to mind a bit. He looked like he was having the time of his life."

"He's always been a circus elephant," Jenny said. "You can't be a coyote if you're a dog. Where's Hector?" From there they went back to real life.

"I promised Mrs. Whitaker two dollars a week to take him until we get a place of our own."

"Frank! Two dollars?"

"All the more reason to get a place right away. Is he going to sign or do we elope?"

Without providing the details, which she never did, Jenny told him her grampa had given in to the point where he'd sign the damn papers and they could both go to the devil as far as he was concerned. But Jenny wouldn't accept that until he'd promised to come to their wedding and give her away.

They were married a month later and my dad came along eight months after that, by which time they had entered into a life that had moved well beyond the boundaries of Frank's

Story. It took Mr. Mac most of that winter to come around but he found it impossible to hold out against Jenny's refusal to stop loving him and the prospect of a grandchild. Frank went back to work at Wilson's lumber yard and they lived in rented rooms on Kootenay St. By April the old man had surrendered unconditionally and arranged for Frank to start learning the hardware business. Jenny insisted on doing the books, despite her other distractions and as a result they managed very well. Frank, of course, was well liked and Jenny kept him focused.

Hector lived to be fourteen years old and when he died, Frank went looking for a relative. He finally tracked one down in Wasa and got a pup whom he named Hector. He had five Hectors in all, all good dogs according to Frank but none better than the first.

My aunt Violet was born in 1929 just in time for The Great Depression. Three more arrived at approximately two year intervals, 1931, 1933, and 1935, all girls. Eight years later, in the middle of the war, a surprise baby came along, my uncle, only seven years older than me, Mike Wilson Burton.

They were hard years, especially with so many mouths to feed but with a little help from Mr. Mac and a small inheritance when he died, they did better than most and were happy. Jenny still sang in the choir so Frank, to his credit, was known as a regular church goer and never let on he went for the music, not the religion. He remained a socialist all his life and kept on good terms with the Rev. Mackay and Mayor Roberts, no mean feat. He never did dance with the mayor's wife.

He and Jenny were invited to supper at the King's whenever the great man was in town. Doc King liked to solicit his opinion on the latest Liberal folly so he could be prepared for the next parliamentary debate. He even tried to get Frank on board for the 1930 election campaign but that became moot when Doc got elevated, or demoted as Frank liked to say, to the Senate. He ended up as Majority Leader and Speaker, dying in office in 1955. Nellie had died a few years before.

In the election, Frances Guimont got the Liberal

nomination but lost by a whisker to the Tory candidate thanks to the bad economic conditions. Since then the riding has gone every which way, sometimes making Frank happy, sometimes breaking his heart.

He would see Ned Harris from time to time but only from a distance, usually on Dominion Day when some Ktunaxa horsemen, dressed in their feathered regalia, would take part in the parade. Their eyes met once and Frank thought he nodded but couldn't be sure. It might have been the movement of his horse.

Frank was pretty sure Doc King never said anything about the pollution in the river and after a while he and Nellie stopped pestering him about it. He told himself he had a business to run and being a socialist was bad enough without getting a reputation as a crank as well. He had a family to support and times were hard. That was true, of course but he was always ashamed of himself for not doing anything more.

When the stories came out about the residential schools, he believed them right away although most didn't. He remembered the nun he'd seen on the front steps that day. He wondered how she had treated the kids and hoped she had been one of the better ones, if there were any. He was glad Ned had grown up before the government made it compulsory to attend and wondered if any of his kids had gone and what had happened to them. It was all something he didn't want to think about but couldn't help sometimes anyway.

Bob and Eileen remained their best friends. They played bridge at least twice a month for years and Bob Jr. married my Aunt Violet the year before I was born. It was Bob Sr. who kickstarted Frank's Story when he and Eileen came back from another weekend in Nelson with a copy of the Daily News.

ELEPHANT SAVED FROM DEATH
Court Order Restrains Execution of Killer
San Francisco June 17, 1935 (AP) A self-styled animal lover saved 'Wally', six ton elephant from a police firing squad

barely 30 minutes before the huge beast was to have been destroyed for killing his keeper, Edward Brown, 45.

Alexander Mooslin, an attorney, obtained a restraining order from Superior Judge Frank T. Deasy and served it upon zoo officials and police marksmen while they were preparing to put Wally to death. Mooslin contended "such dignity should not be destroyed."

The petition asserted the elephant "unavoidably and instinctively killed the keeper because of the cruel and inhuman treatment inflicted by caretakers."

On the same page a second article declared:

ELEPHANT THAT KILLED KEEPER MAY HAVE ROAMED EAST KOOTENAY IN 1926

Possibility that the elephant which on Tuesday trampled and gored a keeper to death at the Fleishhacker zoo in San Francisco was one of those which escaped from the Sells-Floto circus at Cranbrook ten years ago and roamed through the East Kootenay forest for almost six weeks, is suggested by a similarity in names.

The San Francisco elephant was known as Wally but its name previously had been Charlie Ed. One of the six elephants which escaped at Cranbrook was known as Charlie Ed, though after its capture it was announced that he would be known thereafter as Cranbrook Ed.....

Charlie Ed was captured September 15, and was exhibited at the Cranbrook fall fair a few days later. He was shipped south to the circus winter quarters September 20. He was sold to the Fleishhaker Zoo in May of this year.

Frank and Bob had made a tradition of going fishing on Kootenay Lake every year in late June. That particular year they had decided to make it a father and son excursion and my dad, just turned nine, went along. That first night while they were sitting around the campfire, such was Frank's excitement at hearing how Charlie had once again cheated death, he told the boys his story from beginning to end. By which I mean the parts pertaining to elephants. It was such a hit that they had him repeat it the next two nights and by the last night some politics had crept in as well.

And that was how it started. As the years went by, each successive girl got added, along with school friends, then grandkids, cousins, friends, neighbours and, finally, total strangers. Excerpts would pop up as dinner conversation and when he ran for city council in '42 he naturally threw a little into his campaign speech.

He never mentioned what finally happened to Charlie Ed and I wonder if he even knew. As far as I have been able to tell, it didn't get into the local papers and I only discovered it when doing some online research for this book. It was published in the San Francisco Examiner the day after that other story came out in Nelson.

SHOOT ELEPHANT DESPITE PROTEST
Huge Beast That Killed Keeper Put to Death
By Police With Moose Guns

San Francisco, June 18, 1935 (UP) Two police inspectors using moose guns, today executed Wally, a six ton bull elephant who killed his keeper, Edward Brown, 45, in a fit of rage.

The killing was ordered by the San Francisco Park Commission despite widespread protest.

Wally, as if in realization of what was transpiring, strained against heavy chains which held him to stakes. His ponderous head was fettered to his legs so that he could not lift it.

The police marksmen sent their bullets through his heavy hide and the great pachyderm collapsed and fell. Five minutes later veterinarians pronounced him dead.

The Letter

Mike Wilson seldom returned to Cranbrook. He had made a career in the army and spent most of the thirties and the first half of the war as an instructor at the Royal Military College in Kingston. After repeated requests for a transfer, he was sent to England in 1942. A year later and by then a Lt. Colonel in command of an infantry regiment, he took part in the invasion of Sicily. In July he led a small squad towards the mountain town of Aidone in order to reconnoiter German artillery positions. They were about to withdraw when the enemy suddenly counter-attacked and cut off the road behind. The thirty Canadians took shelter in the town and held off repeated attacks for three days. On the last day a German shell struck the wall of a house three men were defending. One was killed and the other two were wounded, stunned by the explosion, and exposed to enemy fire. Mike ran across a hundred yards of open ground, lifted one man onto his shoulders and dragged the other towards shelter. As they reached safety, he was hit by a spray of machine gun fire and killed.

The story of his death and award of a DSO was reported in both local papers along with the news that he had recently married an American woman in England named Dora Vane. Frank was a city councilor at this time and was assigned the task of writing condolences to the widow on behalf of the city. After a delay, a brief acknowledgement was duly received, signed Mrs. Dora Wilson. When the surprise baby was born a month later he was christened Mike Wilson Burton.

After Granny J died, the old house was put up for sale. I took on the job of clearing out the basement. I had my eye on a new snowblower Frank had bought a couple of years before but never used. He liked to pay the grandkids to shovel.

While I was clearing his work bench, I came across a Rowntree Dairy Box tucked in behind a row of old paint cans. Inside was a stack of letters. The one on top had a return address on it from D. Vane, The Priory Cottage, Tadley, Hampshire, England. The letter was dated November 24, 1943.

Dear Frank,

What a crazy old world this is! Never did an official condolence letter ever gladden the heart of a grieving widow as much as yours. Not that most grieving widows were the first lover of the city councilor sending it – and I'm fairly sure it was vice versa too!

I guess you can tell I'm pretty excited right now and just in case you are wondering, it's Mavis Weeks. Your letter caught up with me this afternoon by post – mail I mean – care of the box office manager. And wouldn't you know it, he handed it over just as we were getting our call for places. After I read it and saw the Yours Sincerely, Frank Burton, Cranbrook City Council, I couldn't help grabbing a pen and paper and starting right away. But I have to go now or Mary Wilkinson will miss her entrance!

OK I'm back. The boys and girls all went out for drinks as usual but I told them I had a date with an old lover. In Leicester of all places! So here I am nice and cozy in the little room I share with my mother (in the play) and no air raids. Touch wood.

Explanations! The play is a terrible piece of fluff called The Lend Lease Bride about an English soldier in Washington, DC who falls in love with a Senator's daughter (guess who) whose husband was killed at Pearl Harbour. I think I got the part because I'm a widow myself and they liked the publicity angle. It's a terrible business!

Anyway, to go back about a hundred years, boy did I hate you. I think I called you a skunk. Mike set me straight when I told him about you and me. He told me you got treed by an elephant! We had a good laugh about that and a few tears too. Then he told me how you saved his life. More tears!

I might as well come right out and say it. Mike loved you probably a lot more than I did. I liked you and all that but mostly I needed someone to help me get out of town. Well, you did that! I found someone else right away. And someone else after that and so on. Boohoo poor me. You owe that elephant a lot. I hear you've got a passel of kids. Good old Jenny!

About Mike, you never needed to worry about him. He liked boys even more than I did. Remember George? Jenny was his cover girl and you were the man of his dreams. He told me the three of you sometimes went out to the movies together and you used to sit yourself between him and Jenny. He loved it!

Anyway, moving right along. When I got to Vancouver I found out there was nothing doing. I looked up the piano player from The Green Door. He was playing in a little back-alley club on Water St. but he said having a white girl there would cause trouble. I think he meant with his wife! That's when lover number two came into the picture. A black man (blush blush). He took me down to Hollywood and we lived together for a few months. He was nice but his wife tracked him down and I had to go.

I can see if I go on like this I'll run out of ink. Long story short, I got an agent and some song and dance work in clubs. Then some dance and bit parts in the movies. That's when I changed my name to Dora Vane. Goodbye Mavis Weeks! If you saw any of the more forgettable movies over the past ten years, you probably saw me. I was Claudette Colbert's younger sister in Road House and the dance hall girl Mack Brown didn't marry in The Cattle Rustlers. I followed a fella to New York and started working the clubs there. Then some chorus work and some small parts on Broadway.

When America got into the war and my latest was a distant memory, I joined a second string USO troupe touring England. One night, lo and behold, there was Lt. Col. Mike Wilson standing with a bouquet of flowers outside my stage door! He'd seen me the night before when he went as the guest of a Yankee captain he was pursuing. No luck there so we spent a boozy night catching up on old news – yours included. I didn't see Mike again until the end of the tour when I decided to stay behind. I settled in as the chanteuse in a swank pub equal distance from a Canadian and American camp – not allowed to say where, of course.

How did we end up married I hear you ask. Well, Mike and I hit it off really well and both being between lovers and Mike not being queer to the core (just to the corps, ha ha) – you know how it is. Or probably you don't. Lucky you. Anyway, one night we were talking about what a lovely couple we made when I mentioned how I knew of more than one cover marriage in Hollywood. Big names too, my lips are sealed.

Then a few days later, Mike came over, looking very serious. He said it was our last week together for a long while. Maybe forever. Well, I knew what that meant although he wasn't allowed to say anything about it. But then he proposed to me! He said both his parents were dead and he was - "quite rich" was the way he put it - and if anything happened to him he couldn't think of anyone he'd rather it went to. And if he lived, which he sincerely hoped he would, we could have a jolly old time until we got tired of each other. Well as proposals go that was a very nice one and to be honest it was my first. You didn't propose to me did you, Frank? I'm pretty sure you didn't.

Next day we went to a lawyer – solicitor, I mean - and he drew up a marriage settlement and three days later we went to a registry office in – oops, can't say. Silly rules! And that's how I became Mrs. Lt. Col Mike Wilson. Poor Mike. My first love and my last, both heroes.

Well, sugar, it's been a long day and until my pot of gold turns up Mary Wilkinson still has to make her entrance. She needs to be wide awake and "perky" I think the director said. You have my address. Please write!

Love and kisses and forever yours,
Mavis

Also in the box were the two notes Mavis wrote to Frank on the day she left town – the one in which she called him Sleepy Head and the one she called him a skunk. There was no second letter from Mavis or Mrs. Dora Wilson and of course I have no way of knowing if he answered hers.

That's it. We're all caught up.

Here's something Frank told me once a few years before he died. He was talking about his elephant year, of course. I don't remember it word for word, but it was something like this.

"The thing that stays with me most, clear and sharp, is the sight of that elephant watching over us, me and Hector, in the first light of dawn.

"Anytime things got too hard, money troubles or worries about the kids, I'd think about Tommy, out there where he belonged, quietly chewing away. Then I'd take a deep breath and get back to the business of living."

ABOUT THE AUTHOR

Richard Rowberry

Richard Rowberry was born in England, grew up in Guelph, Ontario, was educated at Queens and York Universities, and attended The National Theatre School of Canada. Over the years he has been a furniture mover, truck driver, newspaper reporter, and arts administrator. He is currently Administrator of Nelson History Theatre. He has four children, four grandchildren, is happily married and has almost always had a dog.

www.ingramcontent.com/pod-product-compliance
Lightning Source LLC
LaVergne TN
LVHW051727080426
835511LV00018B/2924